LAKELAND FE

Near Eastern Fells

Mark Richards

HarperCollins*Publishers*

HarperCollins*Publishers* Ltd
77-85 Fulham Palace Road
London W6 8JB

Everything clicks at www.collins.co.uk

Collins is a registered trademark of
HarperCollins*Publishers* Ltd

10 9 8 7 6 5 4 3 2 1
08 07 06 05 04 03

A catalogue record for this book is available from the
British Library

ISBN 0 00 711366 8

Reproduction by Colourscan, Singapore
Printed and bound in Singapore by Imago

CONTENTS

Key to maps and diagrams GRID NORTH IS TOP OF EVERY MAP

 contours 15metre/30ft intervals, shown only to indicate relief

 crags and scree

 wall boundaries

 fence boundaries

 trees and woodland

 beck or gill

lake or tarn

 road and buildings

 summit cairn

23 car parking, cross-reference number with table on page 10

3 route number as described in the text

 strongly marked path

intermittent path

no path
author's recommended route

The hand-drawn maps and diagrams in this guide are based upon
HARVEY SUPERWALKER: LAKELAND CENTRAL

LAKELAND FELLRANGER

Eight title divisions of the English Lake District

A personal passion

My earliest memories of Lakeland came through studying artistic essays and books of the picturesque that my mother had acquired. They portrayed the romance of a majestic landscape that had formed the backdrop to her youth. Born in north Lancashire she naturally knew of Lakeland as a special place, though she had little opportunity to visit.

At a similar time, through the tales of Black Bob, the Dandy wonder dog, comic strip stories of a shepherd's adventures on the hills about Selkirk, I gained a love of both pen & ink drawing and the hills of the Scottish Borders. All distantly set in a romantic land of my own very youthful dreams, for I was born in rural west Oxfordshire and the magic that my mother clung to was becoming increasingly real to me.

Holidays were always allied to my parents roots. My father's Cornish ancestory gave me early seaside trips to that wonderful coastline and as my teenage years unfolded a regular busman's holiday to a fell farm on Lord Shuttleworth's Leck Hall estate, gave me the hands-on feel and flavour of rough fell country. My first fragmentary taste of what Lakeland itself was all about came, when I was twelve years old, on a day-trip to Ambleside and Great Langdale, when I remember purchasing The Southern Fells, Book Four of Alfred Wainwright's *'A Pictorial Guide to the Lakeland Fells'*. That book was periodically purused as my formative life as a young farmer kept my attention firmly on the needs of a 150-acre farm of cattle and corn. Socially I revelled in the activities of the Young Farmers' movement. I remember an exchange with the Alnwick club gave me a chance to climb The Cheviot in smooth-soled leather shoes, my first real fell climb. After master-minding two ploughing marathons, 100 then 200 acres turned from stubble to tilth in 24 hours, in my early twenties I sought new adventures. I joined the Gloucestershire Mountaineering Club and got to grips with Snowdonia, Scotland and yes, at long last, the Lakeland Fells. Rock climbing and long days in all weathers, ridge walking put me in touch with the thrill of high places.

That first Wainwright guide focused my mind on a love of wild places, Lakeland in particular. Quickly I now acquired the remainder of the series and feeling far removed from the beauty of it all, I took to drawing from my own black & white photographs, mimmicking AW. Within a year of joining the Mountaineering Club I had become a firm friend of the legend himself, spending regular weekends at Kendal Green joining him on his original exploration of the Coast to Coast Walk, The Outlying Fells *(see page 228 for my one moment of recognition)*, Westmorland Heritage and supplying numerous photographs of Scottish mountains he was unable to reach, for his Scottish Mountain Drawings series. As my walking progressed and his faltered, so my trips to Kendal became fewer. Marriage, a family and farming brought responsibilities so time constraints deflected my attention from AW and the Lakeland I loved.

I remained in farming until almost forty during which time I had several walking guides published. AW nurtured my first title, a very pictorial map-guide to The Cotswold Way back in 1973. This was followed by guides to the North Cornwall Coast, Offa's Dyke Path, a three-part exploration of the Peak District National Park and Hadrian's Wall. Many small guides and articles later, including a happy sequence of *Out of the Way* pieces for The Countryman, a journal I had known from childhood being published on my doorstep. All along gnawing at the back of my mind was the sense that someday I should prepare my own complete survey of the Lakeland Fells. Having edited a little magazine, *Walking Wales,* for one year, I found I could ignore it no longer and, with the support and encouragement of *HarperCollins,* to whom I will be forever grateful, I moved to Cumbria to begin Lakeland Fellranger.

Helvellyn from Red Screes

From fireside to fellside

Free time spent out on the fell is always the very best of time. One may sit at home pore over maps and consult guides, letting the imagination run riot, but nothing matches the fun and thrill of actually being out there. To wander by lonely becks and over rough fellsides, to climb to high cairned summits, to sense the freedom, space and sheer beauty of it all is an holistic emotion beyond poetic words and pictorial expression. The contrasts of seasons and time of day, the play of light and shadow, the mischiefous antics of mist and cloud. Coping with wind and rain, snow and ice in an environment that one comes to know by stints and stages. The form and character of each fell becoming like friends from childhood, reliable, happy in reunion whatever the time span since last in their company. One harbours memories of times past and relishes new days of quest in their kinship. The sweat, pain and ache of tired limbs, out scored by pleasurable moments of adventure and sheer elation. Expeditions relished, each new view adored. How grateful we are for their existence, these magicial fells. In small compass, great mountains, deep green dales, wind-whipped lakes, still tarns reflecting the sky, dancing becks, fearsome buttresses, whispering woods and clouds racing across sweeping pastures inhabited by bleating heafed sheep, the air tingling with the rippling call of skylark and the hoarse rasp of raven. And for all our pleasure in solitary wanderings, who has not smiled upon an encounter with the best of all fell creatures, fellow fell-rangers?

This guide

The Helvellyn and Fairfield group forms a sustained high level north to south ridge division through the midriff of Lakeland. The character of the range lends itself supremely well to fellwalking. Crags seldom intervene to hamper ridge walks, and where they do, as upon Striding Edge linking Birkhouse Moor with Helvellyn, given fair weather the adventure can be entertained by the majority of suitably attuned and equipped walkers. The group contains famous fells. Who would not be stirred by the romance in the name Helvellyn, Dollywaggon Pike or Catstycam, or resist the complete fell-day provided by the Fairfield Horseshoe and the circuit of the Dodds, or hold back from wandering up Dovedale bound for Dove Crag, or venture onto the great whale-back of Red Screes to see the wide panorama of fells either side of the Kirkstone Pass? The range has long been renown for its diverse store of superb fell days.

The purpose of this guide is to show the fullest complement of walking routes on each fell. The pressure of boots down the years have taken their toll. Remedial action is costly, for example £60,000 alone has been spent on Dollywaggon Pike by the National Park. Much commendable pitching and paving has been undertaken by The National Trust too, but 'official' advice on your choice of routes has inevitably always been strict. The '*people are sheep*' syndrome sustained by limiting route information to the modern variations of traditional paths. Lakeland Fellranger serves the imperative to provide at least one solid reference to the range of reliable options available, a valuable by-product being to spread the load on the path structure, in this one vital dimension this series is unique.

Each route is identified by a red number which links the diagrams and maps to the adjacent text. The routes themselves recognised in three forms (see preceding key): bold dashes for the principal trails; thin dashes for lesser paths liable to be intermittent or the old green tracks of shepherds' past, and lastly, dots, where there is no path on the ground and represents nothing more than the author's recommended route. No two walkers follow the same treads, neither do they explore with the same plot, so what is revealed in this guide is a very personal expression of the potential route structure. Nonetheless, it is fundamentally reliable and for fellwalkers who love to explore, a rich source of entertaining route planning ideas. A good guide should also be a revelation. Hence for each fell summit or better nearby viewpoint, a full panorama is given, which alone should encourage readers to carry the tome to the top!

The guide may be formally structured to cover important matters such as the nature of the summit, safe lines of descent and the linking ridge routes, sprinkled with a few items of interpretation, but underlying it all is a desire to share the pleasure of exploration which is open to each one of us. Let us long love Lakeland and care for its future. May its magic remain an inspiration for each new generation.

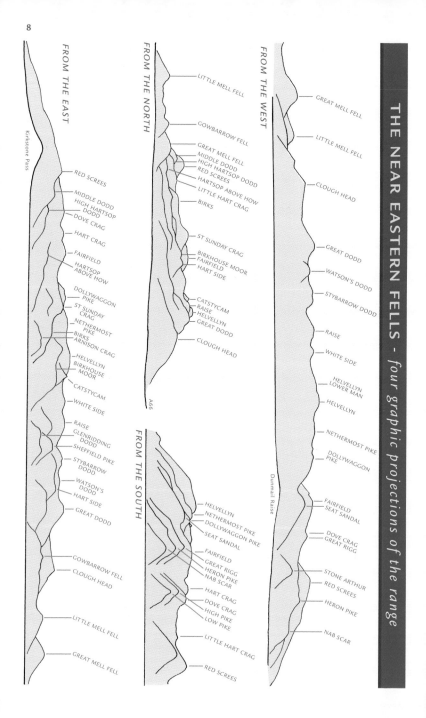

8

THE NEAR EASTERN FELLS - four graphic projections of the range

FROM THE EAST

Kirkstone Pass

- RED SCREES
- MIDDLE DODD
- HIGH HARTSOP DODD
- DOVE CRAG
- HART CRAG
- FAIRFIELD
- HARTSOP ABOVE HOW
- DOLLYWAGGON PIKE
- ST SUNDAY CRAG
- NETHERMOST PIKE
- BIRKS
- ARNISON CRAG
- HELVELLYN
- BIRKHOUSE MOOR
- CATSTYCAM
- WHITE SIDE
- RAISE
- GLENRIDDING DODD
- SHEFFIELD PIKE
- STYBARROW DODD
- WATSON'S DODD
- HART SIDE
- GREAT DODD
- GOWBARROW FELL
- CLOUGH HEAD
- LITTLE MELL FELL
- GREAT MELL FELL

FROM THE NORTH

A66

- LITTLE MELL FELL
- GOWBARROW FELL
- GREAT MELL FELL
- MIDDLE DODD
- HIGH HARTSOP DODD
- RED SCREES
- HARTSOP ABOVE HOW
- LITTLE HART CRAG
- BIRKS
- ST SUNDAY CRAG
- BIRKHOUSE MOOR
- FAIRFIELD
- HART SIDE
- CATSTYCAM
- RAISE
- HELVELLYN
- GREAT DODD
- CLOUGH HEAD

FROM THE SOUTH

- HELVELLYN
- NETHERMOST PIKE
- DOLLYWAGGON PIKE
- SEAT SANDAL
- FAIRFIELD
- GREAT RIGG
- HERON PIKE
- NAB SCAR
- HART CRAG
- DOVE CRAG
- HIGH PIKE
- LOW PIKE
- LITTLE HART CRAG
- RED SCREES

FROM THE WEST

Dunmail Raise

- GREAT MELL FELL
- LITTLE MELL FELL
- CLOUGH HEAD
- GREAT DODD
- WATSON'S DODD
- STYBARROW DODD
- RAISE
- WHITE SIDE
- HELVELLYN LOWER MAN
- HELVELLYN
- NETHERMOST PIKE
- DOLLYWAGGON PIKE
- FAIRFIELD
- SEAT SANDAL
- DOVE CRAG
- GREAT RIGG
- STONE ARTHUR
- RED SCREES
- HERON PIKE
- NAB SCAR

FELL MOSAIC

Chapter and page references providing an overview of adjacent fell range mapping, inevitaby fragmented within this guide, as an aid for planning your liberty on the fells.

Threlkeld

Dockray

Ullswater

Thirlmere

Patterdale

Dunmail Raise

Grasmere

Grasmere

Kirkstone Pass

Rydal Water

Ambleside

GREAT MELL FELL
114-119

LITTLE MELL FELL
192-195

CLOUGH HEAD
48-57

GOWBARROW FELL
94-103

GREAT DODD
104-113

HART SIDE
136-143

WATSON'S DODD
282-285

STYBARROW DODD
272-281

SHEFFIELD PIKE
246-255

RAISE
220-227

WHITE SIDE
286-293

GLENRIDDING DODD
86-93

BIRKHOUSE MOOR
24-33

CATSTYCAM
40-47

HELVELLYN
150-167

BIRKS
34-39

ARNISON CRAG
18-23

NETHERMOST PIKE
212-219

ST SUNDAY CRAG
256-265

HARTSOP ABOVE HOW
144-151

DOLLYWAGGON PIKE
58-65

FAIRFIELD
76-85

HART CRAG
128-135

SEAT SANDAL
238-245

HIGH HARTSOP DODD
178-181

GREAT RIGG
120-127

DOVE CRAG
66-75

MIDDLE DODD
202-205

STONE ARTHUR
266-271

HIGH PIKE
182-185

LITTLE HART CRAG
186-191

HERON PIKE
170-177

RED SCREES
228-237

NAB SCAR
206-211

LOW PIKE
196-201

STARTING POINTS

	LOCATION	GRID REFERENCE	PARKING	BUS STOP
1	Threlkeld	325 254		*
2	Wanthwaite	316 231		
3	Sandbed Gill	319 219		
4	Legburthwaite (NWW)	318 195	P	
5	Stanah	318 189	P	*
6	Thirlspot	317 178	P	
7	Swirls (NWW)	316 169	P	
8	Wythburn Church (NWW)	324 136	P	*
9	Dunmail Raise	327 116		
10	Mill Bridge	335 092		*
11	Stock Lane	339 073	P	*
	Redbank Road (NP Info. Centre)	335 073	P	*
	Broadgate	338 078	P	*
	A591 lay-by	337 086		*
	A591 lay-by	342 076		*
12	White Moss Common	348 064	P	*
13	Pelter Bridge, Rydal	365 059	P	*
	lane to Rydal Mount, Rydal	364 063		*
14	Rydal Road, Ambleside	375 047	P	*
15	The Struggle	397 077		
16	Kirkstone Pass	401 080	P	*
17	Red Pit	403 089	P	
18	Kirkstonefoot lay-by	402 112		*
19	Cowbridge (NT)	402 134	P	
20	Deepdale Bridge	399 143		*
21	Patterdale	396 159	P	*
22	Grisedale Bridge	390 161		
23	Glenridding (NP Info. Centre)	385 169	P	*
24	Stybarrow Crag	387 179		
25	Glencoyne Bridge (NT)	386 189	P	
26	Aira Force (NT)	400 200	P	*
27	Gowbarrow Crag	415 204		
28	Park Brow (NT)	397 204		
29	High Force	397 210		
30	Dockray	392 215		*
31	High Row	380 219		
32	Todgill	400 228		
33	The Hause	423 235		
34	Watermillock Church	431 232		
35	Cove	430 236		
36	Matterdale End	395 235		*
37	Brownrigg	407 247		
38	Troutbeck	390 266		*

P - formal car parking facilities (some with coin meters)
otherwise informal, limited lay-by or private (inn/hotel) parking
* - serviced bus stop close by

Public transport may be a problem elsewhere but here in the heart of Lakeland one may confidently plan a day around a reliable rural service, given a proper study of timetables. The Mountain Goat service is supplimented by a regular bus from Lancaster via Kendal bound for Carlisle. Pertinent to this book buses run along both the A591, via Grasmere and Thirlmere and the A592 via Kirkstone Pass and Patterdale. For current advice contact : TRAVELINE public transport info 0870 608 2 608

Northern Fells

PENRUDDOCK

A66 PENRITH >

< KESWICK A66

THRELKELD

POOLEY
BRIDGE

< KESWICK A591

DOCKRAY

Ullswater

Thirlmere

GLENRIDDING

PATTERDALE

fell above 305m/1,000 feet

38 parking text/map reference

Fell summit/chapter
35

LOW HARTSOP

Brothers
Water

Far Eastern Fells

Dunmail
Raise

A591

Kirkstone
Pass

GRASMERE

RYDAL

Grasmere

Rydal
Water

A592 WINDERMERE

AMBLESIDE

Central Fells

miles 1   2   3   4   5

km 1 2 3 4 5

READY RECKONER *for route planning*

NOTE: Many of these routes have variations, hence the tally relates to the most direct option

start & route	text reference nos.	ascent *(feet)*	distance *(miles)*
1 Arnison Crag 18-23			
21 PATTERDALE			
direct *(3 options)*	1|2|3|4	940	0.8
via Glemara Park	5	1,100	1.9
via Deepdale	6	1,100	3.0
2 Birkhouse Moor 24-33			
23 GLENRIDDING			
via Keldas & Mires Beck	1|4|5|6	1,960	2.2
via NE ridge	2|3|7	1,865	2.1
via N ridge	2|3|8	1,865	2.6
21 PATTERDALE/22 GRISEDALE BRIDGE			
via Hole-in-t'-Wall	9|10	1,900	3.2
via Nethermost Cove wall	9|11	1,900	3.8
3 Birks 34-39			
21 PATTERDALE/22 GRISEDALE BRIDGE			
via Glemara Park	1	1,550	2.0
via Thornhow End	2	1,550	2.1
4 Catstycam 40-47			
23 GLENRIDDING			
via E shoulder	2|3	2,420	3.8
via Swirral Edge col	2|3	2,420	4.0
via NW ridge	1|4	2,440	3.7
5 Clough Head 48-57			
3 SANDBED GILL			
via Fisher's Wife's Rake	1|2	1,900	1.5
2 WANTHWAITE			
via Fisher's Wife's Rake	3|1|2	1,930	2.0
via Wanthwaite Crags	3|4|2	1,900	2.5
1 THRELKELD			
via Threlkeld Knotts	1|2|3|4|5	2,000	3.0
via White Pike	1|2|6	1,900	2.8
6 Dollywaggon Pike 58-65			
9 DUNMAIL RAISE			
via Willie Wife Moor	4|5	2,045	1.8
via Raise Beck	1|2|3	2,050	2.3
via Birkside Gill	6	2,070	2.0
22 GRISEDALE BRIDGE			
via Spout Crag	7|8	2,325	4.3
via Cock Cove	7|9	2,325	4.5

7 Dove Crag 66-75

19 COWBRIDGE

via Houndshope Cove	1|3|4	2,080	3.5

18 KIRKSTONEFOOT

via The Stang	2|4|6	2,060	3.0
via Hogget Gill	2|4|5	2,060	3.1

8 Fairfield 76-85

20 DEEPDALE BRIDGE

via Greenhow End	1|2	2,360	5.0
via Deepdale Hause	1|3	2,360	4.2

21 PATTERDALE/22 GRISEDALE BRIDGE

via Cofa Pike	5	2,380	6.4
via Deepdale Hause	6|7	2,410	7.2

9 Glenridding Dodd 86-93

24 STYBARROW CRAG

via Mossdale	1|3	970	1.0
via lakeside & sylvan path	2	990	2.0

22 GLENRIDDING

via The Rake	4|5	950	1.0

10 Gowbarrow Fell 94-103

33 THE HAUSE

via Little Meldrum	1|2|3	580	2.3
via Great Meldrum	4	530	1.8
via Watermillock path	5	725	2.5

30 DOCKRAY

direct	6	670	1.2
via Ulcat Row	7	690	2.5

26/28/29 AIRA FORCE

via Aira Force *(3 options)*	8|9|10	1,050	1.7
via Green Hill	11	1,080	2.4
via Gowbarrow Park	12	1,060	3.3
via Yew Crag	13	1,100	3.6

27 GOWBARROW CRAG

direct	14	1,100	1.3

11 Great Dodd 104-113

30 DOCKRAY/31 HIGH ROW

via Deepdale & Randerside	1|2|3|4	1,860	3.8
via Mosedale	5	1,480	6.0

4 LEGBURTHWAITE

via Mill Gill	6	2,260	2.4
via Ladknott Gill	7	2,280	2.7
via Beckthorns Gill	8	2,350	3.4

12 Great Mell Fell 114-119

36 MATTERDALE END

approach to Brownrigg	1	130	1.0

37 BROWNRIGG

direct *(3 options)*	2 | 3 | 4	1,240	1.0
circuit of fell		420	3.0

38 TROUTBECK

direct	5	880	1.0

13 Great Rigg 120-127

11 GRASMERE

via Stone Arthur	1	2,260	2.4
via Greenhead Gill	2	2,260	2.5

14 Hart Crag 128-135

20 DEEPDALE BRIDGE

via Link Cove	1 | 3	2,200	4.5
via Dry Gill	1 | 2	2,330	4.0
via Rydale	4	2,500	4.4

15 Hart Side 136-143

28 PARK BROW/29 HIGH FORCE/30 DOCKRAY

via Common Fell *(4 options)*	1 | 2 | 3 | 4 | 6	1,530	3.8
via Dowthwaitehead	5 | 6	1,530	4.3
via Glencoyne balcony path	7	1,530	4.2

16 Hartsop above How 144-151

19 COWBRIDGE

direct	3 | 4	1,400	2.1

20 DEEPDALE BRIDGE

direct	1 | 2	1,410	2.4
via Dry Gill	5	1,410	2.8
via Link Cove	6	1,450	4.2

17 Helvellyn 152-169

6 THIRLSPOT

via Old Pony Route	1	2,500	4.1
via White Stones Routes	2	2,500	3.5

7 SWIRLS

direct	3 | 4 | 5	2,400	2.4
via Helvellyn Screes	6	2,450	2.8

8 WYTHBURN

direct	7	2,520	2.8
via Middle Tongue	8	2,550	2.5
via Whelpside Gill	9	2,530	2.4
via Mines Gill	10	2,520	2.6

23 GLENRIDDING

via Old Pony Route	**11**	2,830	6.0
via Red Tarn Beck	**12**	2,600	5.0
via Mires Beck	**13 | 15**	2,720	4.4

21 PATTERDALE/22 GRISEDALE BRIDGE

via Striding Edge	**14 | 15**	2,700	4.5

18 Heron Pike 170-177

11 GRASMERE

via Town End	**1 | 2 | 3**	1,800	1.9
via Swan Hotel	**4 | 5**	1,790	1.9

12 WHITE MOSS COMMON

via Dunney Beck	**6**	1,840	1.6

13 RYDAL

direct	**6 | 7**	1,840	2.4
via Blind Cove	**8**	1,840	2.3

19 High Hartsop Dodd 178-181

19 COWBRIDGE

direct	**1**	1,180	2.1

20 High Pike 182-185

14 AMBLESIDE

direct	**1**	1,990	3.3

21 Little Hart Crag 186-191

19 COWBRIDGE

direct	**1**	1,570	2.9
via Caiston Glen	**2**	1,570	3.8
via Hogget Gill	**3**	1,570	3.5

22 Little Mell Fell 192-195

33 THE HAUSE

direct	**1 | 3**	410	0.4

35 COVE

direct	**2**	705	0.7

23 Low Pike 196-201

13 RYDAL

via Buckstones Jump	**1**	1,470	1.8

14 AMBLESIDE

via Low Sweden Bridge	**2**	1,500	2.5
via High Sweden Bridge	**3**	1,500	2.7

24 Middle Dodd 202-205

18 KIRKSTONEFOOT

via Caiston Glen	**1**	1,500	2.4
direct	**3**	1,490	1.4

17 RED PIT

direct	**3**	1,000	0.9

25 Nab Scar 206-211

13 RYDAL

direct	1	1,300	1.0
via Dunney Beck	2	1,300	2.5

12 WHITE MOSS COMMON

direct	3	1,300	1.7

26 Nethermost Pike 212-219

8 WYTHBURN

direct	1	2,330	2.0
via Comb Gill	2	2,330	1.8
via Middle Tongue	3	2,330	1.9

21 PATTERDALE

via Nethermost Cove	4 | 5	2,430	4.2
via Ruthwaite Cove	6	2,430	4.8

27 Raise 220-227

5 STANAH

via Sticks Pass	1	2,300	2.5
via Fisher Place Gill	1 | 2 | 3	2,350	2.7

6 THIRLSPOT

via Brund Gill or Sticks Gill	3 | 4 | 5 | 6	2,300	2,5

23 GLENRIDDING

direct	7 | 9	2,400	3.3
via Old Pony Route	7 | 8	2,400	4.8
via Sticks Pass	7 | 10	2,400	4.6

28 Red Screes 228-237

14 AMBLESIDE

via S Ridge	1	2,380	4.1
via Scandale	2	2,400	4.8
via wallers' quarry route	3	2,400	4.3
via Middle Grove	4	2,400	5.0

15 THE STRUGGLE

direct	5	1,365	1.2

16 KIRKSTONE PASS

direct	6	1,060	0.7

17 RED PIT

direct	8 | 9	1,400	0.7

18 KIRKSTONEFOOT

via Middle Dodd	7	1,900	2.0
via Caiston Glen	10	1,890	2.9

29 Seat Sandal 238-245

10 MILL BRIDGE

via Tongue Gill	1 | 2	2,090	2.8
via Little Tongue Gill	1 | 3	2,100	2.9
via S ridge	1 | 3 | 4	2,100	2.9
via Gavel Crag	1 | 3 | 5	2,090	2.4

9 DUNMAIL RAISE

via Raise Beck	**6**	**1,660**	**1.7**
direct	**7**	**1,660**	**1.2**
Achille Ratti direct	**8**	**1,700**	**1.1**

30 Sheffield Pike 246-255

25 GLENCOYNE

via Nick Head	**1|2|3**	**1,720**	**2.5**
via Black Crag	**1|2|4**	**1,720**	**1.9**
via Heron Pike	**1|2|4|5**	**1,720**	**2.1**

23 GLENRIDDING

direct *(options)*	**6|7|9**	**1,750**	**1.8**
via Mossdale	**8**	**1,720**	**1.5**
via Greenside Mine	**10**	**1,720**	**3.0**

31 St Sunday Crag 256-265

21 PATTERDALE

direct	**1**	**2,270**	**3.0**
via Blind Cove	**2**	**2,270**	**4.1**
via Glemara Park	**3**	**2,270**	**3.5**
via Grisedale	**5**	**2,300**	**6.4**

20 DEEPDALE BRIDGE

direct	**4**	**2,270**	**2.9**

32 Stone Arthur 266-271

11 GRASMERE

direct	**1**	**1,320**	**1.4**
via Greenhead Gill	**2|3**	**1,320**	**1.9**

10 MILL BRIDGE

via Tongue Gill	**4|5**	**1,420**	**1.7**

33 Stybarrow Dodd 272-281

5 STANAH

via Sticks Pass	**1|2|4**	**2,180**	**2.5**
via Stanah Gill	**1|3**	**2,200**	**2.0**

31 HIGH ROW

via Dowthwaitehead	**5|6**	**1,520**	**4.0**
via Deepdale	**7|8**	**1,400**	**3.1**
via Miners' Path	**9|10**	**1,550**	**5.4**
via Nick Head	**10**	**1,530**	**5.1**

34 Watson's Dodd 282-285

4 LEGBURTHWAITE

direct	**1**	**1,970**	**2.0**

35 White Side 286-293

7 SWIRLS

direct	**3|5**	**2,100**	**2.9**
via Old Pony Route	**3|5|6**	**2,150**	**3.2**

23 GLENRIDDING

via Old Pony Route	**2**	**2,350**	**1.8**
via E Ridge	**3**	**2,340**	**1.8**

ARNISON CRAG

Approaching the head of Ullswater the traveller cannot help but attend to Arnison Crag, its rugged little ridge climbing directly from the village of Patterdale to an eye-catching rock pulpit. Dwarfed by surrounding heights, yet possessing characteristics many a mightier fell would envy, this is a worthy, yet easily-won fell-walking prize, taking a tad over two hours, there and back.

Tenuously connected to St Sunday Crag it is intimately rooted in the Patterdale fraternity of fells. The fell has two contrasting aspects: Juniper clothed crags and coarse scree fall directly eastward, while to the west sequesters Glemara Park, an old deer preserve, harbouring beautiful oakwood carpeted by bracken and, in their season, bluebells.

In most cases the ascent is but the first stage on the greater climb to St Sunday Crag via Trough Head. For all the simplicity of the ridge there are several subtle varations to the ascent, with a choice of two distinctly different circular walks, both begin with the north ridge and provide attractive return options via either Glemara Park or lower Deepdale.

slopes of PLACE FELL

PATTERDALE 21

Grisedale Beck

Mill Moss

Youth Hostel

Bleaze End

Oxford Crag

Glemara Park

fold

Thornhow End

Black Crag

Greenbank

Goldrill Beck

Deepdale Beck

BIRKS

20 Bridgend

LOW HARTSOP (A592) 1ml >

Trough Head fold

Deepdale Hall

APPROACHES
for diagram see
ST SUNDAY CRAG
page 321

Wall End

Coldcove Beck

Deepdale

The fell-name means *'the crag associated with Arnison'*, a personal-name

434 metres   1,424 feet

ASCENT *from Patterdale*

Pay & Display car park opposite Patterdale Hotel

1 A signed footpath GR 397158 from the vicinity of the public toilets leads up a track. At a stone building the path branches left passing the birchwood environs of Mill Moss to reach a kissing-gate onto the open fell. Three options can be considered from this point. **2** The uncommon way aims for a subsidiary knot on the eastern scarp, crowned with the best cairn on the fell - a pathless route dogged by bracken in summer. Bear left, beside the fence skirting the marshy ground, join a sheep trod crossing to a wall. Go right and, as the wall curves left, continue up the slope trending left, climbing to the stony gully leading to a notch find the cairn up to the left, a superb, little visited, viewpoint above the Goldrill vale. Continue ascending the steep bank to join a ridge path, itself little better than a sheep trod.

3 Alternatively, head straight up the bracken slope to crest Oxford Crag, continuing above the wall.   **4**   The only way when the bracken is king is to follow the footpath to the deer park wall kissing-gate, do not go through, instead ascend left, keeping the wall to the right. High up the wall bends as the gradient eases 100 yards beyond this point either bear left onto a sheep trod then smartly right, up the rocky ridge to the skyline notch between the twin summit outcrops, climbing right to the main top.   Alternatively, continue to the broad ridge-top hollow, slant left up a path to swing round onto the summit from the south.

Bluebell banks of Glemara Park beneath Thornhow End, looking to the summit

5 The north-facing valley of Glemara Park offers a surreptitious approach. Pass through the deer park wall kissing-gate holding to the footpath which fords Hag Beck. After some seventy yards bear off left with a tractor track which winds up the bank, as this diminishes contour left to ford the beck and accompany its east bank up to a metal ladder-stile crossing the deer park wall at the dale-head. Turn left ascending close to the wall, at its high point bear right onto the ridge, climbing to the summit from the broad depression.

Southern approaches may begin from Patterdale following the roadside footway passing Patterdale Youth Hostel, and Bleaze End a name derived from the light grey scree blazened hillside above. Branch onto the bridle-track at the cattle-grid this leads via gates past Greenbank Farm and Lane Head. Alternatively, begin direct from Bridgend (lay-by car parking) following the walled lane to Lane Head. Go left upon the gated track bound for Wall End, passing to the right of Deepdale Hall Farm. Here either **6** follow the steep shepherds' trod, best in winter when the bracken is low, or **7** continue to where the telephone wires cross askew, go right, keeping beneath their line on a ramped green track, go to the right of the wall corner into a confined groove. Gaining height a path materialises, drifting up from the walled enclosures, this fords a gill below a confluence. Continue within the grooved path until bracken intervenes, now bear up right, pathless, towards the ridge top, gradually gaining a sheep trod passing a ruined fold to reach the Trough Head cross-paths, turning north-east (right) along the undulating ridge path.

Ullswater from the head of Glemara Park

The Summit

A place to linger and consider the picturesque qualities of Patterdale, the head of Ullswater (though there are better viewpoints) and the Hartsop vale: green straths bound by high fells - this is beauty distilled. For all the apparent rock there are precious few loose to amalgamate into a cairn, nature preferring the tidiness of glacially smoothed bedrock. A small cairn rests on the ledge visible from the youth hostel, guess who constructed that one. As a perversity, though there is no doubt that this is the summit, the undulating grassy ridge continuing to Trough Head swells over one higher, far less distinguished, grassy knoll.

Safe Descents

The fell-top is marshalled by crags so in mist leave the summit to the S taking an immediate exaggerated sweep right, slanting down to the broad depression. Join the path which leads N accompanying the old deer park wall down tight by Oxford Crag, for the Patterdale footpath.

Ridge Routes to....

BIRKS   DESCENT 260 feet   ASCENT 750 feet   1.2 miles

Follow the ridge path SSW. As it crosses the highest point bear off right to accompany the deer park wall down to the dale-head. Do not cross the metal ladder-stile, instead turn left beside Hag Beck (as to Trough Head), branch steeply right to keep company with the broken wall mounting W onto the top of Birks.

Arnison Crag from the higher ridge-top knoll to the south-west

PANORAMA

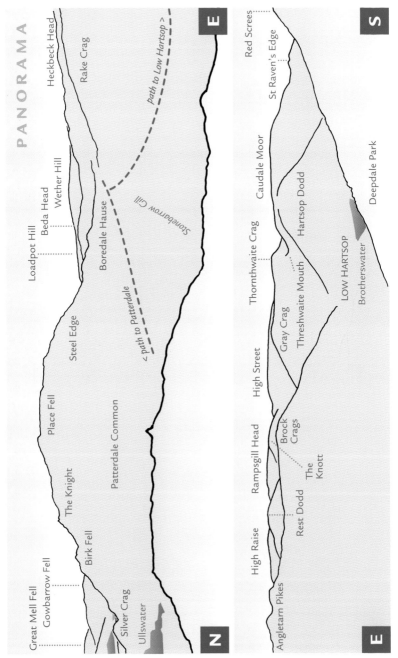

E

Heckbeck Head
Rake Crag
path to Low Hartsop >
Beda Head
Wether Hill
Loadpot Hill
Boredale Hause
Stonebarrow Gill
Steel Edge
< path to Patterdale
Place Fell
The Knight
Patterdale Common
Birk Fell
Great Mell Fell
Gowbarrow Fell
Silver Crag
Ullswater

N

S

Red Screes
St Raven's Edge
Caudale Moor
Hartsop Dodd
Deepdale Park
Thornthwaite Crag
Threshwaite Mouth
LOW HARTSOP
Brotherswater
High Street
Gray Crag
Rampsgill Head
Brock Crags
The Knott
Rest Dodd
High Raise
Angletarn Pikes

E

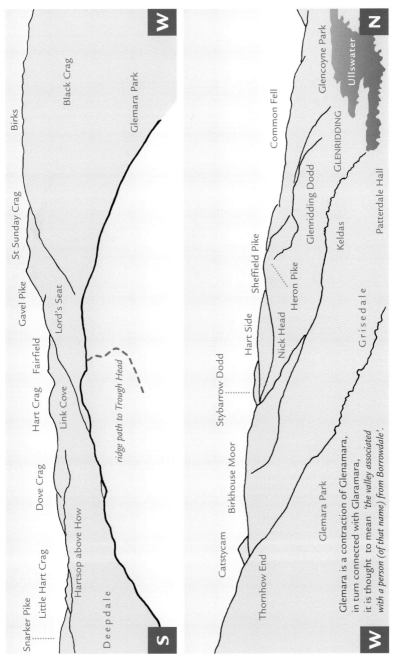

W

Snarker Pike
Little Hart Crag
Harsop above How
Dove Crag
Hart Crag
Fairfield
Link Cove
Lord's Seat
Gavel Pike
St Sunday Crag
Birks

Black Crag

Glemara Park

ridge path to Trough Head

Deepdale

S

N

Catstycam
Thornhow End
Birkhouse Moor
Glemara Park
Stybarrow Dodd
Hart Side
Nick Head
Sheffield Pike
Heron Pike
Glenridding Dodd
Common Fell
Keldas
GLENRIDDING
Glencoyne Park
Ullswater
Patterdale Hall

G r i s e d a l e

Glemara is a contraction of Glenamara,
in turn connected with Glaramara,
it is thought to mean 'the valley associated
with a person (of that name) from Borrowdale'.

W

BIRKHOUSE MOOR

Helvellyn embraces Red Tarn with two striking ridges. To the north Swirral Edge, which culminates with an abrupt flourish upon Catstycam, while Striding Edge, forming the southern wall, forges east over High Spying How to connect with the stately mass of Birkhouse Moor. From this very moor-like summit the ridge falls in steady stages towards Ullswater. The rocky knob of Keldas, the loveliest asset of Birkhouse Moor, adorned with pines and flanked with bluebells, forms the extremity of this ridge and offers the most exquisite imaginable view of the lake's upper reach, especially so when canoes, yachts and the steamer bring colour and life to the scene.

Thus well connected, Birkhouse Moor has inevitably become a means to an end and seldom an end in itself. A staging post to greater things. Nevertheless, the fell has two exclusive ascents, off the main line tracks to Helvellyn. Two ridges rise to the subsidiary summit, north of the ridge wall. The north ridge, climbing directly above the environs of the Greenside Mine, is least defined, while the north-east ridge rising to The Nab is an inviting succession of rocky steps, peering into Blea Cove this is the best route on the fell.

The paucity of silver birch in the area contrasts with the place-name evidence implying the fellsides were once richly clothed with this attractive tree. Indeed, the dale-name Glenridding is further suggestive of the former existence of woodland, being derived from the Celtic 'glyn rhedyn' which translates as 'the valley beset with bracken', a plant which naturally prefers the partial cover of a birch wood.

718 metres   2,356 feet

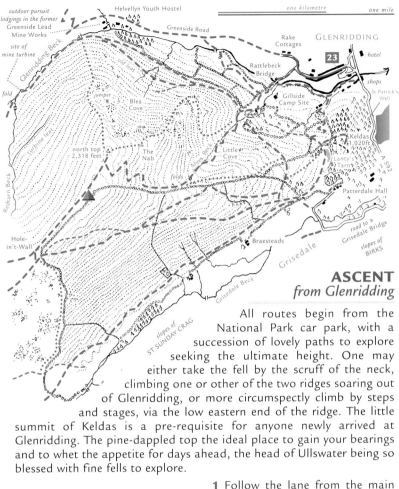

one kilometre

one mile

ASCENT
from Glenridding

All routes begin from the National Park car park, with a succession of lovely paths to explore seeking the ultimate height. One may either take the fell by the scruff of the neck, climbing one or other of the two ridges soaring out of Glenridding, or more circumspectly climb by steps and stages, via the low eastern end of the ridge. The little summit of Keldas is a pre-requisite for anyone newly arrived at Glenridding. The pine-dappled top the ideal place to gain your bearings and to whet the appetite for days ahead, the head of Ullswater being so blessed with fine fells to explore.

Steep ascending wall to the Hole-in't-Wall

1 Follow the lane from the main street on the south bank of Glenridding Beck (signed to *'Gillside Farm, no vehicles'*). This leads by Glenridding Public Hall through Eagle Farm. At the fork keep left with the main track to Westside Cottages, a waymarked and hand-gated path, unnecessarily divided at the beginning, winds up part-pitched to a kissing-gate. Continue the zig-zagging ascent upon, what in

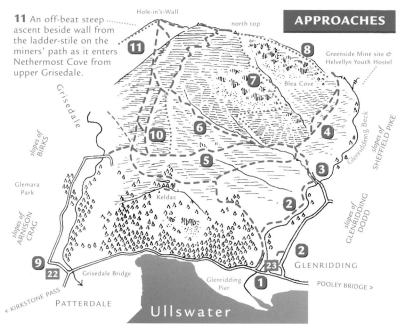

11 An off-beat steep ascent beside wall from the ladder-stile on the miners' path as it enters Nethermost Cove from upper Grisedale.

APPROACHES

Hole-in't-Wall

north top

Greenside Mine site & Helvellyn Youth Hostel

Blea Cove

Grisedale

slopes of BIRKS

Glenridding Beck

slopes of SHEFFIELD PIKE

Glemara Park

Keldas

slopes of ARNISON CRAG

slopes of GLENRIDDING DODD

GLENRIDDING

Grisedale Bridge

Glenridding Pier

POOLEY BRIDGE >

< KIRKSTONE PASS

PATTERDALE

Ullswater

May, is a beautiful bluebell bank, like bracken, another old woodland indicator. Reaching a second kissing-gate in the rising wall, switch left, signed *'Striding Edge, Grisedale'*. Approaching the kissing-gate access to Lanty's Tarn, cross the stile on the left beside a padlocked gate entering the Patterdale Hall estate enclosure. Follow the one permitted path to the summit of Keldas. Backtrack and go through the kissing-gate to visit the conifer screened reservoir Lanty's Tarn *(Lanty being a pet form of the personal name Lancelot)*. As the track breaks to open pasture on the right, one may traverse to Brownend Plantation (an open woodland with kissing-gate in its midst), or pass the dam sweeping down to the enclosure corner, meeting up with the path from Patterdale at a hand-gate.

2 The alternative start from the car park leads to Rattlebeck Bridge. Either follow the path out via the Health Centre onto Greenside Road. Advance beyond The Travellers Rest to where the road forks, turn left down the lane to the bridge or, more pleasantly, follow the track through Eagle Farm, only now bear right at the fork with the bridle-path running beside Glenridding Beck and the camping field.

3 Ascend the track from Rattlebeck Bridge, signed *'Helvellyn via Mires Beck'* passing via a stile/gate up to a fork below 'Miresbeck' cottage.
4 For Keldas go left crossing Mires Beck up the bank to a hand-gate, follow the waymark posts guiding diagonally up the enclosure to a hand-gate, continuing to a kissing-gate onto the main Keldas path.

Blea Cove from Heron Pike, with Catstycam to the right

With Birkhouse Moor to the fore, go right on the stony path to the ladder-stile/gate in the intake wall. Four routes embark from this point.
5 The steadiest of all begins with the Mires Beck path but bears left. Watch for waymarks after the ford on a path that runs above the intake wall to curve up onto the ridge at a gate/stile. This path can be followed over the ridge, through Brownend Plantation, via a kissing-gate, to unite with the throng upon the Patterdale path, going right bound for the Hole-in't-Wall. Better, follow the ridge wall to meet up with the Mires Beck path above the circular sheepfold. Here a wall-stile can also give access to the old Patterdale path on the Grisedale side.

6 Of recent years the Mires Beck path has been elevated in state and status, diverting traffic from the Red Tarn Beck route, a superbly engineered path crafted to minimise the effects of rampant boots bent on Striding Edge. From the top of Mires Beck the path climbs, initially close to the ridge-wall, then drifts away to gain the broad top of the fell, coming close to the wall again at the ragged cairn on the true summit.

7 Direct approaches to the north-east ridge are not encouraged, bracken is a further deterrent. The most efficient route follows the Mires Beck path from the ladder-stile, breaking away right immediately before the ford. Trend up the marshy ground keeping to the bracken fringe seeking a sheep-path traversing right. The clue is the solitary rowan growing from a rock, the trod tops the first outcropped step of the ridge.

Waves of bluebells line the path on the descent from Lanty's Tarn

Substantial pitched path rising from Mires Beck

Passing a second lone roan climb, via juniper shrubs, up a short scree path, then work the natural way with only slight evidence of a path up the outcrop-stepped ridge. On the highest shelf pass a pool (in outline the shape of a bear!) commanding a lovely view over Blea Cove. Ultimately reach the large cairn on the north top, a fine viewpoint to enjoy alone, with the main body of Helvellyn-intent folk content to ignore this peaceful outpost of the massif.

8 Though less attractive the north ridge gives an airy view over the environs of the Greenside Mine from which is may be climbed directly from the foot-bridge, juniper, half way up lending further interest to the stiff pathless grassy ascent. A pleasant green-way leads across the northern flanks of Birkhouse Moor, a

Walkers muse on the serenity of Keldas in gazing over the beautiful upper reach of Ullswater

popular alternative to Greenside Road, this leads off right from the ladder-stile, running just above the intake wall (notice at intervals the vermin trap creeps at the foot of this wall). Part way a path angles half-left up onto the adapted course of a water leat. From the rock-cut shelf where this is joined an old quarry incline trends up into Blea Cove, this is not recommended as a line of ascent; and though one may gain the north-east ridge directly here, via scree, this is certainly inferior to **7**.

ASCENT *from Patterdale*

9 From Grisedale Bridge follow the minor road leading into Grisedale, the road bends right, crosses the valley and as it bends back east, towards the hunt kennels, go through the kissing-gate, rising up the pasture bank to a hand-gate. Take the path left ascending from the wall. This heavily used path climbs, it seems for ever, via two intermediate hand-gates, to the Hole-in't-Wall stile high above Grisedale, a stirring mountain scene. Turn right following the north side of the ridge-top wall to the summit - when all instincts may be pleading with you to cross High Spying How instead!

10 The curious rambler will relish the discovery of the old green path which runs in sympathy with the modern trail. The birth of this little used option can be found by taking the footpath cutting back right after 100 yards along the fringe of old larches towards the kissing-gate in Brownend Plantation, an open sycamore woodland. Here switch back left rising over the brow. Alternatively, follow the main path bearing back right in the hollow short of the first hand-gate, zig-zagging to join the earlier path coming over the brow. The path heads west above a fence and a ragged pine copse. Where the fence turns up the fellside find a stile/hand-gate, continue up the grassy slope merging with the Mires Beck path from over the wall. Crossing a stile some forty yards above the main path, duly drifting down to converge. After a few yards a narrow, unheralded, green path bears up half-right, this is the old path ignored by the modern legions, rising through heather and bilberry. The path is slightly sunken in places, climbing in two zig-zag stages and above stone retaining edges to level approaching the Hole-in't-Wall stile *(seen below looking along the ridge to Birkhouse Moor)* and an earlier ladder-stile.

The Summit

The slender ridge wall crosses the top of the fell in such a manner as to render the actual summit out of reach of all, bar the most dedicated of peak-baggers. The grassy knoll on the south side, unmarked and rarely visited being the true summit for the purest. The loose cairn beside the popular trail to Striding Edge, is an honest and adequate compromise, though most walkers do not deign even to give it second glance as they stride on to loftier endeavours.

Wisely, the excessively worn wall-side path east of the summit has been given an indefinite sabbatical, with a new path pitched to the north. A far better place to deliberate is the north top. A path leads from this made-track, passing pools to the less trammelled and delightfully panoramic environs of the cairn.

High Spying How, Helvellyn and Catstycam from the ridge-top marsh

Safe Descents

The ridge-top wall offers deliverance for both Glenridding and Patterdale. However, do adhere to the newly engineered path east, for the former, to be ushered down Mires Beck, and for the latter, keep beside the wall to a gate/stile, there go right passing down through Brownend Plantation.

Ridge Route to....

HELVELLYN   DESCENT 110 feet   ASCENT 880 feet   2 miles

No more thrilling ridge exists for the Lakeland fell-walker. Follow the ridge wall west, where this breaks left at the Hole-in't-Wall, continue with mounting drama over the rocky crests of Low and High Spying How to test your balance or prudence on the rocky arete of Striding Edge. Put your walking poles in the pack and bring your fingers (white knuckles) into play! In deference to the pounding of incessant erosive boots treat the path with reverence. The final tower perhaps the most trying, with short chimneys down to left and right. In winter with icy rocks and a strong gale the greatest of all care is needed right along the ridge, in summer algae on the rocks has a similar slick effect - caution is valour in mountain terrain. A rough scramble culminates upon the plateau rim.

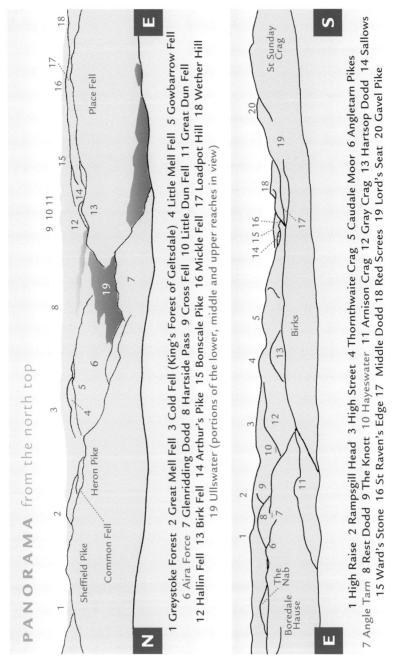

PANORAMA from the north top

N

Sheffield Pike
Common Fell
Heron Pike
Place Fell

E

1 Greystoke Forest 2 Great Mell Fell 3 Cold Fell (King's Forest of Geltsdale) 4 Little Mell Fell 5 Gowbarrow Fell
6 Aira Force 7 Glenridding Dodd 8 Hartside Pass 9 Cross Fell 10 Little Dun Fell 11 Great Dun Fell
12 Hallin Fell 13 Birk Fell 14 Arthur's Pike 15 Bonscale Pike 16 Mickle Fell 17 Loadpot Hill 18 Wether Hill
19 Ullswater (portions of the lower, middle and upper reaches in view)

S

St Sunday Crag
Birks

E

Boredale Hause
The Nab

1 High Raise 2 Rampsgill Head 3 High Street 4 Thornthwaite Crag 5 Caudale Moor 6 Angletarn Pikes
7 Angle Tarn 8 Rest Dodd 9 The Knott 10 Hayeswater 11 Arnison Crag 12 Gray Crag 13 Hartsop Dodd 14 Sallows
15 Ward's Stone 16 St Raven's Edge 17 Middle Dodd 18 Red Screes 19 Lord's Seat 20 Gavel Pike

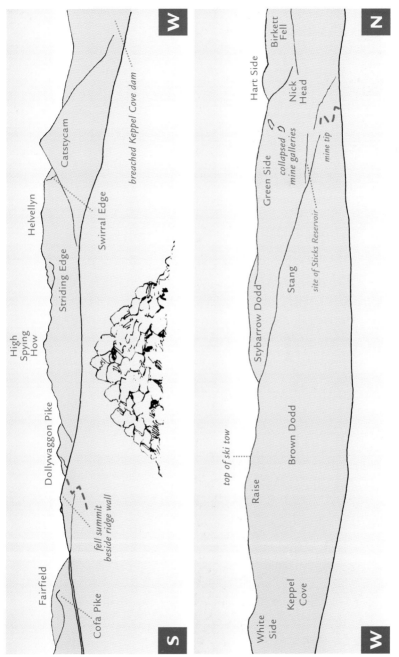

W

S

Fairfield
Cofa Pike
High Spying How
Dollywaggon Pike
fell summit beside ridge wall
Striding Edge
Helvellyn
Catstycam
Swirral Edge
breached Keppel Cove dam

N

W

White Side
Keppel Cove
Raise
top of ski tow
Brown Dodd
Stybarrow Dodd
Stang
site of Sticks Reservoir
Green Side
collapsed mine galleries
mine tip
Hart Side
Nick Head
Birkett Fell

BIRKS

In essence, Birks is little more than the broad shoulder of St Sunday Crag, a rather plain north-easterly ridge stepped down from the higher fell, holding altitude for half-a-mile before plummeting into Grisedale. It is, however, bound by crags to north and east, those frowning over Grisedale, notably the lower glacially smoothed Elmhow Buttress, a playground for eager rock-climbers. Divided from the parent fell by Cold and Blind Coves, neither hanging valleys of scenic note, its charming face being the Black Crag scarp overlooking Glemara Park. Virtually no-one sets out to climb Birks, most commonly its summit is a pleasant incidental, drawn into the descent from St Sunday Crag, even then many walkers pass the summit cairn without faltering their stride, preferring the Thornhow End viewpoint upon the head of Ullswater.

Elmhow Buttress

622 metres   2,241 feet

ASCENT *from Patterdale*

1 Via Thornhow End. Approach from Patterdale, via the Mill Moss footpath, crossing the foot of Glemara Park to meet up with a stiled footpath rising direct from the Grisedale valley road. GR 386157 Bear south climbing the steep Thornhow End ridge, rising above the open woodland skirt a crag to reach a low stile in the park wall. A grooved, heavily worn path continues. Divert almost immediately left onto the leading edge of the fell winding onto the grassy crest above Black Crag, curving south-westward to reach the summit. **2** Via Glemara Park. Initially ascend the open woodland of the Glemara Park valley to the west of Hag Beck, fording half-way up to complete the climb close to its east bank. Cross the metal ladder-stile spanning the dale-headwall, continue to where the broken wall kinks right. Climb the steep grass slope beside the broken wall, which ceases near the top.

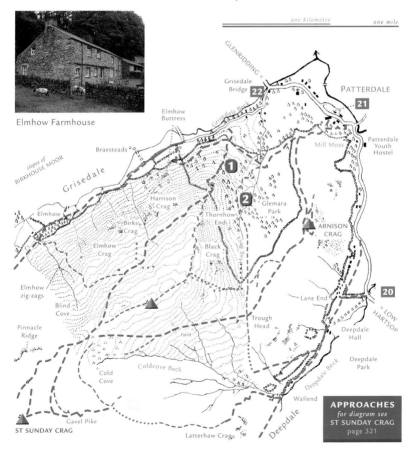

Elmhow Farmhouse

Looking east from the summit

The Summit

A timid huddle of stones marks the summit, all else is grass. If the ground is dry then lodge on the turf and soak in a pleasant enough girdle of friendly fells, particularly of the Far Eastern fells due east *(above)*.

Birks bathed in sunlight backed by St Sunday Crag in this view from Park Brow Foot

Ullswater from Thornhow End... a view to extol

Safe Descents

From this benign crest perilous crags are little suspected, even in clear conditions, but they are very real for anyone who strays north and north-east from the summit. The wisest precaution is to head E off the ridge path passing a large erratic en route to join a broken wall falling (metephorically) to the head-stream of Hag Beck. Bear left to the ladder-stile, crossing the old deer park wall at the head of Glemara Park, and accompany the beck down-dale bound for Patterdale.

Ridge Routes to....

ST SUNDAY CRAG   DESCENT 40 feet   ASCENT 770 feet   1.25 miles

A grassy ridge leads SW to the wet depression above Blind and Cold Coves. Either follow the worn highway up the ridge or ease the gradient by slanting S (half-left) with a path aiming towards the prominent shoulder of Gavel Pike, before turning to the summit on The Cape.

ARNISON CRAG   DESCENT 750 feet   ASCENT 260 feet   1.2 miles

Aim E, on finding a large white erratic boulder descend, quickly picking up a broken wall leading down to Hag Beck. Go left to the deer park wall, at the head of Glemara Park, promptly turn up right and at the wall's high point, bear up onto the grassy ridge which undulates to reach the rocky summit.

PANORAMA

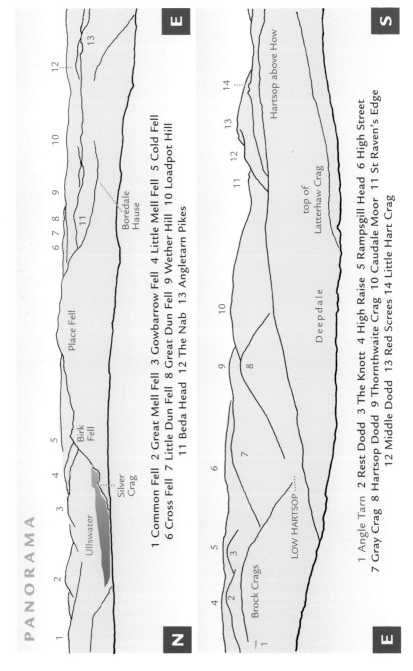

N **E**

Ullswater

1   2   3   4   5

Birk Fell

Place Fell

6 7 8   9   10   12   13

Silver Crag

11

Boredale Hause

1 Common Fell 2 Great Mell Fell 3 Gowbarrow Fell 4 Little Mell Fell 5 Cold Fell
6 Cross Fell 7 Little Dun Fell 8 Great Dun Fell 9 Wether Hill 10 Loadpot Hill
11 Beda Head 12 The Nab 13 Angletarn Pikes

E **S**

Brock Crags

LOW HARTSOP

1   2   3   4   5   6   7   8   9   10   11   12   13   14

Deepdale

top of
Latterhaw Crag

Hartsop above How

1 Angle Tarn 2 Rest Dodd 3 The Knott 4 High Raise 5 Rampsgill Head 6 High Street
7 Gray Crag 8 Hartsop Dodd 9 Thornthwaite Crag 10 Caudale Moor 11 St Raven's Edge
12 Middle Dodd 13 Red Screes 14 Little Hart Crag

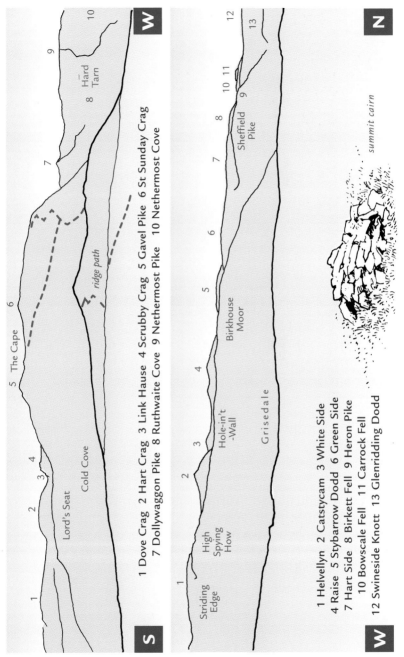

S

W

Lord's Seat

Cold Cove

1 Striding Edge   2   3   4   5 The Cape   6   7   8 Hard Tarn   9   10

ridge path

1 Dove Crag 2 Hart Crag 3 Link Hause 4 Scrubby Crag 5 Gavel Pike 6 St Sunday Crag
7 Dollywaggon Pike 8 Ruthwaite Cove 9 Nethermost Pike 10 Nethermost Cove

W

N

Striding Edge

High Spying How

Hole-in-'t-Wall

Griesdale

Birkhouse Moor

Sheffield Pike

1   2   3   4   5   6   7   8   9   10 11   12   13

summit cairn

1 Helvellyn 2 Catstycam 3 White Side
4 Raise 5 Stybarrow Dodd 6 Green Side
7 Hart Side 8 Birkett Fell 9 Heron Pike
10 Bowscale Fell 11 Carrock Fell
12 Swineside Knott 13 Glenridding Dodd

CATSTYCAM

Catstycam's elegant chiselled proportions, which lend it special distinction when viewed from afar, ensure it merits separate status, a condition denied High Spying How. The hobnail scratched dragon's spine of Swirral Edge plummets from the high plateau of Helvellyn, briefly levels, then with one exuberant leap soars to the tiny crest of Catstycam. In every sense and emotion a zenith, a real mountain peak, culminating like a sharpened Keswick pencil. Given eighty feet and a link to a nether neighbour this would be exalted as one of the finest fells in the district. Deficient of that head of rock and neck of land *(which incidentally is the origin of the name Swirral, a variation being Swirls on the Thirlmere side of the range)* the fell assumes a far more modest place. An outpost of the higher mountain, which is made the mightier for its presence.

Apart from its conical profile the other distinguishing feature is its frowning craggy north face, split by a massive scree filled gully. The dark pointed outline, admired on the long march up Glenridding Beck, is best seen from Birkhouse Moor, from where its relationship to Helvellyn may be judged, while from Raise one may know just how impressively it beetles over Keppel Cove.

Catstycam performs one notable service to the discerning walker. On a day when the top of Helvellyn is teeming, this pin prick of a place is invariably deserted, strange but true. There are three variant spellings in currency Catchedicam, Catstye Cam, and Catstycam, correctly pronounced Cat-stee-cam. The fell-name translating as *'hen-comb shaped crest, with a steep path frequented by wild cat'*. It should be understood that down the ages wild cats were detested for their ferocity towards humans, therefore it can be deduced that this feline abode was avoided!

890 metres   2,920 feet

Water and water-power were in great demand during the latter years of the local lead mining industry and the remains of three dams lie at its foot. As an intriguing quest consider tracking beside the marshy course of the water-race which contours around 730 feet from the breached concrete Keppel Cove dam, in the shadow of the north face. Find several mine rails once re-employed to make tight the leat and much rotting timber shuttering. The race crossed Red Tarn Beck by an elaborate wooden chute (now lost), traversing the slopes of Birkhouse Moor *(see rock-cut section below)* to end at a still intact stone pipe-head, from where the water sped to a turbine house below, the concrete foundations of this building and some of the supporting pillars remain.

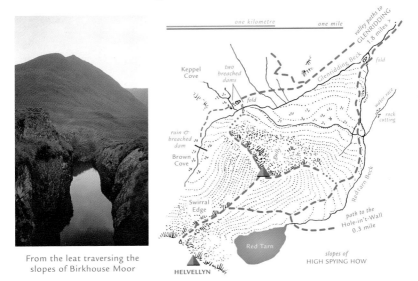

From the leat traversing the
slopes of Birkhouse Moor

Catstycam belongs exclusively to Glenridding, every drop of rain that falls on its slopes (evaporation excepted) gravitates irresistibly into Ullswater. Hence direct ascents naturally begin from the village car park.

ASCENT *from Glenridding*

Follow the tracks either side the of the valley passing beyond Greenside Mine and above a footbridge. **1** The northern route, via Greenside Road, branches left off the Sticks Pass path onto the track signed *'Helvellyn, Brown Cove and Whiteside Bank'*, veering left to cross the footbridge for southern ascents. **2** The green path, traversing the slopes of Birkhouse Moor from Rattlebeck Bridge, comes above this footbridge, the path continuing to a footbridge over Red Tarn Beck, winding up in measured engineered stages, approaching Red Tarn a path bears right to mount directly onto the eastern shoulder of Catstycam.

From the east ridge of White Side, with Brown Cove dam and tarn bottom right

This is joined from route **1** by bearing down left to cross the Glenridding Beck footbridge. The path advances upstream, crossing a footbridge opposite a large sheepfold, beyond the main confluence. A well maintained path climbs towards the corrie tarn, **3** the grassy east shoulder route branching right, becoming clearer as height is gained. The principal path joins the path from the Hole-in't-Wall slanting up to the Swirral Edge col, turning right with the ridge path to the summit.

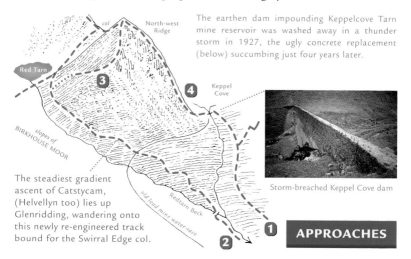

The earthen dam impounding Keppelcove Tarn mine reservoir was washed away in a thunder storm in 1927, the ugly concrete replacement (below) succumbing just four years later.

col

North-west Ridge

Red Tarn

3

4 Keppel Cove

slopes of BIRKHOUSE MOOR

Storm-breached Keppel Cove dam

The steadiest gradient ascent of Catstycam, (Helvellyn too) lies up Glenridding, wandering onto this newly re-engineered track bound for the Swirral Edge col.

old lead mine water-race

Redtarn Beck

2

1

APPROACHES

Catstycam seen as a single peak rising above
Glenridding Beck, in this view from the
Sticks Pass path running beneath Stang End,
the juniper-clothed east ridge-end of Raise.

4 The most challenging line, holds company with the bridle track - kept in good order for mountain rescue vehicles. This route was developed as the main line of ascent for Helvellyn when tourists travelled on pony-back with trusted local guides. Keeping in harmony with the beck, advance to the concrete dam. With alacrity one may stride over the dam, alternatively with a stiff breeze apply a modicum of caution, fording the beck, clambering to the far end, climbing the ensuing bank to a terrace (former dam building track). Now slant up the slope to the right, a scouring of scree intimating the first traces of the path onto the north-west ridge. For all its initial unassailable appearance the ridge (and path) become more sure as height is gained, capitulating relatively meekly, the steady climb duly rewarded by an head in the clouds climax.

From the eastern shoulder of Raise, with St Sunday Crag to the left and Helvellyn in dark silhouette right

Pink-tinted rock at the summit, looking to High Spying How

The Summit

A transitory cairn, as tiny as the summit, confirms the highest point. It is a measure of the place that no sturdy column has been built, for the fell was so fashioned by nature as to render a man-made pile a ridiculous adjunct. Rock and grass fight for every inch yet afford plenty of scope for sitting, as sit you will to feast your eyes on this the most stirring amphitheatre of the fell domain.

Safe Descents

Any lurch to the north is perilous. Both southern approaches are safe enough. For Glenridding choose the eastern shoulder path, ensuring a right-hand bias. For Patterdale, and added indemnity, opt for the ridge path leading south-west down to the col short of Swirral Edge, there track left to ford Red Tarn Beck, contouring to the Hole-in't-Wall.

Ridge Route to....

HELVELLYN   DESCENT 320 feet   ASCENT 516 feet   0.9 miles

Head SW down the ridge to the col. The path now becomes progressively more inveigled with splintered rock and tends to keep to the left of the spine, as rock dominates and hands come into play on this wonderfully simple scramble up Swirral Edge. Notice the fine view of both Helvellyn's shattered east face, Water Crag to the right and the excessive amount of hobnail scratching on the rocks proving the popularity of this route throughout the long age of fellwalking fashion. Reaching the cairn on the scarp brink, turn left SE to reach the triangulation column.

Looking down the jagged arete of Swirral Edge to Catstycam

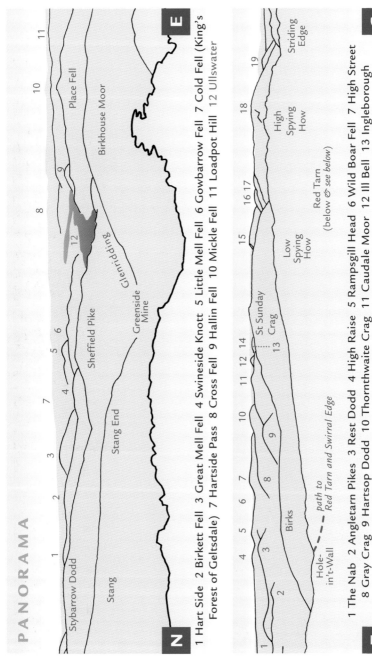

PANORAMA

N / E

Stybarrow Dodd — Stang — Stang End — Sheffield Pike — Greenside Mine — Glenridding — Birkhouse Moor — Place Fell

1 Hart Side 2 Birkett Fell 3 Great Mell Fell 4 Swineside Knott 5 Little Mell Fell 6 Gowbarrow Fell 7 Cold Fell (King's Forest of Geltsdale) 7 Hartside Pass 8 Cross Fell 9 Hallin Fell 10 Mickle Fell 11 Loadpot Hill 12 Ullswater

E / S

Birks — Hole-in't-Wall — path to Red Tarn and Swirral Edge — St Sunday Crag — Low Spying How — High Spying How — Red Tarn (below & see below) — Striding Edge

1 The Nab 2 Angletarn Pikes 3 Rest Dodd 4 High Raise 5 Rampsgill Head 6 Wild Boar Fell 7 High Street 8 Gray Crag 9 Hartsop Dodd 10 Thornthwaite Crag 11 Caudale Moor 12 Ill Bell 13 Ingleborough 14 Yoke 15 Red Screes 16 Dove Crag 17 Hart Crag 18 Fairfield 19 Great Rigg

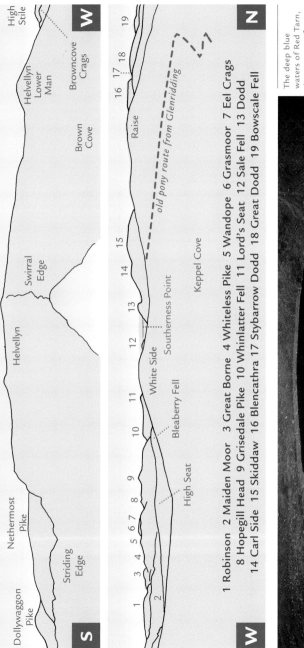

W / S panel (upper skyline): High Stile · Helvellyn Lower Man · Browncove Crags · Brown Cove · Swirral Edge · Helvellyn · Nethermost Pike · Dollywaggon Pike · Striding Edge

N / W panel (lower skyline): Raise · old pony route from Glenridding · White Side · Southerness Point · Keppel Cove · Bleaberry Fell · High Seat

1 Robinson 2 Maiden Moor 3 Great Borne 4 Whiteless Pike 5 Wandope 6 Grasmoor 7 Eel Crags 8 Hopegill Head 9 Grisedale Pike 10 Whinlatter Fell 11 Lord's Seat 12 Sale Fell 13 Dodd 14 Carl Side 15 Skiddaw 16 Blencathra 17 Stybarrow Dodd 18 Great Dodd 19 Bowscale Fell

The deep blue waters of Red Tarn, the name a reference to the pink-hued screes which spill from Catstycam. Its earlier British name was Helfa-llyn 'high lake of the hunting-ground'.

CLOUGH HEAD

The fell-name means *'headland the ravine'*, alluding to either Beckthorns or Sandbed Gills, eye-catching gullies draining the craggy western slopes. Further intriguing local place-names are Threlkeld, which translates as *'the spring of the serf'*, the first element appearing in the modern word enthral *'to hold enslaved'*, and the farm Wanthwaite means *'the clearing where the aromatic herb angelica was grown.*

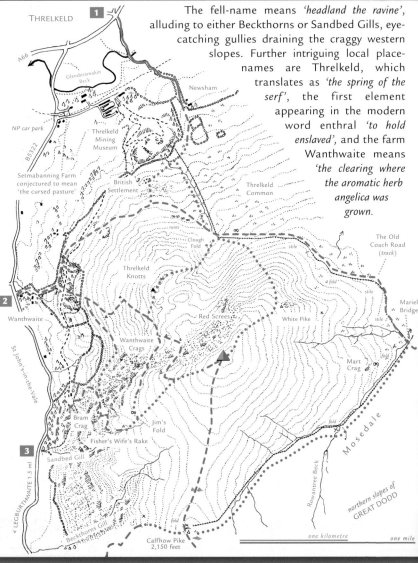

THRELKELD

1

A66

Glenderamakin Beck

Newsham

NP car park

B5322

Threlkeld Mining Museum

Setmabanning Farm conjectured to mean 'the cursed pasture'

British Settlement

Threlkeld Common

The Old Coach Road (track)

ruins

Clough Fold

stile

Threlkeld Knotts

fold

stile

2

Wanthwaite

Red Screes

White Pike

Mariel Bridge

stile

St John's-in-the-Vale

Wanthwaite Crags

Mart Crag

fold

Bram Crag

Jim's Fold

fold

Mosedale

3

Fisher's Wife's Rake

Sandbed Gill

< LEGBURTHWAITE 1.5 ml

Rowantree Beck

northern slopes of GREAT DODD

Beckthorns Gill

fold

one kilometre

one mile

Calfhow Pike 2,150 feet

726 metres   2,386 feet

From Bleaberry Fell

The arresting prow of Clough Head differs from the established pattern of the range in one significant respect, its crags line the western, rather than eastern slopes. These buttresses, forming one side of the dramatic view of Blencathra through St John's Vale, entice paragliders who can frequently be seen chasing along this façade gaining lift from scarp thermals, having launched from the Old Coach Road. Arguably the best fell-walking moments also focus upon these crags, with Fisher's Wife's Rake and the traverse of Buck Castle special delights.

Clough Head is both the final nail on the 20-mile end-to-end ridge walk from either Ambleside or Kirkstone Pass and the first bag on the popular 12-mile grassy round of the Dodd's, destination Dockray, with the promise of a well-earned cask ale crowned with a hearty bar snack at the Royal Hotel.

FISHER'S WIFE'S RAKE
dashes practical route,
dots original route, now degenerated.

Wanthwaite and Bram Crags from above Bridge House

The fell cradles important history too. The Threlkeld British Settlement has survived remarkably intact since desertion soon after the Romano-British period: the inspiration for the Longbarrow project at Flusco. The adjacent Threlkeld Granite Quarry has been re-developed by Ian Hartland and his team of enthusiasts incorporating Ian and Jean Tyler's mining museum from Caldbeck. The combined exhibition vividly reveals the triumphs and tribulations of the diverse quarrying and mining industries central to the economic and social fabric of the district prior to the advent of tourism.

ASCENT *from Wanthwaite*

1 Via Fisher's Wife's Rake. This ingenious route is named after the Fisher's of Rake How. The husband cut peat on the moor above Wanthwaite Crags leaving it to dry, whereupon his wife hauled it down this perilous rock and scree rake upon a hand-sled - hard climbs in harsh climes. The direct approach begins from the valley road at GR 319219. Pass the barrier and follow the old quarry track which promptly switches left, rising by conifer bedecked spoil banks. Take the main track right, aiming towards the dis-used Bramcrag Quarry, after a few yards deflect left on the green path, beneath a shed. Cross the mineral line track-bed; mounting the bank to a hand-gate at the point where the quarry bounding fence meets the intake wall. Avoiding scree trend left just above the wall (the original direct sled-gate is now lost under the scree), until well above the wall junction. Climb directly up to the foot of Wanthwaite Crags. A well defined sheep path converges from the left (this can be adopted as an alternative contouring

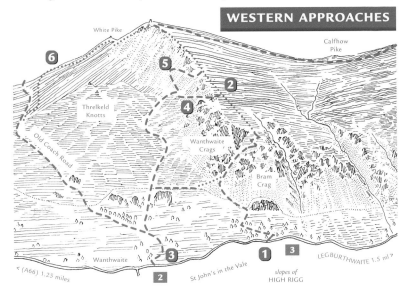

WESTERN APPROACHES

approach from the ladder-stile sited above Hilltop Quarries). Clinging to the under-cliff, the path deftly avoids further scree to re-unite with the original sled-gate in picking up a grass path zig-zagging onto easier ground at the head of Sandbed Gill. The views across the crag face towards Skiddaw and Blencathra well reward the exertion. The path fades into the rushes approaching Jim's Fold.

2 From the vicinity of Jim's Fold a simple grassy plod north-eastward leads to the summit.

3 More orthodox ascents begin from Wanthwaite GR 316231 via the Old Coach Road, signposted *'Matterdale, unsuitable for motor vehicles'*. Follow the gated lane flanked by a shelter belt, rising beyond Hilltop Farm as a walled lane. Watch for the small

The lower section of Fisher's Wife's Rake

Thirlmere from above Beckthorns Gill

stile on the right at the left-hand bend, with the thump-thump of an hydraulic ram over the wall to the left. Clamber up a hollow beside a spoil bank to the level green track, bear half-right after 25 yards cross the second track-bed. Take the path up beside the young conifers and a light fence shielding the edge of Spion Kop Quarry to a ladder-stile, continuing uphill to a ladder-stile in the intake wall. Notice the adjacent sheep-creep in line with the path off the fell which runs on to be lost over the quarry rim. Either contour right, bound for Fisher's Wife's Rake, or ascend the peat sled-gate. At the second bend it splits with two paths running parallel up through a shallow cutting. A thin path bears left aiming for the top of Threlkeld Knotts, a fine viewpoint, while the sled-gate leads on to face two optional lines to the skyline.

4 The first branches off the sled-gate, contouring on a narrow trod to the base of the scree. Upon reaching an eroded section of earthy scree angle left; keep on the top side, clambering up to the prominent stumpy shoulder of Buck Castle, a reminder of the days when goats grazed the crags to discourage sheep from the perilous ledges. Avoid the contouring sheep path, which is consistently less comfortable. From Buck Castle contour above Wanthwaite Crags enjoying exciting views down the gullies into the sylvan strath of St John's-in-the-Vale. On reaching grass the path becomes indistinct on the approach to Jim's Fold.

5 The upper route stays with the cairned path to the foot of the scree. Switching right on a diagonal traverse cross two fans of loose scree to the cairn on the scarp brink. **6** The White Pike route is more commonly the objective of ascents from Threlkeld though the Old Coach Road provides a steadier start to the day from Wanthwaite. This line is perhaps best reserved as a crag-free descent in mist.

Blencathra from White Pike

Ill-suited to modern off-road four-wheel drive traffic the Old Coach Road (track) is badly rutted here at Hause Well Brow and later approaching Mariel Bridge. The principal sufferers from their visitations being the colony of frogs living otherwise contented lives notably along Barbary Rigg.

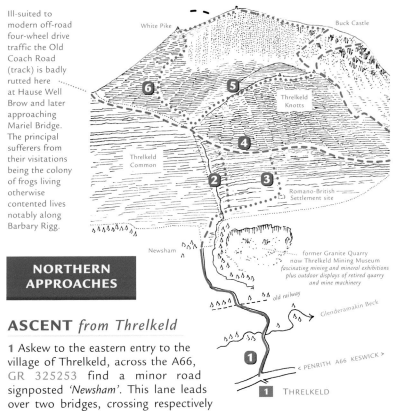

NORTHERN APPROACHES

ASCENT *from Threlkeld*

1 Askew to the eastern entry to the village of Threlkeld, across the A66, GR 325253 find a minor road signposted *'Newsham'*. This lane leads over two bridges, crossing respectively the Glenderamakin and the track-bed of the former Penrith-Cockermouth Railway (which may yet be revived). Short of the entrance to Newsham, go through the fence gate to the right joining a rough track in equally rough pasture. Ascend with the tree-screened Threlkeld Quarry on the right, glancing by a small walled enclosure on damp ground curve right to a gate in the fence.

2 Bear left, ascending to the right of the gill to gain the Old Coach Road. **3** Although the British Settlement site can be visited at this point, many walkers will be more inclined to save the inspection of this fascinating survival for the descent. Lying some 300 yards west on a stony shelf, with what appear contemporary droveways leading to east and west, the Threlkeld Settlement is at least two thousand years old. It functioned as a pastoral farming community, though deserted during Romano-British times, strong outlines of hut circles and stock compounds are still extant. An unruly litter of glacial rocks surrounds the site, a confusion that has contributed to holding its integrity preventing clearance for agricultural improvement. Ascend direct from the site to reach the Old Coach Road.

White Pike, Clough Head and Threlkeld Knotts from Scales

4 Follow the open track left passing the foundations of four stone structures of unknown purpose and date. Approaching a gate two options occur. **5** Either bear right passing Clough Fold, swinging up the stony ridge onto Threlkeld Knotts' northernmost crest. Small cairns mark the two minor tops of this underling height. This sub-edge route connecting in natural fashion to the drove path from Wanthwaite. **6** Alternatively, pass to the right of the gate on a green path angling above the fence parallel with the track. Branch off at personal inclination onto the wide, indefinite ridge keeping left of the scree. The subsidiary outcrop of White Pike can be ignored en route to the summit, though there is no merit in such an action, for this rocky shoulder is a splendid viewpoint, possibly more conducive for a prolonged contemplation than the actual fell top. Travellers, and this includes the now unwelcome four-wheelers wending along the Coach Road, can be surveyed as from a sentry post.

Threlkeld British Settlement looking east

The Summit

A stunted windbreak clings to the stone-built Ordnance Survey pillar marking the summit. To the south the fell drifts gently away as an upland sheep pasture, while northwards, beware, a great scree slope plummets from close to the column. It is largely as a viewpoint that Clough Head excels, offering sneak glimpses of both Morecambe Bay and the Solway Firth, a gracious sweep of central Lakeland and, as its piece de resistance, Blencathra, the one true mountain in the Northern Fells, with a fistful of tempting ridges culminating on Hall's Fell Top. If you have time make a point of visiting White Pike, a far better spot for a quiet comtemplation of all things fell scenic.

Old triangulation column and wind-break

Safe Descents

As a rule of thumb Clough Head is precipitously craggy to the west and crag-free to the east, so the sane course of action in poor visibility is to head for the subsidiary summit of White Pike and the Old Coach Road. NB: there are stiles evenly dispersed along the bounding plain multi-wire fence between Mariel Bridge and Clough Fold to effect access to the track. Western approaches make poor escapes in anything but fine weather, Fisher's Wife's Rake especially difficult to fix even when Jim's Fold has been located. How many fellwalkers have cowered in its crude shelter perplexed their next move? From Calfhow Pike the dreary hollow of Mosedale is an assured line of descent, for all that it puts one some three miles from a motor road, east or west.

Ridge Route to....

GREAT DODD DESCENT 330 feet   ASCENT 755 feet   2 miles

A clear path leads SSW over the grassy prairie bound for the lonely outcrop of Calfhow Pike. As a isle in an ocean this moment of excitement merits a pause in your stride. The place-name means *'rocks where hinds loitered with their calves'* indicative of the historic liberty of red deer. Beyond pass by pools, result of peat extraction, before angling SE on a worn path climbing without distractive interest glancing by the cairn on Little Dodd, curving NE to the cairn on the bald summit GR 342205.

PANORAMA

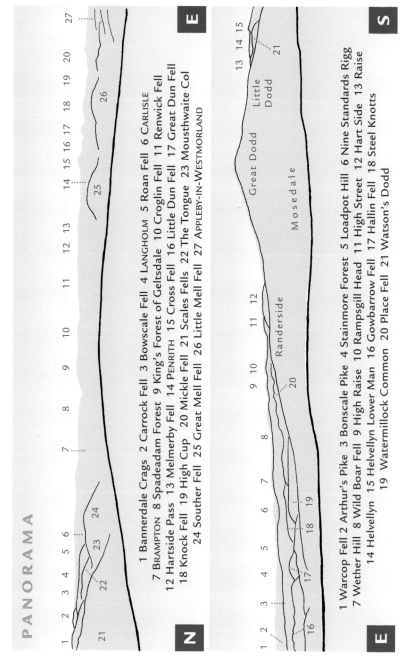

N

1 Bannerdale Crags 2 Carrock Fell 3 Bowscale Fell 4 LANGHOLM 5 Roan Fell 6 CARLISLE
7 BRAMPTON 8 Spadeadam Forest 9 King's Forest of Geltsdale 10 Croglin Fell 11 Renwick Fell
12 Hartside Pass 13 Melmerby Fell 14 PENRITH 15 Cross Fell 16 Little Dun Fell 17 Great Dun Fell
18 Knock Fell 19 High Cup 20 Mickle Fell 21 Scales Fells 22 The Tongue 23 Mousthwaite Col
24 Souther Fell 25 Great Mell Fell 26 Little Mell Fell 27 APPLEBY-IN-WESTMORLAND

E

1 Warcop Fell 2 Arthur's Pike 3 Bonscale Pike 4 Stainmore Forest 5 Loadpot Hill 6 Nine Standards Rigg
7 Wether Hill 8 Wild Boar Fell 9 High Raise 10 Rampsgill Head 11 High Street 12 Hart Side 13 Raise
14 Helvellyn 15 Helvellyn Lower Man 16 Gowbarrow Fell 17 Hallin Fell 18 Steel Knotts
19 Watermillock Common 20 Place Fell 21 Watson's Dodd

S

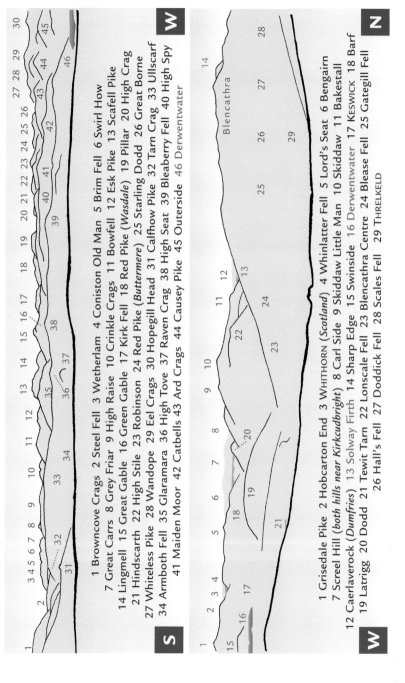

S — **W**

1 Browncove Crags 2 Steel Fell 3 Wetherlam 4 Coniston Old Man 5 Brim Fell 6 Swirl How 7 Great Carrs 8 Grey Friar 9 High Raise 10 Crinkle Crags 11 Bowfell 12 Esk Pike 13 Scafell Pike 14 Lingmell 15 Great Gable 16 Green Gable 17 Kirk Fell 18 Red Pike (*Wasdale*) 19 Pillar 20 High Crag 21 Hindscarth 22 High Stile 23 Robinson 24 Red Pike (*Buttermere*) 25 Starling Dodd 26 Great Borne 27 Whiteless Pike 28 Wandope 29 Eel Crags 30 Hopegill Head 31 Calfhow Pike 32 Tarn Crag 33 Ullscarf 34 Armboth Fell 35 Glaramara 36 High Tove 37 Raven Crag 38 High Seat 39 Bleaberry Fell 40 High Spy 41 Maiden Moor 42 Catbells 43 Ard Crags 44 Causey Pike 45 Outerside 46 Derwentwater

N — **W**

Blencathra

1 GriSedale Pike 2 Hobcarton End 3 WHITHORN (*Scotland*) 4 Whinlatter Fell 5 Lord's Seat 6 Bengairn 7 Screel Hill (*both hills near Kirkcudbright*) 8 Carl Side 9 Skiddaw Little Man 10 Skiddaw 11 Bakestall 12 Caerlaverock (*Dumfries*) 13 Solway Firth 14 Sharp Edge 15 Swinside 16 Derwentwater 17 KESWICK 18 Barf 19 Latrigg 20 Dodd 21 Tewit Tarn 22 Lonscale Fell 23 Blencathra Centre 24 Blease Fell 25 Gategill Fell 26 Hall's Fell 27 Doddick Fell 28 Scales Fell 29 THRELKELD

DOLLYWAGGON PIKE

Place-names normally have descriptive origins, through language and dialect change, the original form alters and the meaning can be lost within a few generations. Hence the crazy form in which this fell-name has been conveyed down the centuries, on face value descriptive of a pram or some small miners' truck. Scandinavian settlers, who gazed up Grisedale, apparently alikened the fell's forbidding headwall to an elevated giant, consequently attributing it the name *'Dolr vegin's peak'*.

While the common frailty of the range, barren western slopes, is sustained, Dollywaggon's eastern facade exhibits great ferocity and, in this dimension, is a fully fledged mountain richly rewarding detailed exploration and respectful admiration.

The east ridge is a walker's delight climbing to the surest of mountain summits. Overlooking the upper section of Grisedale are two mighty cliffs, Falcon and Tarn Crags, split by near vertical gullies, that should not be tested by walkers. Tucked high under the south ridge, Cock Cove is a truly wild sanctuary, the name indicating the former lek or display ground of black grouse. The absence of paths confirm that few walkers venture into this hanging valley.

The fell has suffered in recent years from the sheer volume of pounding feet, especially those chasing off the massif, such short-cuts grossly eroding the path down to Grisedale Tarn. Relays of rock have been hauled and set in the higher scarred sections to give a measure of stability and eventually some hope of recovery, and walkers gently coaxed back onto the old zig-zag path, with judicious pitching securing footing.

858 metres   2,815 feet

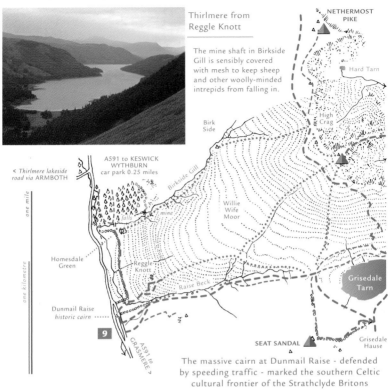

Thirlmere from
Reggle Knott

The mine shaft in Birkside
Gill is sensibly covered
with mesh to keep sheep
and other woolly-minded
intrepids from falling in.

NETHERMOST
PIKE

Hard Tarn

High
Crag

Birk
Side

Birkside Gill

A591 to KESWICK
WYTHBURN
car park 0.25 miles

< Thirlmere lakeside
road via ARMBOTH

one mile

one kilometre

falls · mine

Willie
Wife
Moor

Homesdale
Green

Reggle
Knott

Raise Beck

Grisedale
Tarn

Dunmail Raise
historic cairn · · · · · ·

9

A591 to CRASMERE >

SEAT SANDAL

Grisedale
Hause

The massive cairn at Dunmail Raise - defended
by speeding traffic - marked the southern Celtic
cultural frontier of the Strathclyde Britons

ASCENT *from Dunmail Raise*

Western approaches may be deficient in eye-catching detail, but give quick access to the main ridge. **1** The more usual route keeps close company with Raise Beck. The prime path leads from a ladder-stile at the dual-carriageway section of the A591 *(verge parking or lay-by 400 yards to the south)*. This leads beside the old bed of the beck, which was diverted to enhance the flow into Thirlmere. Brushing through the early bracken, the worn path enters the narrow valley as a sure staircase, with views of several fine cascades en route to the valley head. The valley withers to a nondescript pass, with the sombre bowl of Grisedale Tarn suddenly spread below, the path trends down, keeping above the tarn, across intermittently boggy ground.

Either **2** link up with the popular path out of Grisedale, switching left before the outflow of the tarn. Excessively used as a descent from Helvellyn, the scoured scree section at mid-height has been annexed, with huge boulders forming the basis of a stout path. Coming close to the escarpment, leave the cairned thoroughfare, and follow the edge to the summit. **3** Alternatively, bear off left closer the tarn on a rougher

one kilometre   *one mile*

NETHERMOST PIKE

Grisedale

Ruthwaite Lodge
Climbers' Hut

Hard Tarn

Ruthwaite
Cove

Ruthwaite Beck

High
Crag

The Tongue

Cock Cove

Grisedale Beck

Falcon Crag

Tarn Crag

Brothers' Parting

Grisedale
Tarn

slopes of FAIRFIELD

slopes of
SEAT SANDAL

Grisedale Hause

NETHERMOST PIKE

High
Crag

Falcon
Crag

Tarn
Crag

2

3

Willie Wife
Moor

5

Grisedale Tarn

Birkside Gill

6

4

Raise Beck

< KESWICK
A591

1

9

Dunmail
Raise

GRASMERE >

**WESTERN
APPROACHES**

route clinging to the edge above Tarn Crag. Above this three deep gullies, unsafe as lines of ascent out of Grisedale, give sensational downward views.

4 As a variant start, follow the fence left to a kissing-gate in the wall, close to the road and adjacent the Dunmail Raise cairn. Angle part right to a broad foot-bridge over Raise Beck and as the wall bends left, by a footpath sign, go right, with little better than a sheep path through the bracken. Closing in on the wall watch for a path switching up left this makes quick shrift of the bracken in climbing above Reggle Knott for a pleasing view down to Helm Crag and the Grasmere Vale. There are two old shepherd's paths up to this edge of Willie Wife Moor, as they faint, keep a contouring line with the merest hint of a path, this is lost at the deep tributary. One may continue to the head of Raise Beck or, **5** follow the gill uneventfully due north-east, crossing the Helvellyn path, to reach the summit.

6 Birkside Gill offers a more intriguing and solitary line of ascent. Follow the permissive path which leads north from Dunmail Raise, having crossed the Raise Beck footbridge, this accompanies the intake wall down towards forestry. The green way passes close under a small larch spinney to reach a footbridge spanning Birkside Gill. Deflect up the steep south bank, admiring the succession of falls. As the valley constricts, see the old fern draped

Two graceful waterfalls in Birkside Gill

copper mine adit on the far bank beside the wall corner. Pass a necessarily sturdy net protected shaft on the near bank, perhaps spotting tiny galena chips in the immediate vicinity. Scree on the north slope keeps progress to the south bank. Where the gill kinks left an old cairn is passed. Keep beside the diminishing watercourse rising above its spring, then by the remains of a small bield to the col. Go right, either over the rough intermediary top, or with the broad path to divert up left to the summit.

ASCENT *from Grisedale*

Forming a deep 'U' shaped valley trough, the glacial erosion that fashioned Grisedale conclusively separated the Helvellyn massif from the Fairfield section of the range.

7 Approaches begin from the village of Patterdale, with good tracks running on either side of this handsome valley, converging short of Ruthwaite Lodge (climbers' hut). The upper part of the journey is littered with large erratic boulders. **8** Pass behind the hut finding an old path slanting

Dollywaggon Pike from Brownend Plantation in lower Grisedale

EASTERN APPROACHES

Ruthwaite Lodge - climbers' bothy

up beside Spout Crag to accompany the cascades of Ruthwaite Gill. Find a comparatively early grassy weakness onto the ridge left, do not delay hoping for better ground higher up Ruthwaite Cove, it does not occur. The Tongue ridge is a series of rocky steps, with the hint of a path as assurance. **9** The more adventurous will find Cock Cove worthy of their quest. Continue on the popular path beyond Ruthwaite Lodge passing under Spout Crag, seeking the tumbling Cockcove Gill. This is no ordinary gill climb, the watercourse having spilt over an awesome crag, makes down a boulder slope to the path. Therefore, take a leftward slant to overcome what must be the actual spout crag. Grassy ground can be found leading above the crag and into the narrow defile of the gill, no path. Where the gill seeps out of a peaty hollow (vestige of a tarn), trend right, over the peat hags, to gain The Tongue ridge.

10 The popular and most secure ascent continues above and beyond the Brothers'

Tarn Crag and Falcon Crag from Cofa Pike

Parting Rock and Grisedale Tarn outflow to embark on a steady zig-zag climb (route **2** from Dunmail Raise).

The Summit

A small cairn marks the summit, a larger pile lies some thirty yards to the west on a broadening of the ridge. The view, particularly across Ruthwaite Cove, is stupendiferous - go on tell me there isn't such a word - well there sure is a breathtaking view the stuff of hairy-chested fells!

Safe Descents

There is security in sticking to the main zig-zagging path down to Grisedale Tarn for either Patterdale or Dunmail Raise. A pathless SW line encounters the Raise Beck path. But on no account consider trekking down The Tongue.

Ridge Routes to....

NETHERMOST PIKE   DESCENT 163 feet   ASCENT 170 feet   1 mile

In fair weather follow the edge N over High Crag. In blustery or dismal conditions bear NW to join the broad path ultimately destined for Helvellyn, taking a NE turn after 750 yards passing a wind-break cairn to the summit.

SEAT SANDAL   DESCENT 922 feet   ASCENT 532 feet   1.3 miles

The literal ridge has no form, nor path. The better practise is to descend to the outflow of Grisedale Tarn, follow the path SW to Grisedale Hause and the abrupt ridge, beside the wall, ESE.

Cock & Ruthwaite Coves from St Sunday Crag

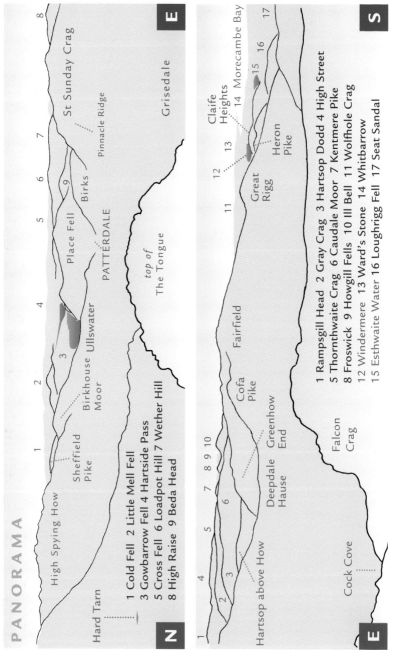

PANORAMA

E

St Sunday Crag

Pinnacle Ridge

Grisedale

8

7

Place Fell

Birks

PATTERDALE

6

5

Birkhouse Moor

Ullswater

4

3

top of The Tongue

2

Sheffield Pike

1

High Spying How

Hard Tarn

N

1 Cold Fell 2 Little Mell Fell
3 Gowbarrow Fell 4 Hartside Pass
5 Cross Fell 6 Loadpot Hill 7 Wether Hill
8 High Raise 9 Beda Head

S

Morecambe Bay

17

16 15

Claife Heights

14

13

12

11

Great Rigg

Heron Pike

Fairfield

Cofa Pike

Greenhow End

Deepdale Hause

10 9 8 7

6

5

4 3 2 1

Hartsop above How

Falcon Crag

Cock Cove

E

1 Rampsgill Head 2 Gray Crag 3 Hartsop Dodd 4 High Street
5 Thornthwaite Crag 6 Caudale Moor 7 Kentmere Pike
8 Froswick 9 Howgill Fells 10 Ill Bell 11 Wolfhole Crag
12 Windermere 13 Ward's Stone 14 Whitbarrow
15 Esthwaite Water 16 Loughrigg Fell 17 Seat Sandal

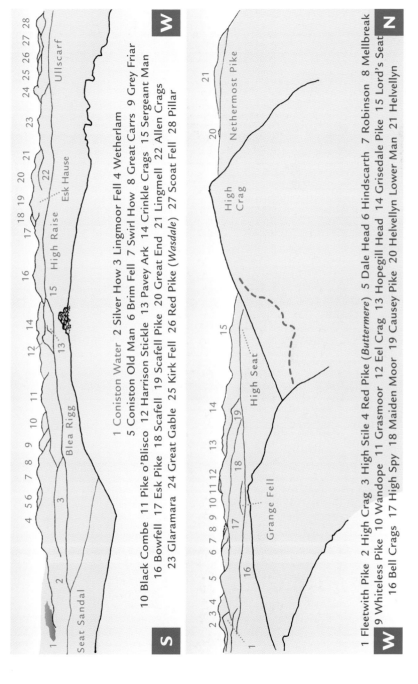

W

N

S

1 Coniston Water 2 Silver How 3 Lingmoor Fell 4 Wetherlam
5 Coniston Old Man 6 Brim Fell 7 Swirl How 8 Great Carrs 9 Grey Friar
10 Black Combe 11 Pike o'Blisco 12 Harrison Stickle 13 Pavey Ark 14 Crinkle Crags 15 Sergeant Man
16 Bowfell 17 Esk Pike 18 Scafell 19 Scafell Pike 20 Great End 21 Lingmell 22 Allen Crags
23 Glaramara 24 Great Gable 25 Kirk Fell 26 Red Pike (Wasdale) 27 Scoat Fell 28 Pillar

Ullscarf

Esk Hause

High Raise

Blea Rigg

Seat Sandal

Nethermost Pike

High Crag

High Seat

Grange Fell

1 Fleetwith Pike 2 High Crag 3 High Stile 4 Red Pike (Buttermere) 5 Dale Head 6 Hindscarth 7 Robinson 8 Mellbreak
9 Whiteless Pike 10 Wandope 11 Grasmoor 12 Eel Crag 13 Hopegill Head 14 Grisedale Pike 15 Lord's Seat
16 Bell Crags 17 High Spy 18 Maiden Moor 19 Causey Pike 20 Helvellyn Lower Man 21 Helvellyn

DOVE CRAG

Familiar to travellers passing the Brotherswater Inn on the Kirkstone road, Dove Crag forms the rugged backdrop to Dovedale. Bestowed a romantic name, symbolising peace, it is one of the fiercest, and therefore to climbers' most compelling crags in Lakeland. Cradling rough coves of stirring beauty, here is a fell with mystique. Akin a hooded monk, head shrouded in a habit, on all other fronts it lacks characterful form. To walkers whose only acquaintance comes during the Fairfield Horseshoe, the rather plain summit is of little moment.

Yet many fells would give their right rigg for Dove Crag's eastern face, guarding a tangle of knobbly ridges. The fell owes its enchanting name to a single crag, renown for its firm rock, a sheer, almost overhanging cliff, invariably shrouded in shadow, hence the name Dove, deriving from the Celtic 'Ddu' for dark place. Unlike almost every other such mighty feature in Lakeland, Dove Crag offers itself, not only to the boldest

792 metres   2,599 feet

climbers, but remarkably too, sure-footed walkers, for, perched high on its northern face, from every angle apparently unassailable, until the approach path out of Houndshope Cove is directly underfoot, is found the Priest's Hole cave *(left)*. Considered of natural origin, this lateral recess offers the most thrilling balcony imaginable peering directly into Hunsett Cove, but its situation is not for the timid. Hunsett Cove is thought to have been the crater of a long silent volcano, and is littered with huge boulders spilt from the crag and henged by knobbly ridges culminating in the upper cleft of Hogget Gill, the principal middle-ground feature in the fell portrait opposite, itself no place for the walker ill-disposed to balancing acts on short rock pitches.

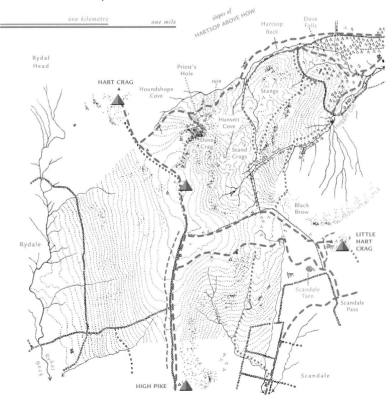

Dovedale from the head of Hogget Gill

ASCENT *from Brothers Water*

There are two starting points. **1** From the Cowbridge car park a delight-ful embowered track leads by Brothers Water, via gates, to pass Hartsop Hall. **2** Alternatively, a bridle-track embarks from the Brotherswater Inn (car parking for patrons) passing through the Sykeside Camping Site,

EASTERN APPROACHES

also via gates. From the Hall a track leads by the outbarn and stock pen. As the larch spinney is passed two options occur. **3** Bear off the track part-right onto the green-way this leads via gates under the spoil banks of the old Hartsop Hall Lead Mine abandoned in 1942 after at least four hundred years exploitation. Running on with a wall left the path rises gently through woodland to emerge at a hand-gate above Dove Falls and almost directly beneath Dovedale Slabs, seen high above.

4 The track may be followed beyond an outbarn, continue across a flat meadow to a plank footbridge spanning Hartsop Beck. A clear path winds up through the bracken, crossing a further small gill, keeping in harmony with the principal beck

to view Dove Falls rising to a hand-gate. Hold by the wall to view the upper falls, then, where the old metal fence meets the wall, go with the fence to pass a large erratic beside the beck and ford joining the main valley path above the north bank *(view right to Dove Crag)*. Showing the pounded effects of its popularity, this path leads steadily up into Hunsett Cove and, as it begins the steeper part of its ascent, portions have been pitched, much work remains. Passing a ruin, thought to have been the retreat of a pillaried religious sect, the path climbs a loose gully, an uncomfortable passage, emerging onto the peaty shoulder close below the precipitous cliff of Dove Crag. In fair weather walkers, with a head of heights, may diverge to inspect

Priest's Hole. The approach path is not too difficult to find. Bear half-left from the solitary erratic boulder, up the grass bank and boulder scree to find a path leading onto the cliff, until underfoot it looks highly improbable, but once begun there are no hazards until the cave is reached: the fore-shelf offers no security to a precipitous six hundred foot! Please respect the climbers' metal casket which holds a visitors book and bare provisions for benighted tigers This should on no account be tampered with. The cave may have been a place of last recourse deep into pre-history, long may it be adored and respected. Retrace your steps to resume the steady ascent of Houndshope Cove to meet the broken wall turning left (SE) to reach the summit.

Bleached splintered plateau outcropping above Dove Crag

There are two further little used lines out of Dovedale. **5** Approaching the Dovedale meadow ford the broad beck on a track which leads to a gate. Pass the old sheep-wash and fold with no sign of a path passing up the flood spill to reach the foot of Hoggett Gill. Unless you have an aptitude for scrambling don't enter the bouldery embowered ravine. Although this begins easily, where a side-gill cleft enters from the south Hoggett Gill encounters a rock-band and tumbles down a sequence of confined falls. To avoid this, keep to the bracken ridge on the right, clamber up the initial outcrop follow the sheep track up the low ridge beside the deeply incised gill (yes, sheep do wander uphill sometimes!). Where the second, open gill enters from the south descend left on a sheep trod and ford Hoggett Gill. Ascend the side gill keeping to the left fork to gain the steeply rising fellside. The blunt rigg, though rocky in parts offers no barrier to a steady climb to the brink of Black Brow. Follow the broken fence right (west) rising onto the main ridge, keeping right upon reaching the ridge wall to the summit. **6** Arguably the best kept secret is the Stand Crags ridge, as secret it must be, with no evidence of a path. Diverge left from the Dove Falls route at the point where the fence meets the wall corner. Follow the wall contouring, then slightly rising, across the shoulder of Stangs. At the point the wall crosses the ridge and shapes to plummet into the Hogget Gill valley, bear right up the ridge, initially with bracken left, weave up by a crag to top a broken wall continuing to crest the Stand Crags ridge on grass. Joining the fence cross the head of the Hogget Gill ravine, marvelling in a fabulous view into Dovedale and towards the white-washed Brotherswater Inn. Follow the old fence to the Black Brow fence junction, again turn right to complete the ascent onto Dove Crag.

Descent towards Hartsop Hall

ASCENT *from Ambleside*

There are two basic lines of approach each beginning from the Rydal Road car park. **7** The principal and most entertaining route, adopted on the eastern out-leg of the Fairfield Horseshoe, climbs via Low Sweden Bridge onto the Low and High Pike ridge (see page 242). The second and distinctly quieter journey advances up Scandale, with two options at the dalehead by Scandale Pass or slightly more adventurously High Bakestones.

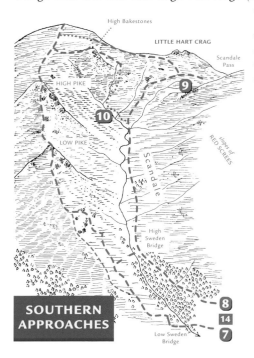

High Bakestones

LITTLE HART CRAG

Scandale Pass

9

HIGH PIKE

10

LOW PIKE

Scandale

slopes of RED SCREES

High Sweden Bridge

SOUTHERN APPROACHES

8

14

Low Sweden Bridge

7

The handsome standard cairn distinguishing High Bakestones

8 From High Sweden Bridge the old valley track wanders into an undulating lane, after a gate traversing Scandale Bottom to reach a sheepfold complex and beyond goes through a gate. **9** At this point either continue up to the Scandale Pass ladder-stile and bear left, then either follow the path above Scandale Tarn which winds up to High Bakestones (Beckstones), or the old ridge-top fence above Black Brow.

10 For an interesting variation go through the gap immediately left of the gate, cross the first beck confluence rising to where a wall and fence meet at the top of the bank above the beck. Keep adjacent and above the beck rising right with the first feeder gill. Above the bracken the ridge steepens, a grooved path winds above the eastern side of the gill and crosses a marsh to join the path from Scandale Tarn. Bear left to gain the distinguished seven-foot tall currick surmounting High Bakestones. The path continues beyond to meet the ridge wall, turn right (north) to reach the acid-rain bleached outcrop and summit cairn *(below)*.

The Summit

A relatively small outcrop forms a plinth for the cairn set two dozen yards east of a deteriorating ridge wall. The plateau has a random scattering of stones, while west of the wall the fell is largely grass. In settled weather one may consider visiting the top of Dove Crag itself, a length of sheep balking wall defining the limit of safe exploration *(see right)*.

Safe Descents

The ridge wall is key, as any vague wandering east will surely end in tears. Either head north to the depression short of Hart Crag, descending Houndshope Cove for Dovedale, or go south 360 yards to the old fence junction, religiously following the fence down to Scandale Pass for both Brothers Water via Caiston Glen and Ambleside via Scandale.

Hartsop above How from the shepherds' wall shielding the top of Dove Crag

Ridge Routes to....

HART CRAG   DESCENT 150 feet   ASCENT 240 feet   0.6 miles

Again it is the ridge wall that acts as the demystify guide, descend easily NE to the shallow depression at the head of Houndshope Cove, clambering to the summit cairn amid an abundance of splintered rock.

HIGH PIKE   DESCENT 450 feet   1 mile

Follow the wall S on a gentle grassy, occasionally peaty path to where the ridge narrows at the summit.

LITTLE HART CRAG   DESCENT 640 feet   ASCENT 130 feet   1.2 miles

Follow the wall S for 360 yards, at which point an old fence diverges east, adhere to this, descending, to run along the undulating peaty moor above Black Brow direct to the twin outcropped summit.

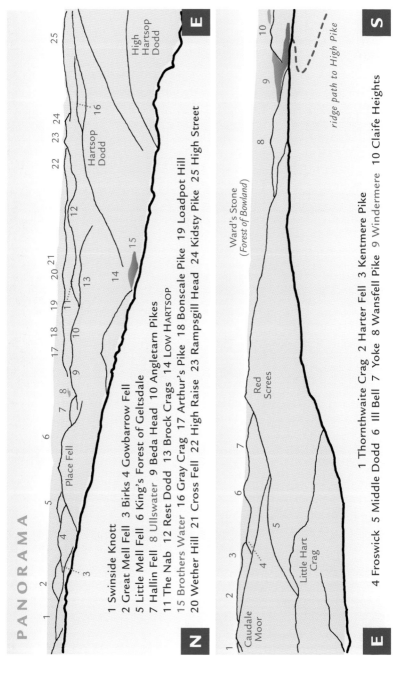

PANORAMA

N / **E**

1 Swinside Knott
2 Great Mell Fell 3 Birks 4 Gowbarrow Fell
5 Little Mell Fell 6 King's Forest of Geltsdale
7 Hallin Fell 8 Ullswater 9 Beda Head 10 Angletarn Pikes
11 The Nab 12 Rest Dodd 13 Brock Crags 14 Low HARTSOP
15 Brothers Water 16 Gray Crag 17 Arthur's Pike 18 Bonscale Pike 19 Loadpot Hill
20 Wether Hill 21 Cross Fell 22 High Raise 23 Rampsgill Head 24 Kidsty Pike 25 High Street

S / **E**

ridge path to High Pike

1 Thornthwaite Crag 2 Harter Fell 3 Kentmere Pike
4 Froswick 5 Middle Dodd 6 Ill Bell 7 Yoke 8 Wansfell Pike 9 Windermere 10 Claife Heights

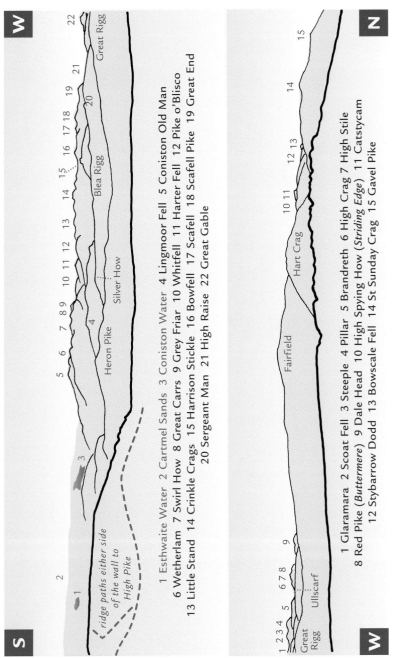

W

S

22 Great Rigg

19 21

20

16 17 18

15

14

Blea Rigg

13

12

11 10

Silver How

8 9

7

6

5 Heron Pike

4

3

2

1

ridge paths either side of the wall to High Pike

1 Esthwaite Water 2 Cartmel Sands 3 Coniston Water 4 Lingmoor Fell 5 Coniston Old Man
6 Wetherlam 7 Swirl How 8 Great Carrs 9 Grey Friar 10 Whitfell 11 Harter Fell 12 Pike o'Blisco
13 Little Stand 14 Crinkle Crags 15 Harrison Stickle 16 Bowfell 17 Scafell 18 Scafell Pike 19 Great End
20 Sergeant Man 21 High Raise 22 Great Gable

N

W

15

14

12 13

Hart Crag

10 11

Fairfield

9

1 2 3 4 5 6 7 8

Great Rigg

Ullscarf

1 Glaramara 2 Scoat Fell 3 Steeple 4 Pillar 5 Brandreth 6 High Crag 7 High Stile
8 Red Pike (*Buttermere*) 9 Dale Head 10 High Spying How (*Striding Edge*) 11 Catstycam
12 Stybarrow Dodd 13 Bowscale Fell 14 St Sunday Crag 15 Gavel Pike

FAIRFIELD

Were this a Scottish hill, then it would have been christened Foinaven 'the bonny mountain', to judge by the only slightly altered contemporary fell-name which should be read 'fair fell' – an alteration on a par with Sheffield Pike. Presiding over the southern corpus of the range and made separate from the Helvellyn massif by the deep trough of Grisedale, Fairfield is indeed a deceptively fine mountain. The Fairfield Horseshoe, on the district's short-list of classic rounds, has given the fell the high status, though adroitly the fell reserves its most stunning qualities to its northern slopes. Observers high on St Sunday Crag, or within the secretive depths of Deepdale, may gaze in awe at a ferocious gallery of crags each interlaced with runs of scree which stream into the barren dale-heads of Link and Cawk Coves. Admittedly, to the greatest extent, the fell falls away as rather feature-less slopes, the daily procession on the Horseshoe, knowing little more than these plainer aspects, must heap the greatest praise on its pre-eminence as a viewpoint, notably the breathtaking view north across the headwall of Grisedale towards Helvellyn. Yet the truncated north-east ridge bracketed by Scrubby and Hutaple Crags and terminated by Greenhow End, is as spectacular as any parade of Lakeland rock.

Of the five natural lines of ascent, the best by far, and understandably the least tested, climbs pathless out of Deepdale into Link Cove to mount The Step. From the vicinity of Mart Crag the forbidding fortress ridge-end of Greenhow End looks unassailable, though succumbs with only steep grass to negotiate. Nonetheless, this is no place for the walker unattuned to wilder fell terrain, nor when cloud swirls and the heavens threaten to open, then the prudent retreat to relish another day.

873 metres   2,864 feet

The 'Horseshoe' ridges rising from the Rothay valley give simple connections from Great Rigg and Hart Crag. A formless scree-infested west shoulder leads up from Grisedale Hause, while the finest ridge, that from St Sunday Crag, mounts from Deepdale Hause over Cofa Pike. Of recent decades three paths have evolved climbing direct from Grisedale Tarn; two lines leading to Deepdale Hause, and one, far from pleasant stony chase, direct to Cofa Pike. So fine a mountain, so varied the routes, with a north/south divide in dramatic quality. Yet, the Horseshoe will always be the popular trail by virtue of its ridge-top symmetry and summits bagged tally - 8.

Bizarre rock tor leading to the piked summit of Cofa Pike, with St Sunday Crag sunlit, background right

ST SUNDAY CRAG

Linkcove Beck is not a place for the average fell wanderer, as it contains pitches suitable for the competent scrambler only.

Mart Crag former haunt of pine marten.

Deepdale Hause

Deepdale

falls

Tarn Crag

Sleet Cove

fold

Mart Crag

Mossydale

< Dunmail Raise via Raise Beck

Grisedale Tarn

Cofa Pike

Cawk Cove

Black Buttress

Hutaple Crag

The Forces

Erne Nest Crag

The Step

Greenhow End

Grisedale Hause

Link Cove

Scrubby Crag

SEAT SANDAL

Rydal Head

Link Hause

HART CRAG

< Grasmere via Old Pony Path descending Little Tongue

< Grasmere via Tongue Gill & Mill Bridge

GREAT RIGG

< valley path to Rydal

Rydal Beck

one kilometre   one mile

Cute eyes might notice - in the title view opposite - that Fairfield bears an uncanny resemblance to a giant lobster, with Greenhow End forming one claw and the top of Scrubby Crag its head, the cloud shadows further adding to the weird impression by adding a tail!

EASTERN APPROACHES

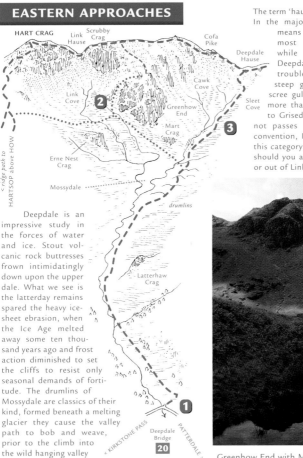

HART CRAG Link Hause Scrubby Crag

Cofa Pike

Deepdale Hause

Cawk Cove

Link Cove **2** Greenhow End

Sleet Cove

Mart Crag **3**

Erne Nest Crag

Mossydale

drumlins

< ridge path to HARTSOP above HOW

Latterhaw Crag

Deepdale is an impressive study in the forces of water and ice. Stout volcanic rock buttresses frown intimidatingly down upon the upper dale. What we see is the latterday remains spared the heavy ice-sheet ebrasion, when the Ice Age melted away some ten thousand years ago and frost action diminished to set the cliffs to resist only seasonal demands of fortitude. The drumlins of Mossydale are classics of their kind, formed beneath a melting glacier they cause the valley path to bob and weave, prior to the climb into the wild hanging valley hollow of Sleet Cove.

< KIRKSTONE PASS Deepdale Bridge PATTERDALE > **1**

20

The term 'hause' can be deceptive. In the majority of instances it means a pass between hills, most give easy passage, while others, such as Deepdale Hause are more troublesome, this offers steep ground and a loose scree gully to the top and a more than rough switch over to Grisedale Tarn. Others are not passes by any measure of convention, Link Hause falls into this category, as fall may you too should you attempt to climb into or out of Link Cove that way!

Greenhow End with Mart Crag at its foot from the drumlins of upper Deepdale

ASCENT *from Deepdale Bridge*

A grand walk which only improves as the drama of the dalehead unfolds.
1 Follow the walled lane to Lane Head. Bear left at the gate along a track which leads on above Deepdale Hall Farm and Wall End - where walls do end. Once Coldcove Beck is crossed the dale's countenance, bereft of trees, turns wilder and in certain lights austere. The valley path diminishes as it advances along the floor of the dale to weave over the drumlin field, with Greenhow End in all its glory looming ahead.

2 Via Greenhow End. To avoid wetting the boots in traversing the Mossydale hollow, pass beyond the moraines and as two becks run parallel on the left of the path, ford, slant up in front of Mart Crag (a sought after retreat test piece for the climber). Hold to the steep pathless grassy slope, to the right of an eroded gill close under Greenhow End. Resist the temptation to step onto a grassy shelf, unless you are a suitably competent scrambler - the broad slabby buttress is a very happy hunting ground for the proficient free-climber, often presaged by scrambling within the challenging recesses of Linkcove Gill. An obvious line of weakness between rock bands permits a steep line up grass and boulders to a point where the rock-band on the right gives way to suitably easier ground, climb to a notch on the skyline. Locate and follow a thin ridge path left ia The Step onto the plateau, with stirring perspectives on impressive rock architecture the rich reward.

3 Via Deepdale Hause, keep to the narrow valley path, climbing on the north side of the ravine to the impressive hanging valley of Sleet Cove. The path slips up past a sheepfold, a good spot to pause and admire the steepling walls of Cofa Pike and Cawk Cove. Cawk was a dialect term for '*a cuckoo*', on the face of it a strange location to find this bird of infamous repute which prefers a wooded environment within which to trade eggs). Cross a marsh to ascend the scored final bank onto Deepdale Hause. Turn left, the ridge path scrambles handsomely onto Cofa Pike (*'the pointed rock of the coves'*), its crest, marked by a cairn, also features a bizarre rock tor reminiscent of the impressive ridges on the Isle of Aran. The final pitch to the summit has the option of an easier path slanting across the scree right to join the path from Grisedale Hause, or up the worn rocks closer the cove rim thus concentrating on the view into Cawk Cove.

Cloud shadows stream across Black Buttress and Hutaple Crag the northern precipices of Fairfield terminating in the sunlit Greenhow End - viewpoint Cofa Pike, with High Street on the far horizon.

WESTERN APPROACHES

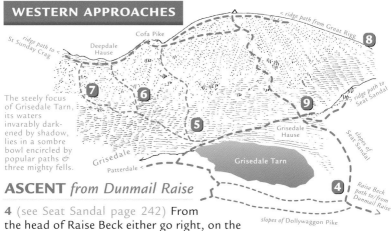

Cofa Pike

St Sunday Crag *ridge path to <*

Deepdale Hause

< ridge path from Great Rigg

8

ridge path to Seat Sandal

7

6

9

The steely focus of Grisedale Tarn, its waters invarably darkened by shadow, lies in a sombre bowl encircled by popular paths & three mighty fells.

5

Grisedale Hause

slopes of Seat Sandal

Grisedale Patterdale <

Grisedale Tarn

4

Raise Beck path to/from Dunmail Raise

ASCENT *from Dunmail Raise*

slopes of Dollywaggon Pike

4 (see Seat Sandal page 242) From the head of Raise Beck either go right, on the contouring path traversing the shadowy north-eastern slope of Seat Sandal to Grisedale Hause, or straight ahead on a wet, intermittent path above the northern shores of Grisedale Tarn. Reaching the outflow, ford and follow the pronounced path, which bears off immediately to the left from the path to Grisedale Hause. There are three options from this path. **5** At the first gill crossing bear up on its right side, a path winds quite steeply over a rocky knot with some loose footing, duly arriving at Cofa Pike - all too often used as a swift descent, hence the pallor state of path. **6** The better line is to keep with the contouring path, beyond the marshy patch at a fork either ascend right, or **7** more comfortably, continue across the shelf climbing in more steady stages to Deepdale Hause. Go right ascending the popular ridge via Cofa Pike.

Arguably the most spectacular view within the range, north from Cofa Pike

The Fairfield Horseshoe from Todd Crag on Loughrigg Fell

Above and below witness southern and eastern perspectives on Fairfield. No two views show more clearly the differing character of the mountain. The gathering embrace of Rydale by a series of eight summits is a fell-walking classic best begun from Ambleside, clockwise via Rydal Park and Nab Scar. While Scrubby Crag, overbearing Link Cove, is wild, inhospitable, and for climbers, difficult both to reach and ascend.

Scrubby Crag from the east ridge of Hart Crag

ASCENT *from Grasmere*

8 (see Great Rigg page 122) Either follow the ridge route, or **9** (see Seat Sandal page 240) to Grisedale Hause. Go right beside the broken wall which falters as scree is encountered, the path winding onto the rocky plateau.

ASCENT *from Rydal*

Fairfield forms the culmination of two striking north/south ridge and valley features each of which may be enjoyed as lines of ascent. **10** The popular horseshoe takes advantage of the ridge crossing three summits northward from the village of Rydal. Begin from Pelter Bridge car park GR 366059, pass up by Rydal Mount onto Nab Sar and over Heron Pike and Great Rigg, a simple energetic four mile trek. **11** For the solitary inquisitive soul the lonesome trail up the Rydal Beck valley will surely appeal on another level - as it is unlikely that you will meet another soul! Again, pass up by Rydal Mount, continuing up the lane and succeeding track via gates. Pass the attractive environs of Buckstone's Jump and beneath Erne Crag by a large erratic incorporated in the wall. From the gate directly below one may make a brief energy-sapping detour up by the winding wall and loose scree to inspect the long abandoned quarry and cave site at the foot of the crag, the haunt of peregrine, a truly wild scene of former industry. The way on up the valley largely adheres to the wall, which has been swept over by gill spillage in two places.

SOUTHERN APPROACHES

continued from above...

As the wall curves to embrace the remote valley pasture, a pathless course is followed across the peaty marsh of Rydal Head. Climb up beside the a curious broken wall enclosure lasooing a portion of the valley head, on a steady plod to the Link Hause saddle. Take heed: this is a pass only in terms of a link between Hart Crag and Fairfield. Do not be tempted to venture straight over into Link Cove, the corrie-name was borrowed wantonly, there is no pedestrian 'link' down. The ridge path leads north-weswards and marches on quite uneventfully to the summit.

Summit wind-break looking north-east

Given calm weather follow the sheep-path along the northern edge. This is far more dramatic and reveals of the fell's most noble precipices.

The Summit

A trio of cairns are grouped about the highest point, two of them fashioned into windbreaks. The cairn nearest the northern brink marks the probable summit. The fell-name suggests a cricket pitch, and while there are areas of open ground, west of the wind swept summit, the plateau simply bristles with rock, sufficient to stifle an easy stride.

Safe Descents

The nature of the summit demands respect. The plethra of cairns is not incidental, but indicative of visitors' caution. Safe ground lies due west and south. To the north lies sure peril, especially in mist.

Ridge Routes to....

GREAT RIGG   DESCENT 490 feet   ASCENT 140 feet   1 mile

A broad trail marked by cairns trends slightly W of S down the ridge.

HART CRAG   DESCENT 320 feet   ASCENT 145 feet   1 mile

A broad, bare path leads across the fair field of Fairfield due E. As the brink of Scrubby Crag draws near the path drifts SE over rocky ground to the small saddle depression of Link Hause, cairns confirming the way.

ST SUNDAY CRAG   DESCENT 650 feet   ASCENT 490 feet   1.5 miles

The pick of the bunch. Either head W over stony ground to where a path angles right, or in good visibility, head directly N, descending to pass over Cofa Pike, scrambling cautiously down to where the ridge constricts at Deepdale Hause. A simple ridge path beyond rises sweetly to the summit.

PANORAMA

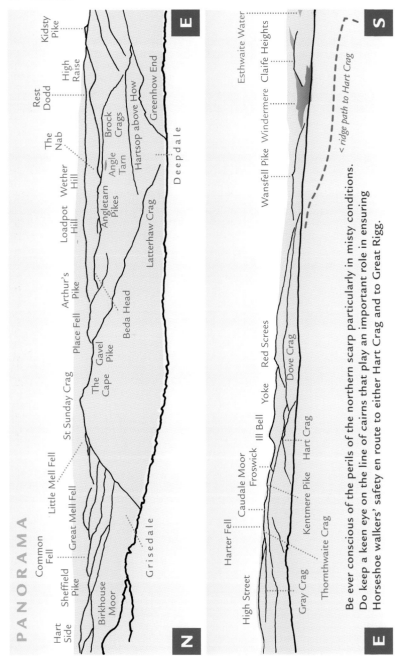

Hart Side — Common Fell — Little Mell Fell — Kidsty Pike — High Raise — Rest Dodd — The Nab — Loadpot Hill — Wether Hill — Arthur's Pike — Place Fell — St Sunday Crag — Great Mell Fell — Sheffield Pike — Birkhouse Moor

Brock Crags — Greenhow End — Hartsop above How — Angle Tarn — Angletarn Pikes — Beda Head — Gavel Pike — The Cape — Latterhaw Crag

Deepdale — Grisedale

N — **E**

Esthwaite Water — Windermere — Claife Heights — Wansfell Pike — Harter Fell — Caudale Moor — Froswick — Ill Bell — Yoke — Red Screes — Dove Crag — Hart Crag — Kentmere Pike — Gray Crag — Thornthwaite Crag — High Street

< *ridge path to Hart Crag*

E — **S**

Be ever conscious of the perils of the northern scarp particularly in misty conditions. Do keep a keen eye on the line of cairns that play an important role in ensuring Horseshoe walkers' safety en route to either Hart Crag and to Great Rigg.

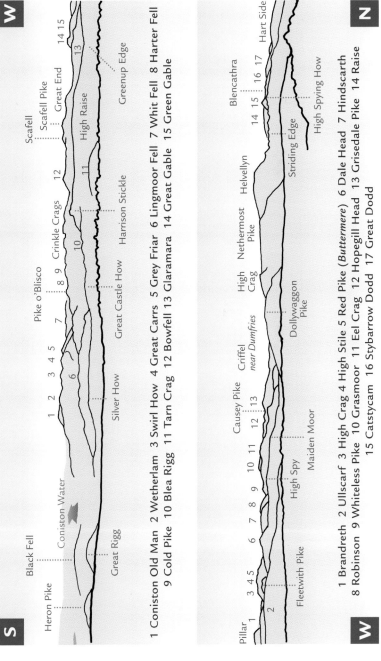

W | **S**

Scafell
Scafell Pike
Great End 14 15
13
Greenup Edge
High Raise
Crinkle Crags 12
11
Harrison Stickle
Pike o'Blisco
8 9
Great Castle How
7
1 2 3 4 5
6
Silver How
Coniston Water
Black Fell
Heron Pike
Great Rigg

1 Coniston Old Man 2 Wetherlam 3 Swirl How 4 Great Carrs 5 Grey Friar 6 Lingmoor Fell 7 Whit Fell 8 Harter Fell 9 Cold Pike 10 Blea Rigg 11 Tarn Crag 12 Bowfell 13 Glaramara 14 Great Gable 15 Green Gable

N | **W**

Blencathra
Hart Side
14 15 16 17
Striding Edge
High Spying How
Helvellyn
Nethermost Pike
High Crag
Dollywaggon Pike
Causey Pike
Criffel
near Dumfries
12 13
Maiden Moor
High Spy
3 4 5 6 7 8 9 10 11
Pillar
1
2
Fleetwith Pike

1 Brandreth 2 Ullscarf 3 High Crag 4 High Stile 5 Red Pike (*Buttermere*) 6 Dale Head 7 Hindscarth 8 Robinson 9 Whiteless Pike 10 Grasmoor 11 Eel Crag 12 Hopegill Head 13 Grisedale Pike 14 Raise 15 Catstycam 16 Stybarrow Dodd 17 Great Dodd

GLENRIDDING DODD

This lowest shoulder of Sheffield Pike falters on most commonly accepted criteria for separate fell status. However, in terms of situation, there can be no denying its individuality, standing proud as punch amid an idyllic arena of lake and fell. A rough top of heather, rock and marsh, crowned by a handsome cairn mimics its higher neighbour. From its southern and eastern edges all the beauties of Ullswater and Glenridding can be surveyed. In former tourist ages it was a prime objective, satisfying all the requirements of a vantage for the romantically picturesque; an essential climb sufficiently removed from the maelstrom about the Greenside Mine. Yet few people trouble to consider its virtues today, which might be seen as a blessing in disguise.

The curious fell-wanderer, eager to discover unusual and sylvan prospects on Ullswater, will adore the old path above Stybarrow Oaks and the intimacies of Mossdale. Yes, Glenridding Dodd is a little gem to savour.

442 metres   1,450 feet

Stybarrow Crag 'the steep brow' bearing down upon the lakeside road, originally the 'road' went up behind the crag

ASCENT *from* Stybarrow Crag

Find a small lay-by (National Trust sign) adjacent to the bolt-pinned rock wall of Stybarrow Crag overbearing the lakeshore road. This is the starting point for a lovely, unvaunted ascent of shy Mossdale.

1 From the post box embark beside the gill, motorist's callous toiletry activities an early hazard on the clamber up beside the garden fence of Hawkhow. Shortly, after glimpsing the veranda of this deliciously sighted house, damper ground intervenes and a more convincing path bears left. This path is a misleading spur to a natural rock cutting and the bilberry and oak crowned top of Stybarrow Crag, a charming spot well worth visiting - backtrack to continue. Keep beside the embowered fence to a stile in a convergent fence, ascending to the Mossdale Beck ravine. Bear up left, without the assurance of a path, up the moss-clothed rocks, close above the tumbling waters within its shaded cleft.

House Holm (Duke of Norfolk Isle) and the middle reach of Ullswater in view from the delectably sylvan path which contours above Stybarrow Oaks towards Mossdale

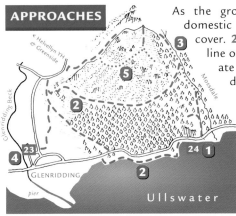

As the ground eases arrive upon a domestic water extraction man-hole cover. **2** There exists an alternative line of approach to this intermediate point. In common with the direct route, never bugled in contemporary guides, yet one to richly savour. It may begin directly from the village car park, but in terms of walking pleasure is better started from the Stybarrow Crag lay-by. Follow the tree-shaded lakeside path, which leaves the vergeless road just beyond the crag. Re-gaining the highway above a boathouse, go right and first left along the lane (footpath sign). Beyond a gate at the wood's end, signed 'How Head', the fenced track heads towards a second gate, just short of the gate go right through the hand-gate (the 'private' notice only bars access via the field-gate).

A permissive path climbs the pasture without the dense bracken, leading via waymark posts and white arrows set on the ground, double

Place Fell from Stybarrow Oaks

zigging to a hand-gate in the intake wall. Go right, in summer fighting back the bracken alongside the wall. Reaching the top corner of the woodland, re-assured by the permissive path signboard, glance back along the wall to see Birkhouse Moor *(see right)*.

The path dips and rises, still close to the wall, then contours along a scree shelf. Watch: bracken can obscure its start. The views from this section, overlooking Stybarrow Oaks, can be matchless, so take your time, stop and gaze often at the upper reaches of Ullswater with its backdrop of fine fells. Shortly notice a cast-iron water pipe at your feet. Rounding a corner this is exposed along a rock. The path is forced briefly

down a few feet, clambering back to the gain the hurdle-gate at the point where the intake wall jumps a rock-step. Securing the hurdle, the path now leads on directly to the man-hole cover beside the juvenile cascades of Mossdale Beck *(drawing left)*.

3 With the startling peak of Heron Pike dead ahead, keep to the left-hand bank. Beat an awkward path through the mature larches, beside the tumbling beck to join a more evident sheep-made path through the bracken. The path leads above a damp hollow (shrunken tarn) unerringly to the hand-gate in the saddle. Go left, curving up beside the wall, branching off right above the scree bank on a path slipping past a stone estate boundary marker in a shallow dip to gain the handsome summit cairn.

ASCENT *from Glenridding*

4 From the National Park car park follow Greenside Road. Passing the Travellers Rest, fork right at the junction, advance to the cattle-grid access to Glenridding Common. Immediately bear right, zig-zagging onto the green track which leads towards the upper terrace. Branch right above the gorse, short of the dwellings; the loose path climbing to the west of Blaes Crag. On gaining a natural respite shelf, either continue up The Rake to the saddle, or **5** indulge in the more interesting lassoing climb. Veer right, traverse below the scree, seeking the one grassy relent, ascend to the prominent vantage cairn, perched on a rock. From this

edge enjoy a splendid bird's eye view over Glenridding. The village owes its origins and growth to centuries-old mining adventure, of recent decades adapting to the economy of the transient tourist and needs of the fellwalker.

Birkhouse Moor from the path to Mossdale east of Blaes Crag

The semblance of a path winds west to the pivotal cairn, alternatively one may choose to keep to the southern edge, via the small TV mast, skirting the marshy hollow before striding across to the reach topmost cairn.

The cairn overlooking Glenridding backed by Place Fell

The Summit

A delectable undulating plateau of rock and heather culminates upon a fine cairn, attributes befitting this cub of the range. For the best view of Glenridding go 200 yards SSE to the southern brink *(see above)*. Larch trees growing high on the northern slopes inhibit an unfettered view of Ullswater, so, for an unforgettable prospect of lake and fell, take the narrow trod east to where the ground plummets sit and enjoy, you will not be the first, nor the last, to love this exhalted spot.

Shirt-sleeves - culmination of a great little climb in any season

Safe Descents

The surest haven is Glenridding. From the summit cairn head west to the saddle and follow The Rake path smartly south to the terrace of old miners' cottages beside Greenside Road.

Patterdale and Arnison Crag from the summit

Ridge Route to....

SHEFFIELD PIKE   DESCENT 140 feet   ASCENT 765 feet   1 mile

Head west, cross The Rake saddle, ignore the gate and subsequent gateway at the wall junction. Ascend to gap in the broken wall climb the magnificent rocky-stepped SE ridge to Heron Pike. The summit lies to the NE beyond a marshy depression. Heather clothing much of the higher ridge and summit approach.

An etymologically apt eagle's-eye view of Glenridding Dodd from Heron Pike

PANORAMA

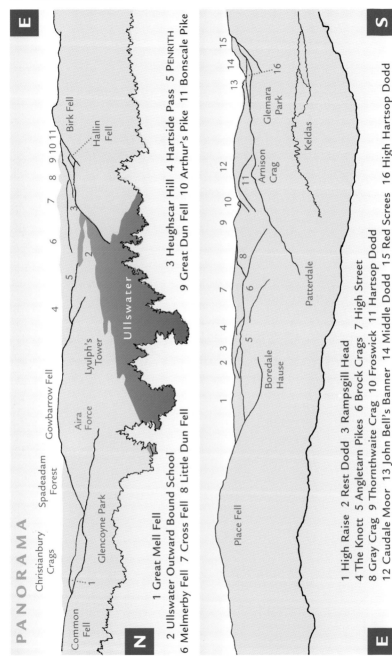

N

Common Fell

Christianbury Crags

Spadeadam Forest

Glencoyne Park

1

Gowbarrow Fell

Aira Force

Lyulph's Tower

Ullswater

4

5

6

7

8 9 10 11

Birk Fell

Hallin Fell

E

1 Great Mell Fell
2 Ullswater Outward Bound School
6 Melmerby Fell 7 Cross Fell 8 Little Dun Fell

3 Heughscar Hill 4 Hartside Pass 5 PENRITH
9 Great Dun Fell 10 Arthur's Pike 11 Bonscale Pike

E

Place Fell

Boredale Hause

1 2 3 4 5 6 7 8 9 10 12 11

Patterdale

Arnison Crag

Glemara Park

Keldas

13 14 15

16

S

1 High Raise 2 Rest Dodd 3 Rampsgill Head
4 The Knott 5 Angletarn Pikes 6 Brock Crags 7 High Street
8 Gray Crag 9 Thornthwaite Crag 10 Froswick 11 Hartsop Dodd
12 Caudale Moor 13 John Bell's Banner 14 Middle Dodd 15 Red Screes 16 High Hartsop Dodd

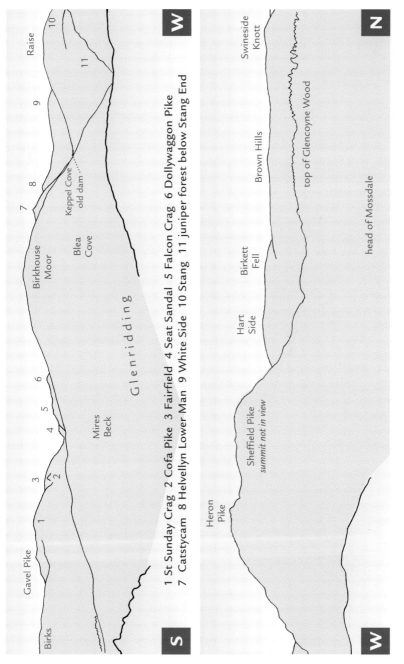

W

S

Gavel Pike
Birks

Raise

10

11

9

8

7

Birkhouse Moor

Keppel Cove old dam

Blea Cove

Glenridding

6
5
4
3
2
1

Mires Beck

1 St Sunday Crag 2 Cofa Pike 3 Fairfield 4 Seat Sandal 5 Falcon Crag 6 Dollywaggon Pike
7 Catstycam 8 Helvellyn Lower Man 9 White Side 10 Stang 11 juniper forest below Stang End

N

W

Swineside Knott

Brown Hills

top of Glencoyne Wood

Birkett Fell

Hart Side

head of Mossdale

Heron Pike

Sheffield Pike
summit not in view

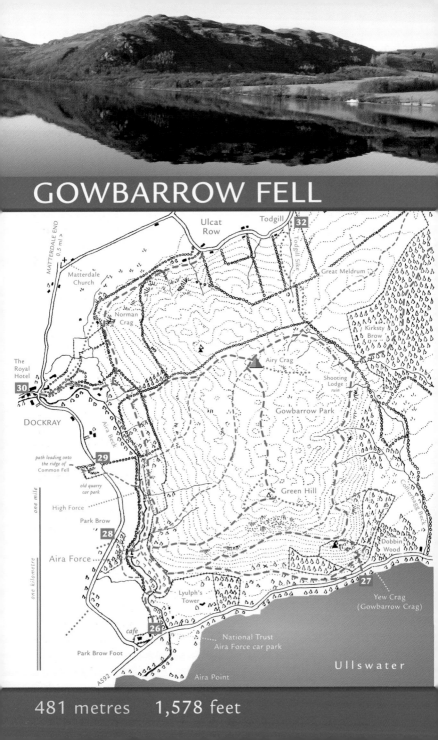

GOWBARROW FELL

481 metres   1,578 feet

Gowbarrow Park is defined by Ullswater to the south, Aira Beck to the west and embraced by a deer park wall to the north and east. The Park, one of a sequence of medieval deer preserves surrounding Ullswater, with Swinburn's Park lying between the two ridges now hosting alien conifers at its head. Under the custodianship of the National Trust the fell habitat is progressively improving, by ensuring an appropriate grazing regime for the resurgent heather swathing its upper slopes, eildlife diversity thus greatly enhanced.

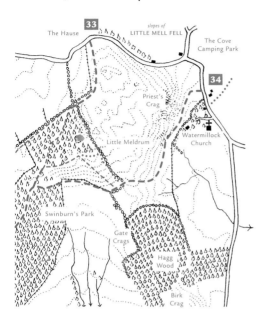

The fell-name derives from the Old Norse terms *gol* gusty + *beorg* defended place.

Walkers quite naturally tend to focus on the romantic environs of Aira Force or trace the old Watermillock path linking Park Brow Foot with Watermillock Church, a scenically rewarding leg stretching three miles. The full ridge can be encircled using the footpath to Ulcat Row and the back road to The Hause, with the Todgill approach to Great Meldrum as a useful means of abbreviating the circuit. Less well known, except by those receiving Outward Bound rock-climbing tuition, is the fascinating stepped path mounting Yew Crag (Gowbarrow Crag to climbers), a stunning approach to the prominent cairns on the Watermillock path and Green Hill, the latter being quite the best viewpoint on the fell.

ASCENT *from The Hause & Watermillock Church*

To the north-east the fell bonds with Little Mell Fell at The Hause GR 424235, suggesting a ridge route, and while it is wholly practical, it is not a holy practise, there being no right-of-way. **1** A tracks leads from the gate to a gate into private forestry. From this point three lines are recommended. **2** Naturalists' will instinctively wish to follow the wall left to peer into the secretive tarn lurking on the ridge at the edge of the conifers, a haven for heron and duck. Where the conifers end bear right

along their fringe to climb over Little Meldrum, a handsome minor viewpoint. **3** Bear half-left, tracing the forestry ride to emerge at the scarp brink, linking to route **2**. The edge path bears right then slants down the scarp along the edge of the larch plantation joining the footpath from Watermillock. Go right, to exit Swinburn's Park plantation via a stile, reaching the ruined shooting box beyond a ladder-stile, go right with the beck.

4 The more direct ridge route follows the wall, with the conifers to the left. Approaching a stile the ground can be marshy, enter the Great Meldrum enclosure. A clear path winds on through the patchy heather pasture rising over Great Meldrum. The name means *'the greater open flat ridge'*, there is no culminating cairn but it is a fine spot to view Great Mell Fell. The path descends to cross a projecting wall corner

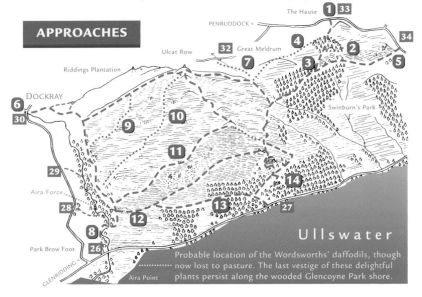

APPROACHES

The Hause **1** **33**

PENRUDDOCK <

34

Ulcat Row **32** Great Meldrum **4** **2**

7 **3** **5**

Riddings Plantation

Swinburn's Park

DOCKRAY **6**

30 **9** **10**

29 **11**

Aira Force.. **14**

28 **13** **27**

12

8

Park Brow Foot **26**

GLENRIDDING

Aira Point

U l l s w a t e r

Probable location of the Wordsworths' daffodils, though
now lost to pasture. The last vestige of these delightful
plants persist along the wooded Glencoyne Park shore.

ladder-stile, thereafter, in unison with the path rise from the old shooting box, mounting to the summit.

5 The conventional eastern approach follows the footpath leading from the minor road above Watermillock church GR 431232. A kissing-gate marks the start of an open path which passes under Priest's Crag before rising, brushing gorse to a hand-gate. Keep the wall left to a stile (before this a minor path climbs the edge right, onto Little Meldrum), hold the fence to the right in reaching a stile into the forestry of Swinburn's Park Plantation. Despite the conifers this section is an enchanting traverse with excellent views over Ullswater to the Far Eastern Fells.

ASCENT *from Dockray*

6 The swiftest route to the top (one mile) begins opposite the Royal Hotel in Dockray GR 393216. A farm lane leads east, becoming an open track after a gate, it passes Millses to merge with a path from Ulcat Row. Keep right, down the valley path. Immediately after passing through a wicket-gate, bear up left to a ladder-stile crossing the intake wall onto the fell. Climb with a wall to the left, via an old fold, ultimately crossing a marshy patch to the summit.   **7** A useful 'back-door' onto the fell begins from the minor road running from Ulcat Row. Embark from Dockray on the signposted footpath leaving the lane left. At a gate, a sequence of gates leads across pastureland to a wall squeeze stile to merge with a path running over the shoulder of Norman Crag. The paths cross a ladder-stile and join a track, passing a whitewashed cottage, to a gate onto the road at Ulcat Row (derived from *'the owl-cottage terrace'*).

Great Mell Fell from above Todgill

Continue east, dipping past the screened cottage Greenbank on the right, to the wooden gate on the right, short of Todgill house, daubed *'Todgill'*.

Ford Todgill Sike (which translates as *'the ditch frequented by foxes'*) and ascend the pasture, thus avoiding the bracken on the east bank, to reach a kissing-gate into the Great Meldrum enclosure. Bear up left to find a sheep path leading south to the ladder-stile into Gowbarrow Park and linking up with the path from the old shooting box, to reach the prominent summit on Airy Crag.

Sandwick *(pronounced 'sanick')* and the Martindale Fells from Green Hill

Environs of **Aira Force**

GR 401200 The principal raison d'etre of the National Trust car park at Park Brow Foot is to serve the huge interest in the far-famed beauties of Aira Force, the centrepiece of Aira Beck's final unfolding drama of turbulent cataracts and charming wooded pathways. **8** A fenced path leads to a hand-gate and entry into a formal glade, overlooked by exotic trees, notably a Monkey Puzzle, the base of its trunk like some monster fowl's claw! Paths split to run either side of the gorge, with steps and bridges strategically placed to assist observation of this beautiful wild water environment. There is no preferred way. Aira Force, a sixty foot crashing cleft, has dainty footbridges above and below. A little further up a fourth bridge aids access to either bank before the crescendo of High Force, a simple shelf of volcanic rock, above which only rock hopping is an option to switch banks. Having given the undoubted charms of the Aira Beck water gymnasium your avid attention, thoughts can turn to loftier matters - the ascent of Gowbarrow Fell, a gorgeous heather landscape brimming with wildlife and superlative views.

ASCENT *from Park Brow Foot*

The direct route crosses the bottom footbridge from the glade and winds up to emerge at a stile immediately above Aira Force. **9** Follow the valley path crossing a fence stile and, prior to the subsequent wicket-gate in a wall, GR 400212 bear up right to a light stile in a fence. A clear path climbs the fell, partially hampered by bracken. The route drifts left to join route **6** - the path beside the ascending fell wall. **10** Some 120 yards from the stile above Aira Force GR 401207 an earlier path has developed, veering from the valley path directly after fording a small gill. Initially rising upon a track, it bears left to lose the open woodland, winds across an indefinite fellside directly to the summit. **11** A popular route, preferably reserved for the descent, begins directly from the stile above Aira Force mounting the bank, climb the edge to gain the cairn on Green Hill. Higher up a secondary path, fashioned by short-cutting descending walkers, bears half-left onto the ridge. It ignores the peerless merits of this headland viewpoint, which surveys a gracious sweep of Ullswater looking into the deeply entrenched Patterdale valley-head and across to the Martindale Fells. The summit of Gowbarrow is in view as a poorly defined ridge path is joined, weave somewhat tediously through the heather to Airy Crag, surmounted by the Ordnance Survey pillar.

12 The Kirkstyle path, the traditional approach, begins from the gate in the bounding fence GR 402204, reached prior to Aira Force. A footpath runs on near the field fence above Lyulph's Tower. This eighteenth century castellated Gothic folly, built by the Dukes of Norfolk, reputedly rests upon the site of an earlier defended structure connected with Lyulph. This old Norse personal-name meaning 'wolf-like', a reference to the first Baron of Greystoke after whom Ullswater was named. This path forks in two, take the left-hand rising line climbing across the rough fell-side beneath Hind Crag. Ignore a secondary path, where heather begins, giving a less than worthy route over a saddle.

Keep to the main path, round the bluff, reaching the slate memorial seat *'a thank offering 1905'*. Across a fence, a cairn enjoys a handsome view over the Ullswater scene; perhaps take time to watch the steamer spreading its wake the width the of lake, as it plies to and fro the

glorious journey between Pooley Bridge and Glenridding Pier *(see illustration left)*. Rounding the hill the path contours, to approach the ruined shooting box, a reminder of the former sporting use of the fell. Cross a footbridge spanning a land-slip gully. The path advancing up the beck, keep back from the bounding wall in ascending to the summit.

ASCENT *via Yew Crag*

13 By keeping to the lower footpath from the start of route **12** a most enjoyable stroll leads through light woodland towards the lakeside road. Nearing the road watch for a path forking half-left, follow this, soon to become a made-path traversing the rocky headland between Yew Crag and climbers' nursery cliff. Notice the stone steps cutting across the line of the path with yew trees visible above and the fine view over Dobbin Wood to the lower reach of Ullswater ahead. Pass on through to a deer-fence gate entering a mature fir and pine enclosure. Advance with the bounding fence to the right, beside a replanted bank, bear half-left to exit the enclosure by the deer-fence gate. Bear sharp left, climbing the combe direct, to meet the contouring Kirkstyle path. Continue up the ridge to gain the cairn on Green Hill, with little hint of a consistent path for encouragement.

14 The more adventurous will relish the stone-stepped path which climbs Yew Crag head-on. This begins from the lay-by at GR 416204. Cross two stiles before mounting left of the bottom crag, slipping through a gap created by a rock flake, keep right, on a path. Cross the traversing path advancing to the cliff. Ignore the older way. Now challenged by brambles, bear right from the overhang, aiming towards the

yew trees; this path switches beneath the yews and has broken away on the cliff so is no longer a safe way for walkers. Instead, from the overhang, keep up left, clamber up a shallow gully, vying with tree roots, at the top bear left and right on a clear path leading past a rocky crest, with fixed belay pegs, to a stile in the cliff bounding fence. Go directly left to meet the Watermillock path at the memorial seat and cairn viewpoint, a suitable spot to stop and admire a marvellous view over the upper reaches of Ullswater.

Summit pillar looking to Great Mell Fell

The Summit

Gowbarrow has a summit and a high place. The latter is Green Hill, a resoundingly good viewpoint. The summit, set well back from the best views, a rocky little ridge buttressed by Airy Crag to the south, is crowned with an old stone-built Ordnance column emblazed with a National Trust emblem. The panorama, though somewhat hindered by foreground heathery knolls, is dominated by the Far and Eastern Fells, with a guest appearance from Blencathra, a mountain in any company.

Safe Descents

The best descents follow the heathery ridge south to Green Hill, then trend easily down the western edge to Aira Force. However, in unfavourable conditions, the wall that runs east to west, 100 yards north of the summit, gives most assurance. Either left on the Dockray route, heading west, which gains the Aira Beck path with little ado, via a ladder-stile in the intake wall, or right, down to the shooting box joining the Watermillock path. The latter option better at keeping bracken at bay.

Ridge Route to....

LITTLE MELL FELL   DESCENT 460 feet   ASCENT 622 feet   2.2 miles

Descend E to the ladder-stile at the wall corner. Traverse Great Meldrum NE upon a clear path finding a stile in the far corner of the enclosure giving access to the wall-side path adjacent to the conifer plantation. This leads to a gate onto a track which swings N to a gate at The Hause. Cross over via the stile, traverse the paddock to a stepped-stile and ascend the obvious fellside path to the summit.

Wordsworth's daffodils *'I wander'd lonely as a cloud'*

Gowbarrow Park has long held a special place in literature. For it was here on 15th April 1802 that William and Dorothy Wordsworth strolled along the Aira Point shore of Ullswater. This was the inspiration for the famous poem penned two years later. Dorothy's Journal entry refers to the simple beauty of these petite, wild narcissus, commenting on their natural vibrance and the sheer number spread along the water's edge, in rocks and among the trees, about the breadth of the turnpike road. See them still along the wooded Glencoyne Park shore *(above)*.

PANORAMA

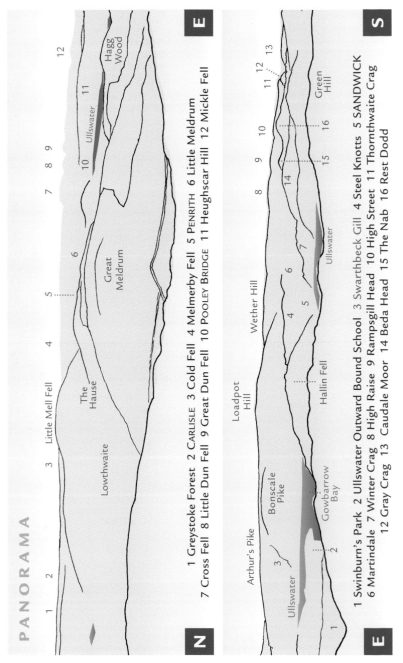

N / **E**

Little Mell Fell

The Hause

Lowthwaite

Great Meldrum

Ullswater

Hagg Wood

1 Greystoke Forest 2 CARLISLE 3 Cold Fell 4 Melmerby Fell 5 PENRITH 6 Little Meldrum
7 Cross Fell 8 Little Dun Fell 9 Great Dun Fell 10 POOLEY BRIDGE 11 Heughscar Hill 12 Mickle Fell

E / **S**

Arthur's Pike

Loadpot Hill

Wether Hill

Green Hill

Boncale Pike

Gowbarrow Bay

Hallin Fell

Ullswater

Ullswater

1 Swinburn's Park 2 Ullswater Outward Bound School 3 Swarthbeck Gill 4 Steel Knotts 5 SANDWICK
6 Martindale 7 Winter Crag 8 High Raise 9 Rampsgill Head 10 High Street 11 Thornthwaite Crag
12 Gray Crag 13 Caudale Moor 14 Beda Head 15 The Nab 16 Rest Dodd

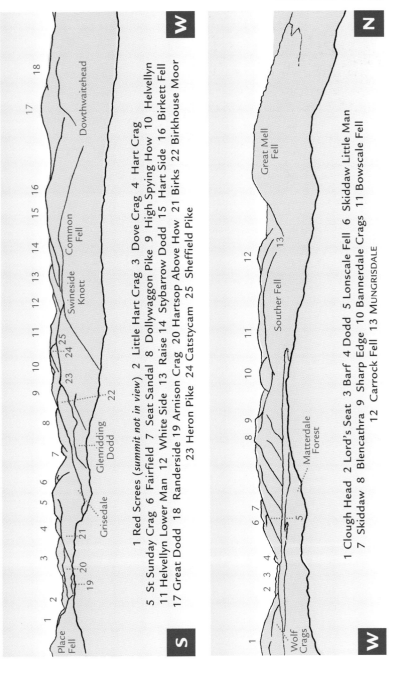

W   **S**

18   17   16   15   14   13   12   11   10   9   8   7   6   5   4   3   2   1

Dowthwaitehead

Common Fell

Swineside Knott

25   24   23   22

Glenridding Dodd

Grisedale

21   20   19

Place Fell

1 Red Screes (*summit not in view*)   2 Little Hart Crag   3 Dove Crag   4 Hart Crag
5 St Sunday Crag   6 Fairfield   7 Seat Sandal   8 Dollywaggon Pike   9 High Spying How   10 Helvellyn
11 Helvellyn Lower Man   12 White Side   13 Raise   14 Stybarrow Dodd   15 Hart Side   16 Birkett Fell
17 Great Dodd   18 Randerside   19 Arnison Crag   20 Hartsop Above How   21 Birks   22 Birkhouse Moor
23 Heron Pike   24 Catstycam   25 Sheffield Pike

N   **W**

13   12   11   10   9   8   7   6   5   4   3   2   1

Great Mell Fell

Souther Fell

Matterdale Forest

Wolf Crags

1 Clough Head   2 Lord's Seat   3 Barf   4 Dodd   5 Lonscale Fell   6 Skiddaw Little Man
7 Skiddaw   8 Blencathra   9 Sharp Edge   10 Bannerdale Crags   11 Bowscale Fell
12 Carrock Fell   13 MUNGRISDALE

GREAT DODD

St John's and Matterdale Commons culminate on Great Dodd, making this the paternal crown of the great sweep of grassy fells north of the Sticks Pass. Rising abruptly from St John's Vale, the convex slope give the illusion of diminished height, while the fell sends out a long eastward limb declining from Randerside in the relaxed manner adored of sphagnum moss. Dowthwaite Crag and Wolf Crags, the abraded the edges of the Matterdale Common ridge, adding much needed visual excitement. Wolf Crags a reminder of a species held vividly in folk memory and hunted to extinction before the advent of the Blencathra Foxhounds. Further evidence of the wolf on the range is intimated by Whelp Side on Helvellyn *'summer-pasture of the wolf cub'*.

Substantial wind-shelter on the south-eastern top

On its short journey to charge the Derwent, Groove Beck undergoes four distinct name changes becoming in turn, Thornsgill Beck, Trout Beck, Glenderamakin Beck and finally the River Greta through Keswick;

857 metres   2,812 feet

Wolf Crags from Mariel Bridge

Glenderamakin would appear to derive from the Cumbrian Celtic elements glyn dwr mochyn '*river valley where domestic pigs forage*'.

Traversing a tough tract of pathless moor, a bridle-way leads north from the Old Coach Road across Sandbeds Moss, bound for Lobbs and Wallthwaite. This route is sometimes adopted by challenge walkers seeking a direct range link to the Northern Fells.

When the Dodds are capped in cloud the 4.5 mile walk from High Row to Wanthwaite along the Old Coach Road is an excellent leg-stretching alternative, with open views to the north across the green desert of Threlkeld Common towards Blencathra.

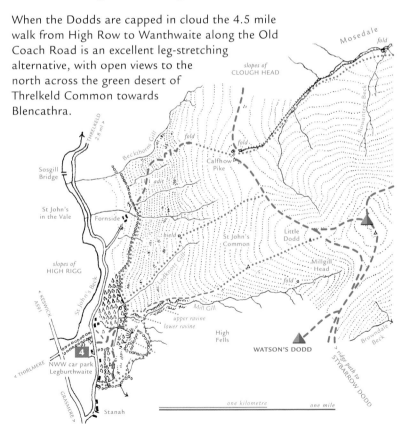

A less orthodox ascent may begin from Mariel Bridge by clambering to the scarp brink of Wolf Crags via Wolfcrags Fold.

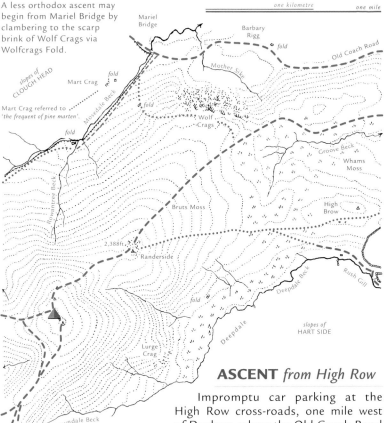

one kilometre *one mile*

Mariel Bridge

Barbary Rigg *fold*

Old Coach Road

slopes of CLOUGH HEAD

Mart Crag *fold*

Mother Side

Mosedale Beck

fold

Mart Crag referred to 'the frequent of pine marten'.

fold Wolf Crags

fold

Rowantree Beck

Groove Beck

Whams Moss

Bruts Moss

High Brow △

2,388ft. △

Randerside

Deepdale Beck

Rush Gill

fold

Deepdale

slopes of HART SIDE

Lurge Crag

Browndale Beck

The summit... it's a breeze!

ASCENT *from High Row*

Impromptu car parking at the High Row cross-roads, one mile west of Dockray, where the Old Coach Road sets course for St John's-in-the-Vale, makes a suitable launch-pad for the ascent of Great Dodd. Two basic lines of attack present themselves via Randerside and Mosedale.

With the former in mind, probably the most pleasing start, features the tiny community of Dowthwaitehead and the Rush Gill section of Deep Dale. **1** Fellwalkers beginning from Dockray may opt for the footpath route signposted within 0.3 mile of the village, traversing the meadows direct to Dowthwaitehead - 'the hill-shaded clearing at the head of the valley'.

2 Embarking from High Row, pass through the gate and follow the coach road track a matter of 110 yards before branching left onto a discernible tractor track winding up the slopes of Low How. Draw right, to a gate in the wall upon a green-way (foopath), which leads down the rocky slopes beneath Dowthwaite Crag to a hand-gate onto the road. Go through the road-gate passing the sheep handling pens. Look right for the permissive path waymarking, guiding, by a brick shed, to a walled lane to the right of Aira Farm. C ontinue via gates with the wall right and stony beck left,

path to Lobbs

Cockley Moor

High Row **31**

Groove Beck

Blake Side

Whams Moss

High Brow ▲ 1,886ft

Low How

Dowthwaite Crag

Rush Gill

Fieldpath to Dockray

Aira Beck

slopes of HART SIDE   DOWTHWAITEHEAD

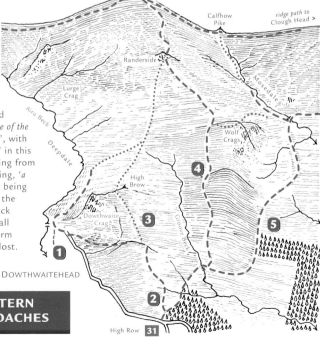

< *ridge path to* Watson's Dodd and Stybarrow Dodd

ridge path to Clough Head >

Calfhow Pike

Randerside

Mosedale

Lurge Crag

Aira Beck

Deepdale

Wolf Crags

High Brow

Dowthwaite Crag

Groove Beck

4

3

5

1

2

DOWTHWAITEHEAD

High Row **31**

Randerside comes from the Nordic and means '*the edge of the summer pasture*', with the term 'side' in this instance deriving from shield or shieling, '*a summer abode*', being transferred to the associated stock grazings with all trace of the farm dwelling now lost.

EASTERN APPROACHES

Calfhow Pike

up to the drove-way. Follow this left, mid attractive surroundings, gradually gaining height above Rush Gill, passing above the waterworks building. Bear half-right where the path merges with the rushes of Dowthwaitehead Moss, aiming for the dry sanctuary of Randerside - there will be moments when you feel you are walking on water!

3 Alternatively, trek straight over High Brow, marked by a small cairn and several large erratic boulders. Wade through the marshes directly to the firm footing of Randerside. **4** The least interesting line keeps with the Old Coach Road to the footbridge/ford of Groove Beck, take a path left, above the sheepfold, popular with skiiers in winter but at other seasons the over-steady spongy climb across Matterdale Common can only be relieved by a detour to inspect the brink of Wolf Crags. The cairn among a loose outcrop of rocks on Randerside offers welcome excuse to pause. A clear path, cairned higher up, leads to the summit.

5 The driest eastern approach holds to the Old Coach Road wandering along the causeway of Barbary Rigg beneath Wolf Crags. The name has nothing to do with pirates on the Barbary coast, rather a late reference to the herb barberry, a plant which may have been inadvertently spilt from a passing stage-coach, and grown wild, for it is rare in northern England outside ornamental garden settings, and is not apparent today. Latterly the track and its ditches can be alive with frog-spawn in early Spring, a scurge on all rogue 4 x 4 joy-riders who fail to heed the notices at either end of the coach road - turning the frogs to frog soup! After the gate, bear left before Mariel Bridge, accompany the fence beside the tumbling Mosedale Beck. From Rowantree Fold either branch left (no path) onto the skyline at Randerside or continue to Calfhow Pike, uniting with the ridge path, thus ensuring a palpable path in poor visibility.

Great Dodd from Troutbeck

Hart Side Raise Stybarrow Dodd Wolf Crags Mosedale

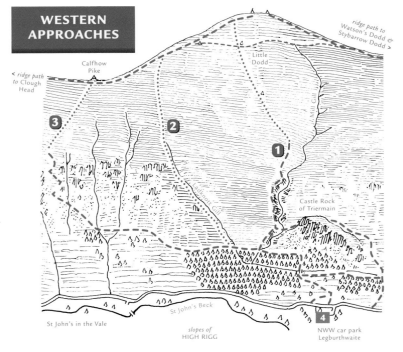

WESTERN APPROACHES

Calfhow Pike

< *ridge path to Clough Head*

Little Dodd

ridge path to Watson's Dodd & Stybarrow Dodd >

Mill Gill

③

②

①

Ladknott Gill

Castle Rock of Triermain

St John's Beck

St John's in the Vale

slopes of HIGH RIGG

NWW car park Legburthwaite

④

ASCENT *from Legburthwaite*

The North West Water car park at Legburthwaite marks a common start for three distinct approaches, only route **1** keeps bracken at bay and sustains interest to any height. Nonetheless, as an opening shot the environs of Castle Rock of Triermain (strictly part of Watson's Dodd) are quite fascinating and go some way to absolve the inevitable tedium of the interminable plod to the top.

See WATSON'S DODD page 283 for the choice of starts converging immediately north of Castle Rock at one or other of the Mill Gill fords.

1 Follow the northern bank above the upper ravine of Mill Gill, a path of diminishing credibility ascends this deeply incised valley. While it is feasible to keep within the gill, a better move, indicated by the last vestige of a path, is to trend onto the open fell at the last rash of stones,

climbing, via an isolated shepherd's cairn *(left)*, over Little Dodd. **2** Mill Gill is not the first watercourse captured by the Thirlmere race, that distinction goes to the neighbouring Ladknott Gill, which tumbles into a pond below the intake wall, before cascading into the channel. Keep to the north side of Ladknott Gill for the least bracken. Climbing onto an indefinite fellside, with the modest interest of a ruined cross-walled bield to inspect, ahead is the ultimate featureless pull to the top.

3 Quite the longest, but by far the best route is the old shepherds' path leading to Calfhow Pike. Follow the intake wall from the foot of the lower ravine in Mill Gill. A word of warning: directly after fording Ladknott Gill be aware that lurking over the wall is the butt of a rifle range, still liable to live firing. The wall dips and rises, with lovely views over the St John's Vale. Coming above Fornside Farm ignore the gate with an inviting green way leading down to the farm, continue, crossing two gills to the point prior to a conifer strip (above a hand-gate). Bear right, onto the clear path rising diagonally up the scree bank, passing close under a small mine adit (beneath a solitary yew) the path zig-zags up a ridge short of the chasm of Beckthorns Gill. The old grooved drove mounts to the remains of a sheepfold set in rushes, either climb direct (no path) to Calfhow Pike passing a spring, or follow the indistinct shepherds' path south-east onto the ridge, continuing, via the cairn on Little Dodd, to the summit.

Hart Side from Randerside

The Summit

A classic 'Dodd', corresponding with the Highland 'Meall', Southern Upland 'Law' and Saxon 'Low' conforms to a gentle dome, bald except for a wind-break cairn on the south-eastern top and a large, but loose amalgam of stones at the true summit *(above)*. The wind-shelter provides the better view, outwith crisp packets and chocolate wrappers!

Safe Descents

There are no crags anywhere near the summit, so descents without a compass are not fraught with stern warnings. However, to the east there is one pitfall to circumnavigate, the soggy morass of Deep Dale; better deserving the name Mosedale than the neighbouring dale. The surest escape in this direction, which also avoids bracken, is along the main ridge path trending west and then north down to Calfhow Pike. From this obvious rock tor follow the fence right, down Mosedale, meeting up with the Old Coach Road, Go left for Threlkeld 3 miles, or right for Dockray 3 miles and perhaps the dry sanctuary of the Royal Hotel bar.

Ridge Routes to....

CLOUGH HEAD DESCENT 755 feet ASCENT 330 feet 2 miles

Take the cairned path W, which angles N from the cairn on Little Dodd descending to Calfhow Pike, avoiding the pools, head N across the depression a clear path rising gently to the old triangulation pillar.

WATSON'S DODD DESCENT 226 feet ASCENT 45 feet 0.8 miles

From the shelter cairn the ridge path runs down the close cropped turf SW, levelling to pass pools on the approach to the solitary summit cairn.

View from the footbridge to the
Old Coach Road fording Groove Beck

Looking to High Rigg from the top of
the Fornside zig-zags overlooking the
deep ravine of Beckthorns Gill

P A N O R A M A

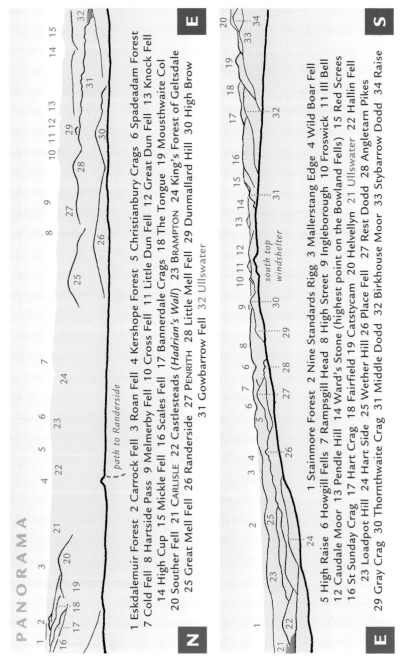

N

1 Eskdalemuir Forest 2 Carrock Fell 3 Roan Fell 4 Kershope Forest 5 Christianbury Crags 6 Spadeadam Forest 7 Cold Fell 8 Hartside Pass 9 Melmerby Fell 10 Cross Fell 11 Little Dun Fell 12 Great Dun Fell 13 Knock Fell 14 High Cup 15 Mickle Fell 16 Scales Fell 17 Bannerdale Crags 18 The Tongue 19 Mousthwaite Col 20 Souther Fell 21 CARLISLE 22 Castlesteads (*Hadrian's Wall*) 23 BRAMPTON 24 King's Forest of Geltsdale 25 Great Mell Fell 26 Randerside 27 PENRITH 28 Little Mell Fell 29 Dunmallard Hill 30 High Brow 31 Gowbarrow Fell 32 Ullswater

E

E

1 Stainmore Forest 2 Nine Standards Rigg 3 Mallerstang Edge 4 Wild Boar Fell 5 High Raise 6 Howgill Fells 7 Rampsgill Head 8 High Street 9 Ingleborough 10 Froswick 11 Ill Bell 12 Caudale Moor 13 Pendle Hill 14 Ward's Stone 15 Red Screes 16 St Sunday Crag 17 Hart Crag 18 Fairfield 19 Catstycam 20 Helvellyn 21 Ullswater 22 Hallin Fell 23 Loadpot Hill 24 Hart Side 25 Wether Hill 26 Place Fell 27 Rest Dodd 28 Angletarn Pikes 29 Gray Crag 30 Thornthwaite Crag 31 Middle Dodd 32 Birkhouse Moor 33 Stybarrow Dodd 34 Raise

S

path to Randerside

south top
windshelter

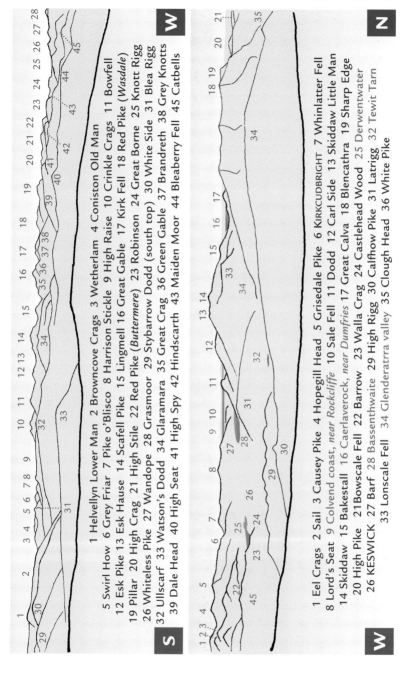

W **S**

1 Helvellyn Lower Man 2 Browncove Crags 3 Wetherlam 4 Coniston Old Man
5 Swirl How 6 Grey Friar 7 Pike o'Blisco 8 Harrison Stickle 9 High Raise 10 Crinkle Crags 11 Bowfell
12 Esk Pike 13 Esk Hause 14 Scafell Pike 15 Lingmell 16 Great Gable 17 Kirk Fell 18 Red Pike (*Wasdale*)
19 Pillar 20 High Crag 21 High Stile 22 Red Pike (*Buttermere*) 23 Robinson 24 Great Borne 25 Knott Rigg
26 Whiteless Pike 27 Wandope 28 Grasmoor 29 Stybarrow Dodd (south top) 30 White Side 31 Blea Rigg
32 Ullscarf 33 Watson's Dodd 34 Glaramara 35 Great Crag 36 Green Gable 37 Brandreth 38 Grey Knotts
39 Dale Head 40 High Seat 41 High Spy 42 Hindscarth 43 Maiden Moor 44 Bleaberry Fell 45 Catbells

N **W**

1 Eel Crags 2 Sail 3 Causey Pike 4 Hopegill Head 5 Grisedale Pike 6 KIRKCUDBRIGHT 7 Whinlatter Fell
8 Lord's Seat 9 Colvend coast, *near Rockcliffe* 10 Sale Fell 11 Dodd 12 Carl Side 13 Skiddaw Little Man
14 Skiddaw 15 Bakestall 16 Caerlaverock, *near Dumfries* 17 Great Calva 18 Blencathra 19 Sharp Edge
20 High Pike 21 Bowscale Fell 22 Barrow 23 Walla Crag 24 Castlehead Wood 25 Derwentwater
26 KESWICK 27 Barf 28 Bassenthwaite 29 High Rigg 30 Calfhow Pike 31 Latrigg 32 Tewit Tarn
33 Lonscale Fell 34 Glenderaterra valley 35 Clough Head 36 White Pike

GREAT MELL FELL

Great Mell is untypical of the range. Conforming to the shape of a giant cheese set upon a dish, akin to some grand designer's trial casting knocked out on the margin of the massif, or a slipper carelessly discarded. Being a loner and something of an exhibitionist, it catches the eye, especially from the A66 corridor, in a way that summits 'on the shoulders of giants' can not. Indeed, descending the Kirkstone Pass it contrives to look like the final swelling of some great distant mountain.

Trees mantle the fell, lending a parkland ornamentation. Though consciously contrived it is a window on a long lost, more general fell verdancy. The fell-name has its roots in the Celtic 'Moel'/Gaelic 'Meall' meaning bald or windswept, suggesting that, when coined, the hill was actually bereft of trees. A shawl of Scots pines drape the east ridge and a few weirdly contorted larches persist almost to the summit. Sheltering from the full force of prevailing weather, the eastern slopes are richly wooded, little disturbed it is a haven for wildlife. Indeed, in the mid-nineteenth century it is claimed that the last wild cat in Cumberland was slain here. There are no crags to mention, though there is a notable erratic boulder, the Cloven Stone, resting near an outbarn on farmland beside Mellfell Beck.

Great Mell is a fell to 'have up one's sleeve' when perhaps the higher fells are wreathed in mist, a new perspective on old fell friends is sought or you wish to mix summiteering with a spot of quiet nature study. Although the 'there and back' ascent may barely dint two hours this can be augmented with a preliminary circuit of the ring fence, by which novel device one may happily consume a full afternoon absorbed in all aspects of this happy little spaniel of a hill, and be well pleased you did!

537 metres   1,762 feet

ASCENT *from Matterdale End and Brownrigg*

Although the majority of ascents begin from the lane-end near Brownrigg Farm, a very pleasant approach may be entertained from Matterdale End, adding a mere mile and a quarter to the climb. **1** Follow the road rising east from the hamlet, branching left into the bridle-lane GR 397236, recently drained, this leads north-west-ward up to the A5091 near Rushmire. Turn immediately right, following the roughly surfaced lane heading north-west. Fording Mellfell Beck the lane rises to a

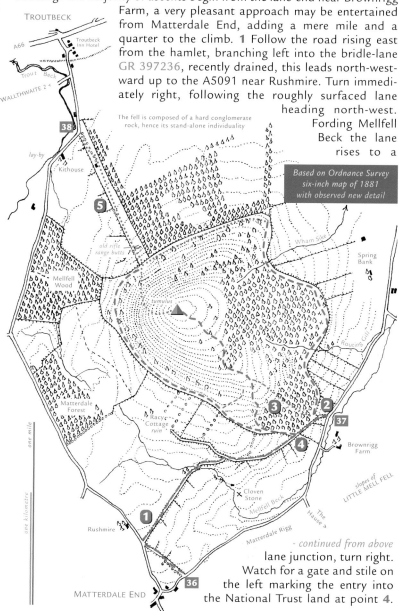

TROUTBECK

A66

Troutbeck
Inn Hotel

Trout Beck

WALLTHWAITE 2 ◁

38

lay-by

Kithouse

The fell is composed of a hard conglomerate
rock, hence its stand-alone individuality

5

old rifle
range butts

Mellfell
Wood

Wham Sike

Spring
Bank

tumulus

Routing Gill

Matterdale
Forest

Racy
Cottage
ruin

3

2

37

4

Brownrigg
Farm

one mile

slopes of
LITTLE MELL FELL

one kilometre

Cloven
Stone

Mellfell Beck

The
Hause ▷

Rushmire

Matterdale Rigg

*Based on Ordnance Survey
six-inch map of 1881
with observed new detail*

1

36

MATTERDALE END

- continued from above
lane junction, turn right.
Watch for a gate and stile on
the left marking the entry into
the National Trust land at point **4**.

Conventional approaches reach this spot from the lane-end located one mile from Matterdale End along the minor road. **2** GR 407246 Park with due care on the verge and follow the lane. **3** At the first bend an inviting gate/stile, with National Trust sign, erroneously suggests the main access point. The obvious path, leading on from here, only follows the ring fence, though a pathless ascent can be made straight up the steep wooded bank from the stile. Emerging from the trees a path materialises, swiftly breaking through the bracken onto the ridge-top pasture. The better option continues in the lane to the stile on the right after 180 yards. **4** Cross the stile, keep the bounding fence to the left, as the trees relent a path branches right, winding up the bracken slope to pass onto the ridge via a solitary tree bent double. The path is joined from the left by a tractor track as it enters the Scots pine spinney and switches right emerging onto the rough pasture and heathery summit.

Typical fell-top larch

ASCENT *from Troutbeck*

Either follow the A5091 south from the Troutbeck Inn for 600 yards, or park on the verge at GR 388264. **5** At the main road bend, cross the stile and follow an old lane to a tin hovel, continue within the old rifle range pasture rising past the redundant butt and target-control shelter, now more steeply, to a gate. There is no pre-ordained path to the summit, so take a natural sweep right and left up the steep western scarp, with up-draught easing elevation.

North-eastern aspect from Penruddock

South-eastern aspect from Great Meldrum

The Summit

A place of splendid isolation, marked by a tiny cairn perched upon a shrunken Bronze Age burial mound. Heather fights the tough moor-grass for supremacy and provides a haunt for the occasional pair of nesting red grouse. Searches for other interest are disappointing, though an odd trench slants east off the scarp brink. The larches, which feature on the northern scarp and on the broad rising east ridge, have a certain entertainment value in their many manifestations, and at least serve as excellent sheep shelters. Given the visibility, the view is rewarding. The Dodds and Blencathra are clearly seen. Lakes are poorly represented with Ullswater making a grudging appearance due south. The artificial tarn behind Brownrigg, the only other water feature, coming into view during the descent of the ridge beyond the ragged belt of pines.

Western aspect from Mellfell Wood, now part of the coniferous Matterdale Forest

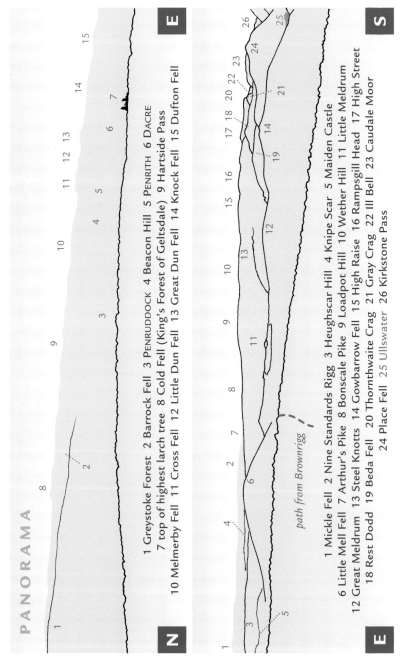

PANORAMA

N **E**

1 Greystoke Forest 2 Barrock Fell 3 PENRUDDOCK 4 Beacon Hill 5 PENRITH 6 DACRE
7 top of highest larch tree 8 Cold Fell (King's Forest of Geltsdale) 9 Hartside Pass
10 Melmerby Fell 11 Cross Fell 12 Little Dun Fell 13 Great Dun Fell 14 Knock Fell 15 Dufton Fell

E **S**

path from Brownrigg

1 Mickle Fell 2 Nine Standards Rigg 3 Heughscar Hill 4 Knipe Scar 5 Maiden Castle
6 Little Mell Fell 7 Arthur's Pike 8 Bonscale Pike 9 Loadpot Hill 10 Wether Hill 11 Little Meldrum
12 Great Meldrum 13 Steel Knotts 14 Gowbarrow Fell 15 High Raise 16 Rampsgill Head 17 High Street
18 Rest Dodd 19 Beda Fell 20 Thornthwaite Crag 21 Gray Crag 22 Ill Bell 23 Caudale Moor
24 Place Fell 25 Ullswater 26 Kirkstone Pass

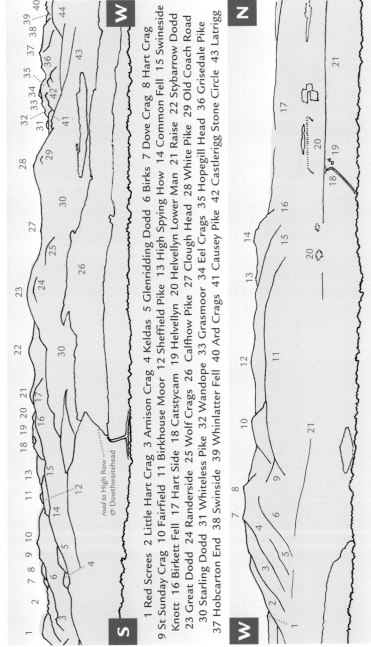

S / **W**

1 Red Screes 2 Little Hart Crag 3 Arnison Crag 4 Keldas 5 Glenridding Dodd 6 Birks 7 Dove Crag 8 Hart Crag 9 St Sunday Crag 10 Fairfield 11 Birkhouse Moor 12 Sheffield Pike 13 High Spying How 14 Common Fell 15 Swineside Knott 16 Birkett Fell 17 Hart Side 18 Catstycam 19 Helvellyn 20 Helvellyn Lower Man 21 Raise 22 Stybarrow Dodd 23 Great Dodd 24 Randerside 25 Wolf Crags 26 Calfhow Pike 27 Clough Head 28 White Pike 29 Old Coach Road 30 Starling Dodd 31 Whiteless Pike 32 Wandope 33 Grasmoor 34 Eel Crags 35 Hopegill Head 36 Grisedale Pike 37 Hobcarton End 38 Swinside 39 Whinlatter Fell 40 Ard Crags 41 Causey Pike 42 Castlerigg Stone Circle 43 Latrigg

road to High Row
& Dowthwaitehead

N / **W**

1 Lord's Seat 2 Blease Fell 3 Gategill Fell 4 Hall's Fell 5 Doddick Fell 6 Scales Fell 7 Blencathra 8 Sharp Edge 9 Mousthwaite Col 10 Bannerdale Crags 11 Souther Fell 12 Bowscale Fell 13 High Pike 14 Carrock Fell 15 MUNGRISDALE 16 MOSEDALE 17 Naddle Crags 18 TROUTBECK 19 old sheep auction ring 20 Roman marching camps (x3) 21 A66

GREAT RIGG

Rising between the deep valleys of Tongue Gill and Rydal Beck and drained by Greenhead Gill, Great Rigg is the concordance of three notable ridges, hence the fell-name, which simply means '*the prominent ridge*'. Walkers converge upon the rounded top, a generous viewpoint, with evident delight, for it is a beautiful place to be. Most frequently they will be involved in a grander endeavour, the Fairfield Horseshoe. Others find their way up more directly from Grasmere, via the Stone Arthur ridge, though may still be lured on consider Fairfield the natural conclusion of their climb.

The fell is best appreciated from the vicinity of Alcock Tarn (*see above*). The south-eastern ridge shoulders on the outcrops of Stone Arthur, the prim, domed summit seen as the neat culmination of Greenhead Gill, a shy re-entrant whose slopes are lined with strongly marked sheep-tracks and dense bracken. The gill itself offers an interesting off-beat line to the top. Tracing a fell beck is always fun, though may appeal more for walkers in need of a sheltered line of descent when a strong westerly makes downward progress difficult.

On the Rydale flank the fell is steep and unwelcoming. The rough, shallow scooped, combes known as coves, offering no attraction for ascent. The term cove is interesting, it derives from the British language which gave us Helvellyn, yet that mountain has not one cove to its name. Here a sequence of coves line the Rydale valley, with Stone Cove tucked under the southern rim and Calf Cove the northern rim of the fell.

767 metres   2,516 feet

From Alcock Tarn, looking up Greenhead Gill
with Stone Arthur sunlit left and Butter Crags near right

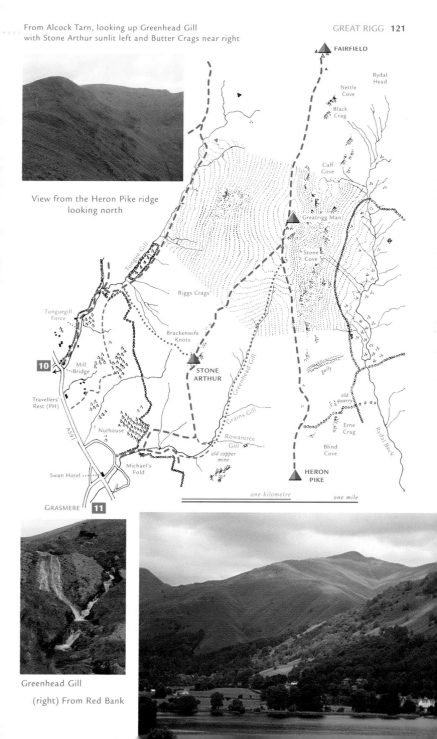

FAIRFIELD

Rydal
Head

Nettle
Cove

Black
Crag

Calf
Cove

Greatrigg Man

Stone
Cove

Rydal Beck

View from the Heron Pike ridge
looking north

Tongue Gill

Riggs Crags

Tonguegill
Force

Brackenwife
Knots

10

Mill
Bridge

STONE
ARTHUR

Greenhead Gill

gully

old
quarry

Travellers'
Rest (PH)

Grains Gill

A591

Nuthouse

Rowantree
Gill

old copper
mine

Erne
Crag

Swan Hotel

Michael's
Fold

Blind
Cove

HERON
PIKE

GRASMERE **11**

one kilometre   one mile

Greenhead Gill

(right) From Red Bank

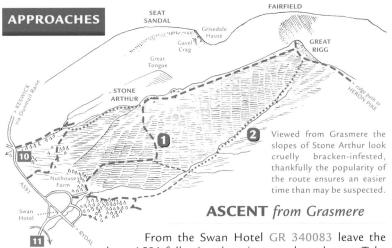

APPROACHES

FAIRFIELD

SEAT SANDAL

Grisedale Hause

Gavel Crag

GREAT RIGG

Great Tongue

KESWICK via Dunmail Raise

STONE ARTHUR

ridge path to HERON PIKE

1

2

10

Nuthouse Farm

A591

Swan Hotel

11

GRASMERE

RYDAL

Viewed from Grasmere the slopes of Stone Arthur look cruelly bracken-infested, thankfully the popularity of the route ensures an easier time than may be suspected.

ASCENT *from Grasmere*

From the Swan Hotel GR 340083 leave the busy A591 following the minor road north-east. Take the second turning right with footpath sign 'Greenhead Gill, Allcock Tarn (sic)'. Where the tarmac ends pass through the gate onto the fell. There are two options to consider - via Stone Arthur and the south-west ridge, or a valley route within Greenhead Gill. **1** See STONE ARTHUR pages 266/271 for a complete picture of the options from the Grasmere vale, suffice to say, the ridge is tempting and well worth the effort. The regular route to the top keeps left, climbing first with the enclosure wall left, then within the old walled lane which sweeps across the slope right, a welcome turf trail wrestling with the ubiquitous bracken. Coming above the Greenhead valley it meets an old path coming sharply out of the gill, here switching left, climb the broadening ridge to clear the bracken with some glee. The path wanders up through the ruined battlements of Stone Arthur and onto the grassy ridge beyond. Half-a-mile of steady tramping leads to a cairn linking to the watershed path, go left to complete the ascent.

2 The secrets of Greenhead Gill are known only to those who are prepared to give it a go! From the gate go right crossing the wooden footbridge, initially winding up the hugely popular Alcock Tarn path. See below the point where the Thirlmere aqueduct crosses the deep ravine. Watch for and join the contouring path leading off the pounded trail leading into the gill bottom. The diminishing path skips and stumbles past the remains of a copper mine to be lost. Henceforth an eagerness to see the next playful act of the beck distracts attention from the deficiencies of steady footing. Waterfalls shrink as height is gained, the banks are just that bit more troublesome. Cross two strong sheep-walks contouring the valley-head, though either might be found welcome respite leftward onto the south-west ridge, from the stiff direct line, which duly eases at the meeting with the 'Horseshoe' ridge path.

Helm Crag from Greenhead Gill

Greenhead Gill - described by Wordsworth as "the tumuluous brook"- from Alcock Tarn

The Summit

Unusually, the summit cairn - a sorry heap, ravaged by many visitations - is identified by name, Greatrigg Man. The latter term contracted from the British 'maen', meaning stone, which might suggest a single ancient marker rock of lost significance. It is a fine place to rest and peer inquisitively down through Nettle Cove into the lonely pastured depths of Rydal Head. Perhaps also spotting walkers dotted along the bounding ridges at other stages of the Horseshoe trail. By some quirk Rydale, the mountain-locked valley to the east, is not identified by name on official maps, the valley pasture being broadly referred to as Rydal Fell.

The long strath of Rydale from Hart Crag looking to Heron Pike and Great Rigg

Great Rigg from Gavel Crag

Safe Descents

The ridge paths leading south (particularly) and south-west are reliable guides, though in really adverse weather consider dropping into the pathless, but sheltered valley of Greenhead Gill for Grasmere. The south-west ridge is fine until the dense bracken is encountered all too soon beneath the outcropping of Stone Arthur. One of the blessings of winter being the bracken's seasonal demise.

Ridge Routes to....

FAIRFIELD   DESCENT 100 feet
ASCENT 450 feet   1 mile

A plainer route does not exist. The wide path descends to a shallow depression ahead of climbing onto the plateau, to be greeted by an excess of cairns, which direct to the summit wind-shelters.

HERON PIKE   DESCENT 580 feet   ASCENT 150 feet   1.5 miles

The undulations of the ridge with several small pools give character to the trail. The top of Erne Crag with its wall-end cairn, merits the title Heron Pike, which has instead been bestowed upon the second slightly higher top due south, deficient of a standard cairn the abundance of quartz suffices.

from Rydal Park

Heron Pike
Erne Crag
Great Rigg
Fairfield

PANORAMA

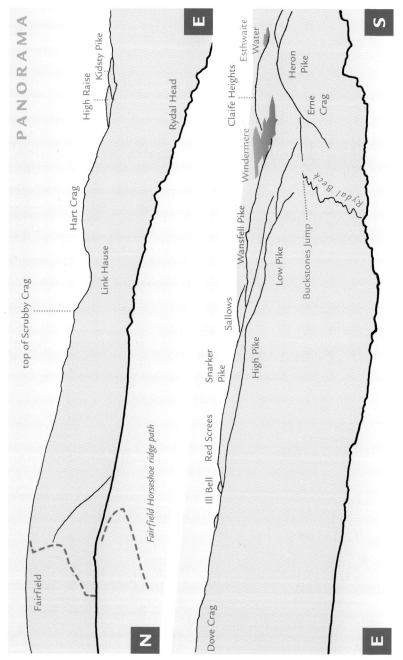

E

top of Scrubby Crag

Hart Crag

Link Hause

High Raise

Kidsty Pike

Rydal Head

Fairfield

Fairfield Horseshoe ridge path

N

S

Esthwaite Water

Claife Heights

Heron Pike

Erne Crag

Windermere

Wansfell Pike

Low Pike

Buckstones Jump

Rydal Beck

Sallows

High Pike

Snarker Pike

Red Screes

Ill Bell

Dove Crag

E

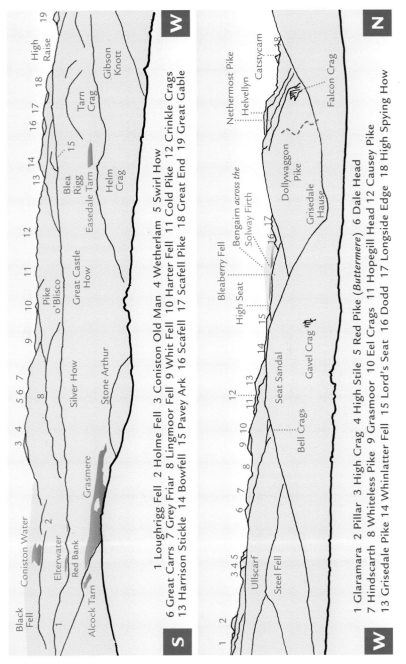

W

1 Loughrigg Fell 2 Holme Fell 3 Coniston Old Man 4 Wetherlam 5 Swirl How
6 Great Carrs 7 Grey Friar 8 Lingmoor Fell 9 Whit Fell 10 Harter Fell 11 Cold Pike 12 Crinkle Crags
13 Harrison Stickle 14 Bowfell 15 Pavey Ark 16 Scafell 17 Scafell Pike 18 Great End 19 Great Gable

Black Fell · Coniston Water · Elterwater · Red Bank · Grasmere · Alcock Tarn · Silver How · Stone Arthur · Pike o'Blisco · Great Castle How · Blea Rigg · Easedale Tarn · Tarn Crag · Gibson Knott · Helm Crag

S

N

Nethermost Pike · Helvellyn · Catstycam · Falcon Crag · Bengairn *across the* Solway Firth · Bleaberry Fell · High Seat · Dollywaggon Pike · Grisedale Hause · Seat Sandal · Gavel Crag · Bell Crags · Ullscarf · Steel Fell

1 Glaramara 2 Pillar 3 High Crag 4 High Stile 5 Red Pike (*Buttermere*) 6 Dale Head
7 Hindscarth 8 Whiteless Pike 9 Grasmoor 10 Eel Crags 11 Hopegill Head 12 Causey Pike
13 Grisedale Pike 14 Whinlatter Fell 15 Lord's Seat 16 Dodd 17 Longside Edge 18 High Spying How

W

HART CRAG

Seen to perfection from Gavel Pike where its brooding north face, standing shoulder to shoulder with Scrubby Crag, looms imperiously above the wild corrie of Link Cove. Elsewhere the fell is less convincing, though small in extent, whether seen from Rydal Head, Dovedale or Deepdale it is uniformly rough in character. The extended arm of the north-east ridge is strictly part and parcel of Hart Crag, though relinquished by custom to Hartsop above How. In full extent it forms the sturdy side-screen separating desolate Deepdale and adorable Dovedale.

Visitors usually arrive along the main ridge firmly focused on the Fairfield Horseshoe, its summit being by far the most rock-infected on that perennially popular round. It can be 'taken' as the culmination of the wild trek up Deepdale, most frequently, however, it forms the natural fulfilment of that superb fellwalkers' ridge, Hartsop above How, stemming from either Cowbridge or Bridgend.

Those who find inspiration from lonely places will love plodding the extent of Rydale to mount pathless Rydal Head onto Link Hause. A word of warning here, a conventional 'hause' it is not! In fact, the north-facing hanging valley of Link Cove might be thought explanatory, for Link Hause is a ridge-top link only between Hart Crag and Fairfield.

The fell sits tantalisingly high and dry being deficient of significant watercourses of its own and, for all its name, no clean face of tempting rock to rival Scrubby Crag for the attentions of dedicated crag rats.

822 metres   2,697 feet

See the maps in the Arnison Crag
and St Sunday Crag chapters
for the Deepdale approach.

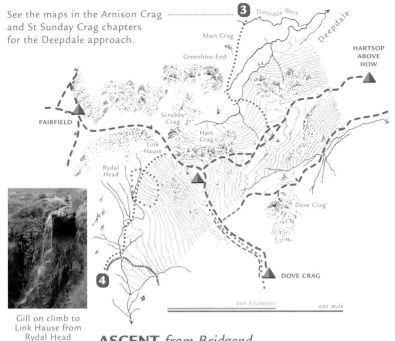

Gill on climb to
Link Hause from
Rydal Head

ASCENT *from Bridgend*

1 Follow the narrow lane to Lane End and the succeeding track via gates above Deepdale Hall. Beyond Wall End cross the clapper-bridge spanning Coldcove Beck and follow the irregular dale-bottom track into the wilds of Deepdale. Passing beneath Latterhaw Crag one may 'dive off' the track south, **2** fording the valley beck, eyeing the skyline nick fashioned by Dry Gill, this gives a neat untrammelled line onto the Hartsop above How ridge. **3** For the greater thrills of Link Cove continue up the dale to the drumlin field. Skirt around the western edge of the aptly named Mossydale hollow, passing up beneath Mart Crag then, more steeply, close under Greenhow End, avoiding the difficulties within the Linkcove Gill ravine. The cove has lower and upper sections, only climbers on a mission to scale Scrubby Crag set foot in the loft corrie. Cross the adjacent gill passing a large erratic to ford Linkcove Gill above its topmost

**EASTERN
APPROACHES**

waterfall. Make up the easy slopes south-south-east to meet with one of two ridge paths above Blake Brow. These paths converge only to divide again when Hart Crag's east ridge steepens, the more entertaining line keeping to the leading scrambly edge. The left-hand path avoids rock, but succumbs to a loose scree gully in climbing to join the edge path on a higher shelf, thereafter jink through the rocks via a welcome grassy strip to the final bouldery ground at the top.

Link Cove from Gavel Pike

Scrubby Crag

Hart Crag

Dove Crag

Greenhow End

Erne Nest Crag

Mart Crag

Mossydale

ASCENT *from Rydal*

But for the cries from the occasional walker along the skyline ridges, one might feel transported into some distant Highland glen when engaged in the three-mile trek up lonely Rydale. This cul-de-sac valley is remarkably peaceful and it is uncommon to meet another soul - a definite plus for those of a solitary inclination. **4** The lane leading up by Rydal Mount gives the one line of entry. A gated track leads into the dale with an enclosure wall never far to the right. The first excitement comes in the form of a cataract and subsequent rockband waterfall feature, Buckstones Jump (access hindered by fencing at the wall gap). The track leads on to a gate where a down wall intervenes (with a large erratic built into the adjacent wall). High above rises Erne Crag at its foot of spoil

scree and retaining walls associated with the long abandoned Erne Crag Quarry. Hereon the track dwindles to a turf trod, one may contour, or dip closer to the wall, passing beneath a gully running off the Heron Pike ridge. Further on the wall has been assailed by gill spillage beneath the steep slopes of Great Rigg, it does not hinder progress. As the Dalehead Close wall swings right, all trace of a path are lost. Follow the valley beck into the mossy interior of Rydal Head (the older name for Fairfield). A walled enclosure once lassoed the lower slopes of Hart Crag its broken remnants are an early guide. Keep to the western side, climbing on above, with just steepness as a handicap to the eventual achievement of the ridge-top saddle at Link Hause. Turn right (south-east) to complete the ascent.

Looking across Link Hause from the Fairfield plateau

The Summit

The summit ridge is a mixture of splintered bedrock and grass. The main ridge path contrives to weave an efficient slalom-course, that is until the very last moment when a few determined boulders intervene and separate the path from the summit cairn (*see above*). There are cairns at either end of a short summit rigg. The ultimate goal, at the south-eastern end is sadly no Shangri-la viewpoint, inevitably playing second fiddle to Fairfield. While the view is hampered by neighbouring fells, to east and west some well-known fells raise their familiar heads to entertain a brief contemplative visit; empty Rydale can soak up any gaze.

Safe Descents

The surest option is S upon the main ridge path (Fairfield Horseshoe), keeping stoically to the ridge wall over Dove Crag. Below High Pike the ridge narrows and takes rocky, frequently eroded steps, but is otherwise a sure guide to Ambleside. For Hartsop and Patterdale the NE ridge, via Hartsop above How, requires care at the outset, being poorly defined as it approaches the precipitous northern edge of Hart Crag. In deteriorating conditions it is better to head S to the first depression beside the broken ridge wall before diverting NNE from the marker cairn, though this has one uncomfortable section, the gully out of Houndshope Cove which is sorely in need of repair. One could also contemplate going W from this point into Rydale, but the joys are few and the miles long to civilisation in distant Rydal. Whatever you do, give no second thought to Link Cove, there is no safe route for the walker into the upper cove even in perfect weather.

Ridge Routes to....

DOVE CRAG   DESCENT 240 feet   ASCENT 150 feet   0.6 miles

The path leaves the eastern brink over rocky ground. As the ground eases, so begins the now intermittently broken ridge wall. The majority of striders abide to the east side in crossing the depression and rising without incident to the summit cairn, set upon a neat rock table.

FAIRFIELD   DESCENT 150 feet   ASCENT 350 feet   1 mile

Head to the northern of the two summit cairns and angle half-right the few paces to join the main ridge path. To enjoy the full grandeur of Scrubby Crag one may cautiously wander across by the solitary cairn set off to north of the path. Otherwise keep rigidly to the well trod way into the narrow saddle of Link Hause and up the rocky step onto the wide, well cairned, plateau. With the privilege of a good day, one may indulge in a spot of edge walking to glimpse the best of this fine mountain clinging to the sheep trods above Scrubby Crag and the northern precipices.

HIGH HARTSOP DODD DESCENT 980 feet   ASCENT 90 feet 1.4 miles

The early stages are not gifted by a cairned path, in mist this can be treacherous. Head NE, a grass strip leads to an area of scree glitter, either hold to the rocky edge, or slip down the unruly scree gully right. Once the steep ground is cleared, a largely grassy rolling ridge ensues, the path taking two lines to Blake Brow, that to the north avoids a final rocky step down. Peat hags are encountered in the depression before the little pull to the cairnless top. For all the simplicity of the ridge, crags abound on either flank making it imperative that the ridge path is adhered to. If an alternative into Dovedale is to be considered, then do so only at the foot of the steep descent from Hart Crag, traversing right into Houndshope Cove.

Hart Crag across Link Cove from Greenhow End

PANORAMA

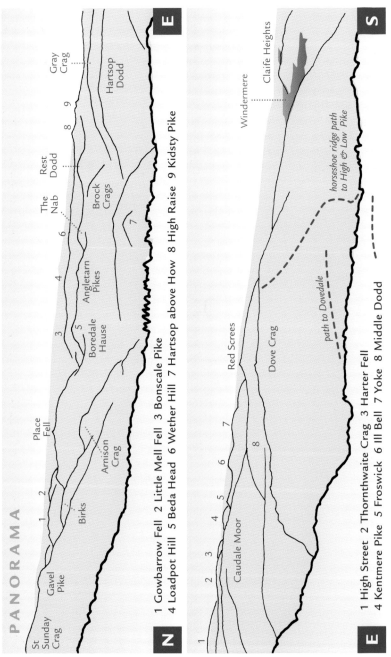

St Sunday Crag Gavel Pike 1 2 Place Fell 3 5 4 6 The Nab Rest Dodd 8 9 Gray Crag

Birks Arnison Crag Boredale Hause Angletarn Pikes Brock Crags 7 Hartsop Dodd

E

N

1 Gowbarrow Fell 2 Little Mell Fell 3 Bonscale Pike
4 Loadpot Hill 5 Beda Head 6 Wether Hill 7 Hartsop above How 8 High Raise 9 Kidsty Pike

Windermere Claife Heights

Red Screes 1 2 3 4 5 6 7 8 Dove Crag Caudale Moor

horseshoe ridge path to High & Low Pike

path to Dovedale

S

E

1 High Street 2 Thornthwaite Crag 3 Harter Fell
4 Kentmere Pike 5 Froswick 6 Ill Bell 7 Yoke 8 Middle Dodd

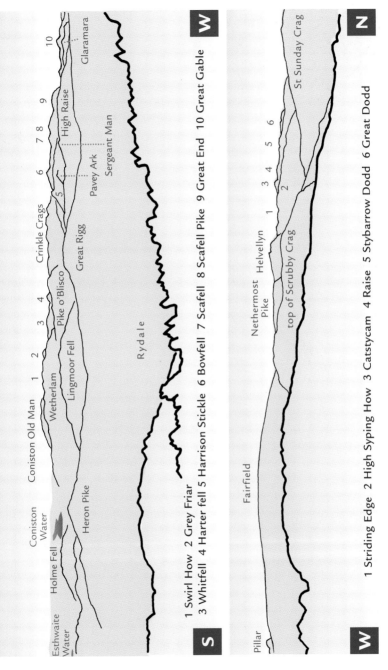

W

Glaramara
10
High Raise
9
Sergeant Man
8
7
Pavey Ark
6
Crinkle Crags
5
Great Rigg
Pike o'Blisco
4
3
Wetherlam
2
Lingmoor Fell
1
Coniston Old Man
Heron Pike
Holme Fell
Coniston Water
Esthwaite Water
Rydale

S

1 Swirl How 2 Grey Friar
3 Whitfell 4 Harter fell 5 Harrison Stickle 6 Bowfell 7 Scafell 8 Scafell Pike 9 Great End 10 Great Gable

N

St Sunday Crag
6
5
4
3
Helvellyn
2
1
Nethermost Pike
top of Scrubby Crag
Fairfield
Pillar

W

1 Striding Edge 2 High Syping How 3 Catstycam 4 Raise 5 Stybarrow Dodd 6 Great Dodd

HART SIDE

It would be all too easy to be dismissive of Hart Side's qualities, over-looking the dreary hollow of Deep Dale and overbearing Dowthwaite-head. But in tandem with its shoulder viewpoint, Birkett Fell, this is a summit, pleasantly set apart from the main thrust of the range, where the fellwalking connoisseur may quietly linger and soak up the good fell air. The fell's health giving qualities acknowledged in times past by herds of red deer at least, hence its name '*summer pasture of the rutting stag*'.

Along its southern flanks runs an old miners' trail, engineered for work convenience and sometimes known as the Miners' Balcony Path - a fine parade contouring above the barren glacial hollow of Glencoyne Head - this forms the focus of approaches. Dockray frequently is the end-point of the popular round of the 'Dodds'. This may begin at Wanthwaite or, when taken as an energetic 12-mile horseshoe, lead off from High Row upon the Old Coach Road.

Uniformly the fairest aspects of Hart Side, and its dependant Watermillock Common ridge, spill down the eastern slopes, indeed, no more sumptuous prospect of Ullswater exists than from Swineside Knott on Brown Hills.

The portion of fell drained by Coegill and Little Aira Becks was chris-tened Birkett Fell in 1963, in memory of the greatly revered advocate, Lord Birkett of Ulverston. Norman Birkett was brought up within a

758 metres   2,487 feet

strong Methodist family, the bedrock of a man of compassion which underpinned a distinguished legal career. His adoration of Lakeland made him an impassioned fighter on its behalf. His crowning triumph was to avert the plan to convert Ullswater into a reservoir. The inquiry ended little more than a week before his death! Such threats never really go away, a guarded vigilance is ever needed. The cairn is composed of stones brought up from the shores of Ullswater by members of the Outward Bound School, it seconds a memorial plaque set on Kailpot Crag with its simple inscription :

*"He loved Ullswater.
He strove to maintain its
beauty for all to enjoy".*

Birkett Fell
Memorial Cairn

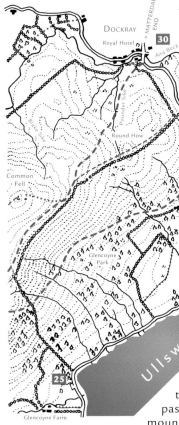

DOCKRAY
Royal Hotel
30
29
High Force
28
Aira Force
Park Brow
Common Fell
Round How
Pounder Side
Black Side
cafe
Glencoyne Park
Ullswater
25
Glencoyne Farm
> MATTERDALE END
Aira Beck

ASCENT *from Dockray*

There are three early lines to consider, each with their own intrinsic merit. **1** The primary route begins from the village immediately south of the bridge, where there is scope for half a dozen cars to park beside the beck. Follow the short lane to a gate entering Watermillock Common (*National Trust*).

A clear track leads off, though be watchful to bear left just before the ford. The path rises to join and accompany the boundary wall above Glencoyne Park, providing an unrivalled vista across the mid-reaches of Ullswater backed by the Far Eastern Fells. **2** Walkers susceptible to ridge routes however damp, may choose to take the scalp of Common Fell, by branching right (no path) at the point of contact with the wall; passing the solitary erratic to reach the mound-top cairn, a prime viewpoint for Dowthwaitehead. The ridge, which can be more a wade than a walk, concludes at Swineside Knott, Ullswater aficionados will love this superlative and unvaunted viewpoint.

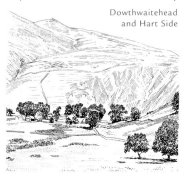

Dowthwaitehead and Hart Side

3 A charming start point is the lower of the two Aira Force access car parks down the road from Dockray. Cross the road to the light stile and follow the clear path through Glencoyne Park, so named as it was once a deer sanctuary. Bracken lined, fording shallow gills this wonderful ascent provides lovely views over the spinney dappled fell-side upon Ullswater. A ladder-stile heralds a wooded passage ahead of

Glencoyne Park and the middle reach of Ullswater from the slopes of Swineside Knott

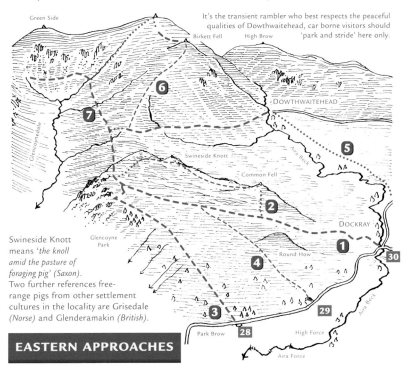

Green Side

It's the transient rambler who best respects the peaceful qualities of Dowthwaitehead, car borne visitors should 'park and stride' here only.

Birkett Fell   High Brow

6

DOWTHWAITEHEAD

7

Glencoynedale

5

Swineside Knott

Aira Beck

Common Fell

2

DOCKRAY

1

30

Swineside Knott means 'the knoll amid the pasture of foraging pig' (Saxon). Two further references free-range pigs from other settlement cultures in the locality are Grisedale (Norse) and Glenderamakin (British).

Glencoyne Park

Round How

4

3

29

Park Brow   28   High Force

EASTERN APPROACHES

Aira Force

breached dam in Glencoynedale

Glencoyne Level

the scenic ascent of Glencoyne Brow to the stile in the wall. These three options converge on the miners' path from Dockray, advancing to a stile in the newly restored wall which runs in a beeline, across the north-eastern slopes of Birkett Fell.

4 A noteworthy alternative start, clings to the ridge climbing directly out of the upper quarry car park (more usually used as an access to High Force down in the wooded Aira Beck valley) via ladder-stiles to follow the ridge wall by Round How, linking to the miners' path from Dockray asit meets the wall.

5 A footpath can be adopted through the meadows to Dowthwaite-head, signposted off the Dockray to High Row road, within 0.4 mile of the Royal Hotel junction. The continuing miners' path is signposted from the Rush Beck footbridge. It climbs the damp intake, crossing gills to a kissing-gate in the fence, before mounting the slope crossing the head-stream of Little Aira Beck to the skyline wall (currently undergoing restoration). A matter of twenty yards south of this spot find a curious composite stone cross laid out beside the wall. **6** From this point either ascend directly, with the wall to the right, to reach the Birkett Fell cairn, or **7** follow the indistinct path dipping over the ridge to join the balcony path where it negotiates a small gill. Contour with this narrow path crossing Wintergroove Gill, wandering under the broken outcrop of Scot Crag before reaching the cascading Deepdale Slack. Ahead notice the spoil and entrance to Glencoyne Level which connects to Greenside Mine's deep labyrinth of shafts and galleries - resist the temptation to venture in. Leave the path climbing on hands and knees steeply beside the joyous tumblings of Deepdale Slack.

Prospectors' trial trench on the summit

The Summit

A cluster of cairns among a ruckle of rocks marks the summit. The curious east/west trench a few yards south suggests a prospecting dig, an evidently vain search for the rich seam of lead due north from the Greenside Mine. Prior to the leisurely age of fellwalking, these fells were the domain of the mining prospector and every single outcrop will have been meticulously scrutinised in the search for rich pickings. North of the summit a shallow hollow measuring 7 yards x 4 yards suggests the site of some rude shelter which certainly had an enviable prospect.

As a viewpoint, Hart Side permits a somewhat distant glimpse of Catstycam, Helvellyn, Helvellyn Lower Man and, in the dip between Green Side and Stybarrow Dodd, the very summit of Scafell Pike piercing the skyline. East of the summit, across marshy ground, stands a proud little cairn, currently in some need of repair. This is Birkett Fell, and is, by some measure, a far better viewpoint, hence it naturally takes precedence as the place to 'stand and stare' (see overleaf).

Safe Descents

Innocuous as this outpost may appear, there are crags to be avoided. The one sure line is east, picking up the wall beyond the cairn on Birkett Fell, follow this right, making the valley by either of the old miners' paths to Dowthwaitehead or Dockray.

Ridge Routes to....

SHEFFIELD PIKE   DESCENT 689 feet   ASCENT 394 feet   1.3 miles

Follow narrow path WSW which 'dissolves' on the gently rising ridge to Green Side. Descend from the cairns SE, curving down, cautious of the presence of an exposed hollow after 550 yards on the southern slope of the ridge. From the lip of this quarried mine, a path angles down, over blanket peat to Nick Head, crossing the depression, rise E over further spongy ground to the summit cairn, proud as punch on its shattered rock plinth.

STYBARROW DODD   DESCENT 164 feet   ASCENT 486 feet   1.7 miles

Advance WSW to the cairns on Green Side, head W, from the shallow dip on a diminishing path, curving NW in mounting onto the breezy summit.

PANORAMA from the Lord Birkett Memorial Cairn on Birkett Fell

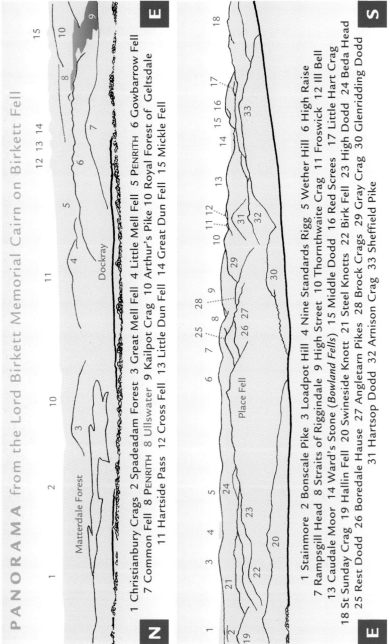

E

N

1 Christianbury Crags 2 Spadeadam Forest 3 Great Mell Fell 4 Little Mell Fell 5 PENRITH 6 Gowbarrow Fell
7 Common Fell 8 PENRITH 9 Ullswater 10 Arthur's Pike 10 Royal Forest of Geltsdale
11 Hartside Pass 12 Cross Fell 13 Little Dun Fell 14 Great Dun Fell 15 Mickle Fell

Matterdale Forest

Dockray

S

E

1 Stainmore 2 Bonscale Pike 3 Loadpot Hill 4 Nine Standards Rigg 5 Wether Hill 6 High Raise
7 Rampsgill Head 8 Straits of Riggindale 9 High Street 10 Thornthwaite Crag 11 Froswick 12 Ill Bell
13 Caudale Moor 14 Ward's Stone (*Bowland Fells*) 15 Middle Dodd 16 Red Screes 17 Little Hart Crag
18 St Sunday Crag 19 Hallin Fell 20 Swineside Knott 21 Steel Knotts 22 Birk Fell 23 High Dodd 24 Beda Head
25 Rest Dodd 26 Boredale Hause 27 Angletarn Pikes 28 Brock Crags 29 Gray Crag 30 Glenridding Dodd
31 Hartsop Dodd 32 Arnison Crag 33 Sheffield Pike

Place Fell

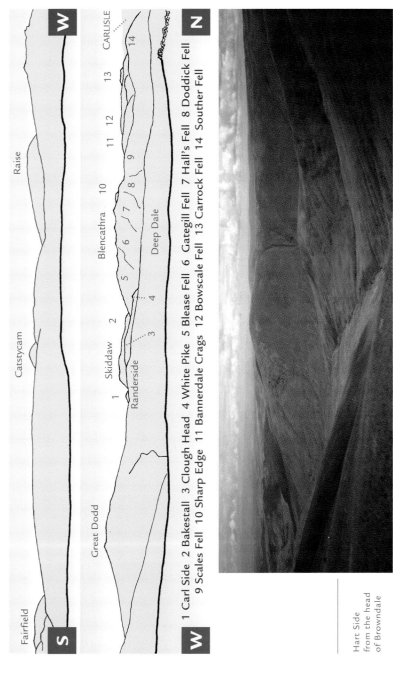

W

Fairfield — Fairfield · Catstycam · Raise

S

N

Great Dodd · Skiddaw · Randerside · Blencathra · Deep Dale · Raise · CARLISLE

1 Skiddaw 2 3 4 5 6 7 8 9 10 Blencathra 11 12 13 14

W

1 Carl Side 2 Bakestall 3 Clough Head 4 White Pike 5 Blease Fell 6 Gategill Fell 7 Hall's Fell 8 Doddick Fell 9 Scales Fell 10 Sharp Edge 11 Bannerdale Crags 12 Bowscale Fell 13 Carrock Fell 14 Souther Fell

Hart Side
from the head
of Browndale

HARTSOP ABOVE HOW

A curious name which might best be translated as '*the rough hill above Low Hartsop*'. It belongs assuredly to Hart Crag. From the foot of Deepdale it rises, curving in sympathy with the dale, to a modest grassy crest, the ridge then dips to a shallow depression before mounting Hart Crag, the rugged culmination of some three and a half miles of very rewarding fell-walking. The ridge is a popular return leg to Dovedale ascents, especially enjoyed for its out-sights of the adjacent craggy Hunsett and Link Coves. Visually, the fell naturally serves the dual function of contrasting sidewalls to the sylvan beauties of Dovedale and shy wildness of Deepdale. The valley traveller will take pleasure from the now, all too rare, natural woodland swarming high above Hartsop Hall and Brothers Water, the lake reflecting exquisitely the old coppiced banks of Low Wood. Once much of the Patterdale glen was similarly richly adorned. How one regrets the massive loss of native woodland throughout the district, primarily forfeit over recent centuries. The culprits: hefted flocks of Herdwick and Swaledale - John Muir's 'hooved locusts'.

Brothers Water and Low Wood

586 metres   1,923 feet

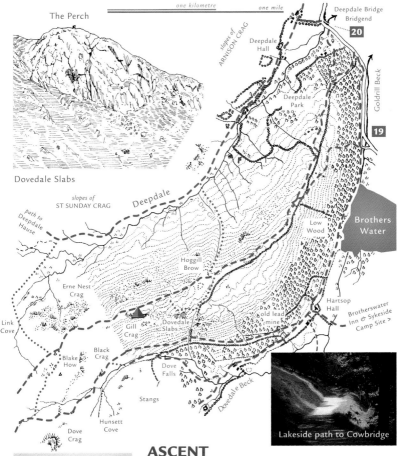

The Perch

one kilometre   *one mile*

Deepdale Bridge
Bridgend

20

slopes of
ARNISON CRAG

Deepdale
Hall

Goldrill Beck

Deepdale
Park

19

Dovedale Slabs

slopes of
ST SUNDAY CRAG

Deepdale

path to
Deepdale
Hause

Dry Gill

Low
Wood

Brothers
Water

Hoggill
Brow

Erne Nest
Crag

Hartsop
Hall

Brotherswater
Inn & Sykeside
Camp Site >

old lead
mine

Link
Cove

Gill
Crag

Dovedale
Slabs

Black
Crag

Blake
How

Dove
Falls

Dovedale Beck

Stangs

Hunsett
Cove

Dove
Crag

Lakeside path to Cowbridge

ASCENT
from Deepdale Bridge & Cowbridge

At either end of the hamlet of Bridgend at Deepdale Bridge (and yes, for pedants, there are two bridges!) lay-by parking may be used. That to the south, beside the telephone kiosk and bus stop, being the key point of embarkation. **1** A gated wall-stile beside the field-gate is crossed to follow the cart track up the pasture to a waymark post which guides left to a cross a ladder-stile - thereby deflecting unwelcome visits to the vernacular barn lying in the vicinity of a Dark Age settlement site. Enter Low Wood, an important woodland habitat extending all

Ridge-top ladder-stile

Low Hartsop and Pasture Beck from the path directly above Cowbridge

along the eastern slopes of Hartsop above How into Dovedale. The path winds gently up to a fence stile, latterly a path joins from the left. **2** This path begins from the road at a stile some 350 yards south-east from the lay-by, crosses a small meadow to via a fence stile entering the woodland to ascend to this point. Leaving the wood, enter the more open pasture of Deepdale Park, steadily ascending with the ridge wall close by.

Deepdale's impressive surround of fells in view from Deepdale Park

Houndshope Cove

Link Cove

path to Deepdale Hause

Erne Nest Crag

6

Dovedale Slabs

EASTERN APPROACHES

4

slopes of ST SUNDAY CRAG

Dry Gill

5

Deepdale

Deepdale Beck

Deepdale Park

Low Wood

3

Brothers Water

2

20

19

1

Goldrill Beck

Remains of Hartsop Hall Lead Mine

Early strides given added impetus from the stirring views up Deepdale, focussed upon the gabled peak of Gavel Pike on St Sunday Crag to the right and the craggy headwall of Fairfield. The path rounds a knoll to a wall-stile now, upon a pronounced grassy ridge.

3 From the Cowbridge car park a path climbs directly from the gate, passing through a deer-excluding fenced section of woodland by weighted gates. The path comes above Low Wood, slanting left to gain a cairn and a fine view over Brothers Water with the steep fells above Hartsop forming a striking backdrop. The path mounts onto the fell's edge, passing cairns and crossing an old wall to reach a ladder-stile, short of the rock step. The ridge path joined, faithfully follow alongside the wall. As the wall drifts left, one may either stick rigidly to the rising ridge, or **4** choose to accompany the wall by the pools. Contour across the grassy slope above the bracken line to stand beside The Perch, a distinctive pinnacle topping sheer Dovedale Slabs, an airy spot well suited for aviarian rest, the breathtaking view of Hunsett Cove and Dove Crag it is well worth the deviation. Cut back up to join the ridge path finding the summit just beyond a gully notch. Two alternative and pathless approaches lie up Deepdale. **5** Passing beneath Latterhaw Crag leave the valley track and ford the Deepdale Beck following Dry Gill direct to Hoggill Brow. Or **6** continue updale, bearing left under Mart Crag climbing into the lower section of Link Cove. Cross Link Cove Gill at the top waterfall, slanting up the eastern slopes to join the ridge path on Blake Brow. Heading north-east along the ridge, cross the peat-hag depression to reach the summit.

Scrubby Crag

Cofa Pike

The Step

Deep
Ha

Link Cove

Cawk
Cove

Greenhow
End

Looking west from the summit

The Summit

Rising from the Hartsop vale the ridge wall swings south-westward as the fell draws to a definite crest, with the actual summit a less than flamboyant terminating flourish. A few stones may lie on the small top which is set above a notch overlooking Hunsett Cove. Many walkers slip by on the eroded peat path, quite oblivious of the ultimate moment, their attention on the peak of Hart Crag as the real objective summit.

Safe Descents

The one line is ENE along the ridge, descending with the security of the wall for company, for either Deepdale Bridge, or, via the first ladder-stile, the National Trust's car park at Cowbridge.

Looking south-west along the summit ridge

High Raise   Rampsgill Head   High Street

The Knott   Gray Crag

Hartsop Dodd

Erne Nest Crag

Hartsop above How from the prow of Greenhow End

Ridge Route to....

HART CRAG   DESCENT 90 feet   ASCENT 980 feet   1.4 miles

A clear path leads SW. Descend to cross an area of eroded peat in the depression. Rise easily on grass beyond, either via a small step in the ridge, or pass to its right. If Dove Crag intrigues then a pathless traverse can be made across Houndshope Cove from this point. Out of preference - in fair weather - tackle Hart Crag's eastern ridge, via the leading scrambly edge. The left-hand path avoids rock, but succumbs to a loose scree gully in climbing to join the edge path on a higher shelf, thereafter jink through the rocks to the summit cairn.

PANORAMA

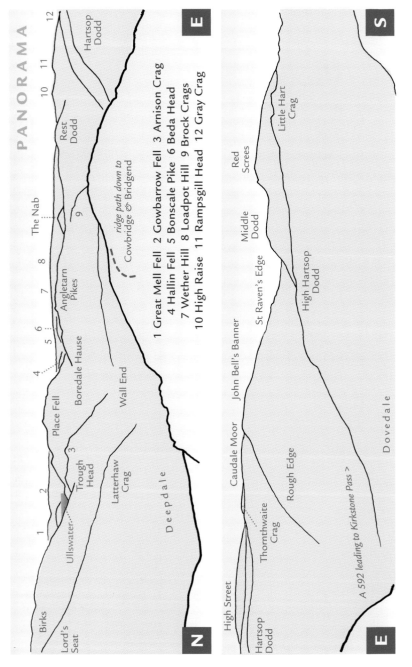

E

Birks

Lord's Seat

Ullswater

1 2 3 4 5 6 7 8 9 10 11 12

Place Fell

The Nab

Rest Dodd

Hartsop Dodd

Trough Head

Boredale Hause

Angletarn Pikes

Latterhaw Crag

Wall End

ridge path down to
Cowbridge & Bridgend

Deepdale

1 Great Mell Fell 2 Gowbarrow Fell 3 Arnison Crag
4 Hallin Fell 5 Bonscale Pike 6 Beda Head
7 Wether Hill 8 Loadpot Hill 9 Brock Crags
10 High Raise 11 Rampsgill Head 12 Gray Crag

N

S

Red Screens

Little Hart Crag

Middle Dodd

St Raven's Edge

High Hartsop Dodd

John Bell's Banner

Caudale Moor

Rough Edge

Thornthwaite Crag

Dovedale

A 592 leading to Kirkstone Pass >

High Street

Hartsop Dodd

E

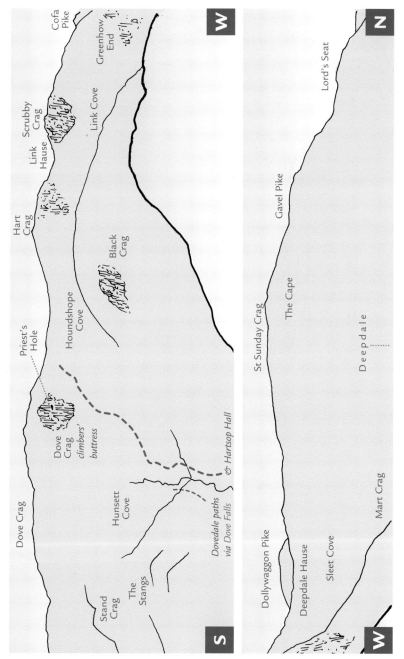

W

Cofa Pike

Greenhow End

Scrubby Crag

Link Hause

Link Cove

Hart Crag

Black Crag

Houndshope Cove

Priest's Hole

Dove Crag

climbers' buttress

Dove Crag

Hunsett Cove

Stand Crag

The Stangs

to Hartsop Hall

Dovedale paths via Dove Falls

S

N

Lord's Seat

Gavel Pike

The Cape

St Sunday Crag

Deepdale

Dollywaggon Pike

Deepdale Hause

Sleet Cove

Mart Crag

W

HELVELLYN

The most visited of the major fells, Helvellyn holds an abiding affection among the widest section of fell-walking society. A place of pilgrimage for lovers of fine mountain scenery. The reason for this devotion? Crowning the highest range in the district, the broad summit stands witness to probably the most complete panorama of Lakeland. Nonetheless, it is a mountain with a split personality. The bulky western slopes fall sharply from high pastures interspersed with scree and minor crags reaching down to the conifer fringed shores of Thirlmere. In striking contrast, the eastern face, featuring towering ridges, serrated and sleek, dividing high glaciated corries, is a mountain environment simply bursting with fun and adventure, epitomising all that is best for the fellwalker.

There is history in the name itself. For, in common with Lochnagar in the Grampians, the fell-name is transposed from the corrie lake cradled in its lofty lap. Pure Celtic in origin, spelt in modern Welsh Helfa-llyn 'the lake of the hunting ground', a clear reference to Red Tarn, transferring to the backing mountain when the meaning was linguistically lost with Viking settlement. The hunting ground in question, Glenridding and Wythburn Commons, will have been frequented by red deer, wild boar and wolf.

Those walkers wishing to climb exclusively for the view, and this includes the moonlight wanderer and sunrise seeker, will come up from Swirls or Wythburn. Whereas the walker determined to gather the fullest day-time mountain experience, will head west from Patterdale or Glenridding, tempted by Striding Edge's razor rocks and the perfect mountain form of Catstycam.

950 metres   3,116 feet

Boot-slicked and eroding paths coalesce along the crest of Striding Edge

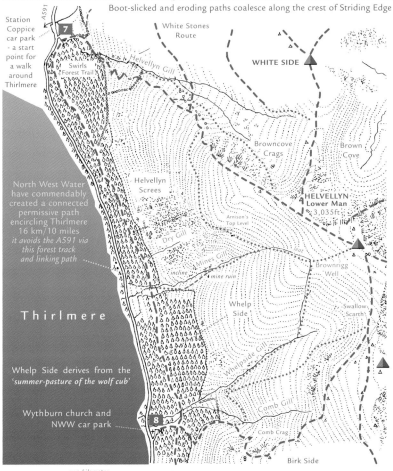

Station
Coppice
car park
- a start
point for
a walk
around
Thirlmere

7

White Stones
Route

WHITE SIDE

Swirls
Forest Trail

Helvellyn Gill

Browncove
Crags

Brown
Cove

North West Water
have commendably
created a connected
permissive path
encircling Thirlmere
16 km/10 miles
*it avoids the A591 via
this forest track
and linking path*

Helvellyn
Screes

HELVELLYN
Lower Man
3,035ft

Arnison's
Top Level

Dry Gill

Mines Gill

incline

mine ruin

Brownrigg
Well

Swallow
Scarth

Whelp
Side

Thirlmere

Whelpside Gill

Whelp Side derives from the
'summer-pasture of the wolf cub'

Comb Gill

Wythburn church and
NWW car park

8

Comb Crag

Birk Side

one kilometre   *one mile*

At the turn of the new millennium a mercy mission of path restoration on a grand scale is visibly bringing stability and longevity to the heavily pounded approach system to this famous and dearly loved mountain...
...now this truly is a feat of 'mountain rescue'.

The Skiddaw massif from the point where the White Stones Route and the Swirls path meet

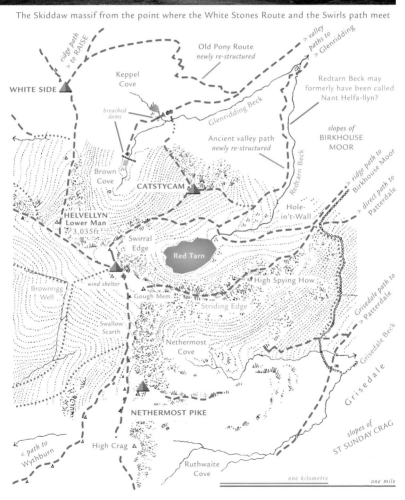

ridge path > to RAISE

WHITE SIDE

Keppel Cove

breached dams

Brown Cove

CATSTYCAM

HELVELLYN Lower Man 3,035ft

Swirral Edge

Brownrigg Well

wind shelter

Gough Mem.

Swallow Scarth

Nethermost Cove

NETHERMOST PIKE

High Crag

Ruthwaite Cove

Old Pony Route *newly re-structured*

> valley paths to > Glenridding

Redtarn Beck may formerly have been called Nant Helfa-llyn?

Glenridding Beck

Ancient valley path *newly re-structured*

Redtarn Beck

slopes of BIRKHOUSE MOOR

> ridge path to Birkhouse Moor

> direct path to Patterdale

Hole-in't-Wall

Red Tarn

High Spying How

Striding Edge

Grisedale path to > Patterdale

Grisedale Beck

G r i s e d a l e

slopes of ST SUNDAY CRAG

< path to Wythburn

one kilometre   one mile

ASCENT *from Thirlspot*

1 The Old Pony Route:

The passage of time has witnessed subtle changes of emphasis in the style of north-western approaches. The first recreational visitors, small in number, took to saddle-back and were guided by a stout local in the service of the Kings Head. Their route can be traced today. However, across the higher flanks of White Side its state is little greater than that of a strong sheep path and becomes lost on the rise to the saddle below Lower Man. 'Steady as you go', were the orders so the trail takes, what to modern tastes would be deemed, a circuitous,

NORTH-WESTERN APPROACHES

over cautious line. The course to the saddle is described on WHITE SIDE (routes **3** & **4**). The path climbs south from this broad gap, attention switching over the ridge to the empty bowl of Brown Cove and the startling peak of Catstycam. Mounting onto the summit of Helvellyn Lower Man the path is never in doubt. Long northern sightings are deceptive, this peak is but a subsidiary height, inferior to Helvellyn by just eighty-two feet. The term Man, deriving from the Celtic maen meaning *stone-marker*, suggests that an important boundary stone once stood here, more ancient than the county march of Cumberland and Westmorland and a landmark from the dale.

Helvellyn from Lower Man

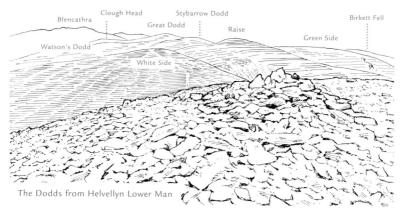

Blencathra | Clough Head | Stybarrow Dodd | Birkett Fell
Great Dodd | Raise
Watson's Dodd | Green Side
White Side

The Dodds from Helvellyn Lower Man

2 White Stones Route : To park at the King's Head it is necessary to collect a permit from the hotel reception, currently a deposit of £5 is levied, redeemable at the bar at the end of the walk (*open all day*).

Go through the gated farmyard behind the hotel, pass the caravan park, by the gate over a channelled ditch. Pass straight up to gate and bridge over the Thirlmere Leat, bearing half-left to an intake wall gate.

Spring 1999 - a week-long helicopter shuttle relaying rock, part of the costly but vital restoration project on the hugely popular Swirls path leading up over Browncove Crags.

Lower down the path has bedded-in and is already proving a practical and aesthetic product of a sensitive mountain path building programme - avoid trappling the edges.

The pitched path follows the wall uphill, at top bear left, fording the gill to the slate sign. Ascend by the gill, fording above the holly bush trending up the rough bank. Once the hotel management white-washed rocks to define the route, but no more. Cairns mercifully do not abound along this well defined path, though several are passed as the path crosses over the brow, by evidence of bields. Cross an open slope, heading for a ford of Helvellyn Gill, with Browncove Crags looming impressively. The White Stones Route crosses the second gill and an old wall before joining the newly pitched path rising from The Swirls car park.

ASCENT *from Swirls*

3 The modern trade route : From the Swirls North West Water car park cross Helvellyn Gill passing up through the gates, take the path right, signed '*Helvellyn*'. With conifers right rise to re-cross Helvellyn Gill, just below its scenic lower ravine. The recently re-aligned path has received considerable pitching and paving repair high onto Browncove Crags, a very necessary, expensive, labour-intensive process, hats off to all involved. Zig-zagging three times to reach the higher intake wall. The boulder paved path ploughs on close to an ascending broken wall mounting the spur of Browncove Crags. The name seems misplaced as the actual Brown Cove lies out of sight to the east of the ridge. As a rustic staircase, the path climbs onto the crest of the crags, an exciting promenade to the top. 4 An intriguing route, seldom undertaken, but one that may interest the non-conformist explorer, leaves the path half-left at the broken wall; though one may delay until the ground steepens, following a sheep path directly under the dark crags.

North West Water
Swirls car park
and information
point for forest
trails and the
Helvellyn path

< KESWICK 5 ml A591

Station
Coppice
car park

Brownrigg
Well

Whelpside Gill

Browncove
Crags

Mines Gill

Helvellyn Gill

Helvellyn
Screes

Thirlmere

**NORTH-WESTERN
APPROACHES**

This crosses the line of the White Stones Route and promptly dissolves. Pass a rain gauge and walk on beneath the towering wall of Browncove Crags, with the merest hint of path for comfort. Some rock from this site was lifted to supplement the huge quantities of stone carried by helicopter across Thirlmere from a site beyond Raven Crag, during the restoration of Browncove Crags path. Keep to the edge of the boulders and right of the massive glacier smoothed outcrop. With the crags well to the right, seek the one clear mossy green strip that runs up the predominantly scree slope, making steady, determined progress to the skyline. This is a fair weather ascent, but one that has appeal on a day when the ridges are teeming with folk.

Either follow the ridge proper to claim the scalp of Helvellyn Lower Man or, keep to the one pedestrian highway which touches the brink above Brown Cove and then forges on to the pillar on Helvellyn.

5 The first of two off-beat routes requiring less intrepid endeavour than may be expected. Delve into Helvellyn Gill, breaking from the formal path at the wall gap, slanting into the pathless bouldery ravine. Climb to the right of the top falls, keeping beside the right-hand fork in the gill to join the White Stones path leading right, over the broken wall, to regain the main path. **6** In fair weather, sustain the pioneering spirit. Branch right from the cobbled path a little higher up, at a large split boulder, aim for a second large boulder peeping over the near brow, now contour directly south upon a modest path fashioned by the cloven hoof of the native Herdwick. Sheep have a hard enough life without wasting effort in moving between good grazings, their trods leading

Whelpside Gill

Thirlmere from above Dry Gill

economically across the slope. The sheep walk rises, then contours along the brink of Helvellyn Screes above the cleft of Dry Gill, with handsome views over Thirlmere. The edge-top trod curves into the upper Mines Gill valley skipping over the topmost screes to bull's-eye on Arnison's Top Level *(see below)*. Continue, on a slightly rising line, into the upper reaches of this side valley, aiming for the foot of the water-cut. Ascend onto Whelp Side beside the narrow groove. This dry leat, no wider than a boot, was etched out by miners to provide a flow of flushing water from Brownrigg Well when the elements conspired to deny them a stream of water in Mines Gill itself. Passing a small wind-shelter, the ground levels arriving at Brownrigg Well, at 2,822 feet the highest spring in Lakeland. An ideal place for an high-level camp, you'll know the respect others have shown this pitch by its pristine state. The summit lies a precise 500 paces east-north-east, up the frost-fretted gritty tundra slope. Whelp Side harbouring folk links with the ancient *'rearing ground of wolf cubs'*.

Arnison Top Level

Mines Gill Spring

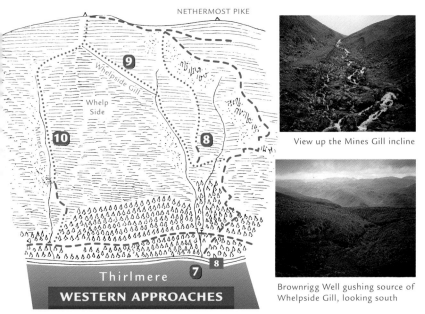

NETHERMOST PIKE

Whelpside Gill

Whelp Side

Mines Gill

9

10

8

Thirlmere **7**

8

WESTERN APPROACHES

View up the Mines Gill incline

Brownrigg Well gushing source of Whelpside Gill, looking south

ASCENT *from Wythburn*

7 Start from the NWW car park, located behind Wythburn Church (access via a track 70 yards south of church, off the A591 Keswick/Grasmere road). Pass through the kissing-gate onto a part pitched path ascending beside fenced gill. Cross the forestry track (a permissive path between The Swirls and Dunmail Raise), signed *'Helvellyn'*. At a gate/stile emerging from the mature forestry, the path keeps to the edge of a fenced enclosure protecting young deciduous growth. Gaining height, enjoy the views behind to Steel Fell and up Wythburn Dale. An intermittently pitched path leads up onto the ridge above Comb Crags, its course never in doubt up the gravelly way over Birk Side and across the western slope of Nethermost Pike to join the main ridge at Swallow Scarth.

8 For the individualist looking for a forgotten route, overlooked by the twentieth century invention of fell-walking, seek out the old shepherd's path winding up Middle Tongue. A pragmatic route to the high pastures, lost when Wythburn Dale was flooded to form Thirlmere and plantations completed the isolation of the high fells. Begin with the Wythburn approach, breaking left to ford Combs Gill as the bracken diminishes beyond the forestry wall. A strongly marked sheep path in the bracken slants over the Middle Tongue ridge towards Whelpside Gill. At midpoint take the grooved path, climbing directly up the bracken-infested ridge, soon splitting in two. The way emerges from the bracken, crests

the ridge, passing what appears to be the base of an old cairn, hereon the path is lost in the rough upper pasture rising steadily towards the base of High Crags. Keep left, with faint evidence of a path, climb the uneventful headwall slope to Swallow Scarth.

The head of Thirlmere from Middle Tongue

A useful tip on just such a climb, look at the sheep, they give both assurance of safe ground and scale in judging progress.

For an utterly peaceful experience all the way to the summit, then choose either Whelpside or Mines Gills, which have a common conclusion. Rough, pathless gill climbs are not everyone's cup of tea, but they do provide an intimacy lacking on open fell paths.

9 Whelpside Gill is the most convenient and is quickly reached from Middle Tongue. There is one fine cascade soon after entering, in tune with most of Helvellyn's dip slope gills, scree and boulders adorn the northern slope, so progress is held to the south bank. As the beck forks, follow the northern branch which rises to Brownrigg Well, a gushing issue; the lush growth akin to an oasis in a desert.

10 Mines Gill, more laborious to find and follow, borders on an adventure, tinged with history. From Wythburn Church rise to the forestry track, and follow this left (north) from the gate/stile. Cross a stile in an intervening fence and, short of the Mines Gill footbridge, bear up the rough bank right, to a stile in the fence. Ascend within the deep trench (former course of incline), with the forestry fence right. The mine incline runs over the gill no more, so at this point the path is forced up

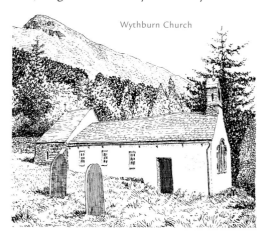

Wythburn Church

on the south side climbing tight to the fence to where the old miners' path emerges from the currently cleared plantation enclosure on the right. The path slants up left passing the ruined mine terrace, smithy and bothy. The mist of past endeavours hang in the air. Imagine the life-style of those, whose daily labour in the bowels of Helvellyn for lead, saw brief relief in this blinkered outlook of the world. Leaving these ghosts behind, climb by a rocky path, listen to the gurgling gill issuing from beneath the spoil, deposited, for lack of option, as a crudely culverted dam in the ravine itself. Continue beside the diminishing gill, higher this becomes dry-bedded to join the leat slanting steeply up to Brownrigg Well (all trace of the necessary dam, thankfully gone).

ASCENT *from Glenridding*

Dramatic glacial corries and finely chiselled ridges heighten the emotions providing thrilling crescendos to all eastern approaches.

Pedestrian traffic is shared between three main routes.

11 Old Pony Route : Follow Greenside Road passing through the old Greenside Mine complex, bear off the Sticks Pass route onto the rough track leading up the west side of the Glenridding Beck valley. As the juniper is passed beyond Rowten Gill, a small outcrop looms. Take the newly restored zig-zagging trail right, climbing above Keppel Cove to the col and join the ridge path. Head south via the two summits of White Side and Helvellyn Lower Man, each distinguished by solitary cairns.

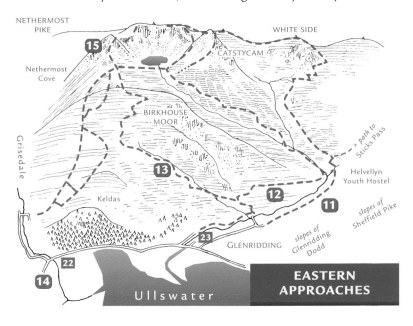

Rattlebeck Bridge is the key to two popular lines of ascent. Approach either from the village street on the south side of the bridge, following the lane through Eagle Farm, taking the bridle-path right, by Gillside camping ground. Alternatively, walk out of the car park at the upper end, following Greenside Road beyond the Travellers Rest (public house), bearing left at the road fork.

12 Red Tarn Beck : Follow the path up to the ladder-stile above Miresbeck Cottage. Go right, taking either of the paths crossing the northern slopes of Birkhouse Moor. Ignore the first footbridge just above the Greenside Mine, continue to cross the footbridge spanning Red Tarn Beck. The path, well-engineered to cope with heavy use, winds up towards the outflow of Red Tarn. One may include Catstycam, the eastern shoulder route being the natural line, alternatively simply continue onto Swirral Edge, or bear left contouring back east to the Hole-in't-Wall for Striding Edge.

13 Mires Beck : Unrelenting pressures on the Helvellyn path infra-structure have led to the creation of a tailor-made 'highway' from Glenridding. A durable pitched path now leads up the eastern side of Mires Beck to the ridge wall, climbing onto Birkhouse Moor it steers right to relieve the scoured ground close to the wall on the upper slope. Passing the summit cairn alongside the tall wall the path undulates to the wall corner at the Hole-in't-Wall path junction.

The impressive final tower of Striding Edge

14 The Patterdale Path :

With car parking in the village of Patterdale at a premium, it never ceases to amaze me the sheer number of walkers on this path out of Grisedale. Embarking from Grisedale Bridge the route follows the minor road into the dale, bear right with the road, cross the beck, branching left at a kissing-gate, as the road bends back east towards the hunt kennels. The path runs up a pasture bank to a hand-gate, then slants half-left, on what can seem an interminable grind, diagonally across the flanks of Birkhouse Moor to the Hole-in't-Wall stile. Two hand-gates in intermediate fences are negotiated en route, on a path that is being quite literally beaten to death - a prime candidate for restorative pitching. The old path described on BIRKHOUSE MOOR *pp35/36* might appeal to the walker seeking to 'tread softly on their hills'. The views into Grisedale, to the gullies of St Sunday Crag and the craggy corries of Nethermost and Ruthwaite Coves are ample compensation for the effort and cause of frequent, appreciative pauses, bordering on dalliance!

15 Striding Edge : The path runs on the north side of Low Spying How to reach the crest on High Spying How, with its striated rocks and stunning views down into Nethermost Cove and over the remains of the Eagle Crag mine. Pass the memorial to Robert Dixon. In need of a lick

of paint and easily missed, this cast iron plate records the unfortunate death of a stalwart member of the Patterdale Foxhounds who fell here during the heat of a chase in November 1858.

From this point either follow the bare rocky spine or the sorely eroding path which teeters first on the northern side then switches to the south side. Though neither route avoids the final twin chimney descent of the ultimate tower buttress. Cross the gap, the easier way is right, up the loose scree of a gully, thereon the choice to the plateau rim is ever more impetuous. Pass the Gough Memorial and the cross-wall wind-shelter to crest the summit... alone?... not likely!

The view into the gap from the top of the final tower on Striding Edge

The next generation finds excitement and fulfilment on the grand old mountain

The Summit

The moment of arrival is euphoric. Even the most taciturn can slip into hearty conversation with complete strangers, the summit of Helvellyn is that kind of place. Incidents recounted, the view extolled, or the vagaries of the mist reviled, the whole mad world put to rights, all in the spirit of kinship unique to such 'summit conferences'.

In profile the highest ground is a truncated dome - west to east, the dip slope tumbling almost sheer into the vast bowl occupied by Red Tarn. The triangulation pillar sits at mid-point on the north-west axis summit ridge, with the actual summit on the projecting knob to the south - viewpoint for the PANORAMA. The combined effect of a myriad frosts

and feet has given the surface of Helvellyn the appearance of a quarry floor, flora restricted to a tiny rare lichen and a thin tundra grass. Cute sheep finding greatest nourishment from lunchbox slippage.

Below this stands the wind-shelter, a place of great society and bleak refreshment. Two Mancunian memorials lie beyond. The sturdy Gough Memorial *(see next page)* stands just out of sight, on the brink above the Striding Edge path. Charles Gough died in 1805 falling in this vicinity, his faithful terrier keeping vigil with his remains for three months until discovery - casual fellwanderers were rare. While beside the Wythburn path a small slate stone records the one occasion a light aircraft landed on Helvellyn on 22nd December 1926. A publicity stunt encouraged by the Manchester Evening News, an Avro 585 Gosport flying out of Woodford in Cheshire. It might never have been believed, for all that a staff photographer partnered the pilot, had it not been that a university professor chanced to be on the summit to witness the whole crazy and unique event.

Safe Descents

Only Striding Edge should be avoided in poor weather. But caution must be applied in reversing all ascents as fierce escarpments line the higher ground and crags lurk at lower levels, particularly to the west.

The rusting cast-iron Dixon Memorial precariously perched on Striding Edge

Ridge Routes to....

BIRKHOUSE MOOR

DESCENT 790ft ASCENT 110ft 2 miles

From the wind-shelter head SE passing the Gough Memorial. The discomforts of the steep path down to the gap impossible to avoid. Clamber out of the gap onto Striding Edge by either of the two chimneys; ignore the flawed path skirting low to the right. This marvellous, all too brief, rocky ridge is reminiscent of such stirring mountain crests as Crib Goch, the A'chir and the Aonach Eagach. The path declines to pass the Hole-in't-Wall, keep the undulating ridge wall close to the right to reach the ragged summit cairn.

CATSTYCAM   DESCENT 516 feet   ASCENT 320 feet   0.9 miles

A cairn at the NW brink marks the departure from the summit plateau. Aim NE down Swirral Edge, which, while steep, seldom taxes hands or posterior in normal conditions. Levelling at 2,600 feet the ridge loses its craggy demeanour and begins a grass and gritty climb to the conical top.

Hobnail-etched arete of Swirral Edge looking up to the summit

NETHERMOST PIKE   DESCENT 297 feet   ASCENT 103 feet   0.8 miles

Aim S from the wind shelter upon the wide Wythburn path. The ridge dips at Swallow Scarth, a place to linger to enjoy a truly stunning view across the head of Nethermost Cove. The path splits three ways, follow the least obvious, left-hand, path holding to the escarpment edge, onto the stony summit plateau.

WHITE SIDE   DESCENT 225 feet   ASCENT 570 feet   1.4 miles

Follow the escarpment edge or The Swirls path NW from the old Ordnance Survey pillar. Directly after the point where this dips, with a glimpse into Brown Cove, bear right re-joining edge to reach the summit cairn on Helvellyn Lower Man. A key point on the ridge. From here the spine of the range heads N, a shale path leading down to a broad saddle, before rising with no complications to the summit of White Side.

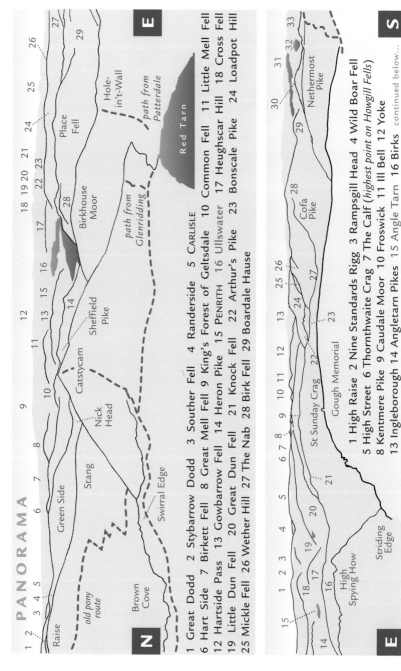

PANORAMA

N

E

Raise, Green Side, Stang, Brown Cove, old pony route, Nick Head, Catstycam, Swirral Edge, Hart Side, Sheffield Pike, Birkhouse Moor, Place Fell, Hole-in't-Wall, Red Tarn, path from Glenridding, path from Patterdale

1 Great Dodd 2 Stybarrow Dodd 3 Souther Fell 4 Randerside 5 CARLISLE
6 Hart Side 7 Birkett Fell 8 Great Mell Fell 9 King's Forest of Geltsdale 10 Common Fell 11 Little Mell Fell
12 Hartside Pass 13 Gowbarrow Fell 14 Heron Pike 15 PENRITH 16 Ullswater 17 Heughscar Hill 18 Cross Fell
19 Little Dun Fell 20 Great Dun Fell 21 Knock Fell 22 Arthur's Pike 23 Bonscale Pike 24 Loadpot Hill
25 Mickle Fell 26 Wether Hill 27 The Nab 28 Birk Fell 29 Boardale Hause

S

E

Striding Edge, High Spying How, St Sunday Crag, Gough Memorial, Cofa Pike, Nethermost Pike

1 High Raise 2 Nine Standards Rigg 3 Rampsgill Head 4 Wild Boar Fell
5 High Street 6 Thornthwaite Crag 7 The Calf *(highest point on Howgill Fells)*
8 Kentmere Pike 9 Caudale Moor 10 Froswick 11 Ill Bell 12 Yoke
13 Ingleborough 14 Angletarn Pikes 15 Angle Tarn 16 Birks continued below...

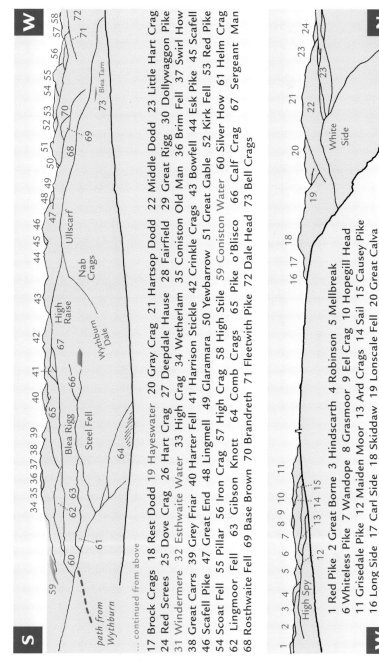

W

S

34 35 36 37 38 39   40   41   42   43   44 45 46   47   48 49   50 51   52 53   54 55   56   57 58

59   60   61   62 63   64   65   66   67   68   69   70   71   72   73

path from
Wythburn

... continued from above

High Spy   Blea Rigg   Steel Fell   Wythburn Dale   High Raise   Nab Crags   Ullscarf   Blea Tarn

17 Brock Crags   18 Rest Dodd   19 Hayeswater   20 Gray Crag   21 Hartsop Dodd   22 Middle Dodd   23 Little Hart Crag
24 Red Screes   25 Dove Crag   26 Hart Crag   27 Deepdale Hause   28 Fairfield   29 Great Rigg   30 Dollywaggon Pike
31 Windermere   32 Esthwaite Water   33 High Crag   34 Wetherlam   35 Coniston Old Man   36 Brim Fell   37 Swirl How
38 Great Carrs   39 Grey Friar   40 Harter Fell   41 Harrison Stickle   42 Crinkle Crags   43 Bowfell   44 Esk Pike   45 Scafell
46 Scafell Pike   47 Great End   48 Lingmell   49 Glaramara   50 Yewbarrow   51 Great Gable   52 Kirk Fell   53 Red Pike
54 Scoat Fell   55 Pillar   56 Iron Crag   57 High Crag   58 High Stile   59 Coniston Water   60 Silver How   61 Helm Crag
62 Lingmoor Fell   63 Gibson Knott   64 Comb Crags   65 Pike o'Blisco   66 Calf Crag   67 Sergeant Man
68 Rosthwaite Fell   69 Base Brown   70 Brandreth   71 Fleetwith Pike   72 Dale Head   73 Bell Crags

N

W

1 2   3 4   5   6   7   8 9 10   11   12   13 14 15   16 17 18   19   20   21   22   23   24

High Spy   White Side

1 Red Pike   2 Great Borne   3 Hindscarth   4 Robinson   5 Mellbreak
6 Whiteless Pike   7 Wandope   8 Grasmoor   9 Eel Crag   10 Hopegill Head
11 Grisedale Pike   12 Maiden Moor   13 Ard Crags   14 Sail   15 Causey Pike
16 Long Side   17 Carl Side   18 Skiddaw   19 Lonscale Fell   20 Great Calva
21 Blencathra   22 Calfhow Pike   23 Watson's Dodd   24 Bowscale Fell

HERON PIKE

A sleek ridge sweeps south from Great Rigg, gently rising and falling between pooled hollows to crest upon the twin-topped Heron Pike. Eastward scree and broken outcrops spill into Rydale with two striking features, a gully, which offers no inducement to novel ascent, while from the summit, steep ground terminates abruptly with a fierce buttress. This is Erne Crag, frequent of peregrine and at its base the former work-place of quarrymen. The fell-name derives from 'peak of sea eagle's eyrie' – whereas Heron Island, within Rydal Water, is a later name and actually does refer to the nesting site of grey heron.

Many walkers stand on the bare quartz south top, rest their limbs content that the summit has been achieved, this is not so. For although it offers marginally the better all round view (hence it features as the station for the fell panorama), looking north even the most amateur of surveyors will notice that the ground rises appreciably to the north-top. This might be disturbing for Wainwright-baggers resting on their laurels having well and truly hung up their boots. They are far from certain to have covered their options in their chase around the Fairfield Horseshoe by stepping aside to touch the cairn, after all the sage of the hills strangely dismissed it as a subsidiary top!

The ridge forms a conclusive division between the deeply entrenched and reclusive Rydale and the verdant, populated loveliness of the vale of Grasmere. Heron Pike claims many summiteers, but precious few exclusive ascents. For all that many amblers from Grasmere venture to Alcock Tarn, they culminate, as do the famous Grasmere Sports fell-race contestants upon nearby Butter Crag, at that 1,200 foot shoulder and think nothing of the ultimate height, their attention sufficiently rewarded

621 metres   2,037 feet

by the westward prospect from this elevation. Rather plain slopes fall into the Greenhead Gill valley, though even they have interest in a series of strongly marked sheep-trods which are fun to trace when the ridge-top trail is over-run with Horseshoe nailers!

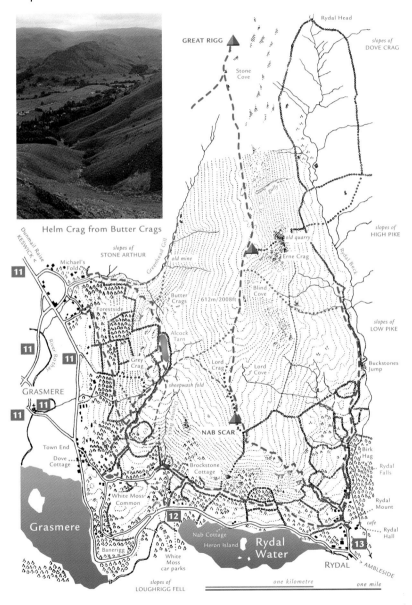

Helm Crag from Butter Crags

WESTERN APPROACHES

Butter Crags

south top

Alcock Tarn

NAB SCAR

Grasmere

White Moss car parks

River Rothay

Rydal Water

slopes of LOUGHRIGG FELL

Rydal Mount

Rydal Hall

RYDAL

The old 'road' from Rydal to Grasmere begins directly above Rydal Mount and leads delightfully by pasture and woodland, becoming a road beyond Brockstone Cottage it slips down by How Top to Grasmere Town End.

ASCENT *from Grasmere*

From Town End. **1** Follow lane by Dove Cottage to How Top where a footpath is signposted, pass round to the left of the small tarn. Hitting the road again, switch immediately left into the lane signposted *'Alcock Tarn'*. Reaching a gate optional paths may be considered. Either **2** go through the gate signed *'Bracken Fell'* climbing an old ornamental drive exiting the woodland at a gate, pass a memorial seat enjoying a fine view across the lake to Silver How. Take a path rising from the left, this is the attractive permissive footpath from Forestside. The path zig-zags by a pool and leads through a hand-gate *(Alcock Tarn plaque)* in a rising wall, an engineered path climbing the steep fellside delivering precisely upon Alcock Tarn. Named after the Victorian owner of The Hollens (recently The National Trust regional office), who fashioned the reservoir from a marshy pool stockingit with trout for sport. As a 'shining level', it is made popular by its qualities as a generous viewpoint. The nearby Butter Crags, an intriguingly pitched outcrop worth a pottering visit, is the high point of the Grasmere Sports Guides Race each August - known as Bitter Crags to flagging runners! Turn right, passing the low dam to reach a stile deporting onto the fell. **3** Alternatively, stay with the steepening lane to a gate, bear left rising to a

Morecambe Bay

Loughrigg Fell

Alcock Tarn from Stone Arthur

kissing-gate where the walls constrict. Above this the path opens with a wall left till the stile accessing the Alcock Tarn enclosure on the left. Continue up the obvious path, at a tiny ford the path bears right destined for Nab Scar. So head on up the damp, pathless slope to crest the ridge path on the approach to the south top.

From Swan Lane. **4** Follow the lane up from the Swan Hotel. The first turning right leads to Forestside where a permissive path is waymarked left. Skirting round a tall wall a sylvan trail leads easily uphill passing a memorial seat and an intriguing section of Thirlmere Aqueduct to meet the path from How Top. **5** The second turning leads to a gate and entry to the open fell at the foot of Greenhead Gill. Go right, crossing the footbridge winding up the consolidated path, with splendid views into the deep valley below. Gaining the shoulder of the fell curve right, by a marsh, to enter the Alcock Tarn enclosure at a stile. The shortcomings of the tarn are more than adequately compensated by the breadth and wealth of the view, particularly from the knoll just beyond the wall to the west. Soak in the scene across Easedale to the mighty fells crowding in about Great Langdale and south-west to the Coniston Fells. Pass the long, shallow pool, beyond the dam cross a plank bridge to reach a fence stile linking up with the ascents from How Top and White Moss.

ASCENT *from White Moss*

6 Cross over the A591 from the main car park. Find two tracks leading north either side of Dunney Beck. The right-hand way, by the quarry-sheltered Coach House, soon constricts into a rough lane climbing to Brockstone Cottage, go left. The other track climbs to the open road beside White Moss Common and a pool filled with flag iris, go right. Passing Dunnabeck reach a kissing-gate on the left where the track bends. Enter the fell proper ascending a narrow path with a wall close left and Dunney Beck right, to a leaking section of the otherwise well-hidden Thirlmere Aqueduct bridging the beck. With bracken continuing to be something of a hindrance, either drift half-left over the hillside above the wall corner, coming to the higher wall bear right, or simply climb directly towards the metal hand-gate on the skyline, joining the same path a little higher, bearing right. The path keeps the enclosure wall close left, then mounts the ridge to pass an old sheepwash dip and twin fold. Beyond the sheepfold encountering the path climbing from Town End, go right, pass the stile entry into the Alcock Tarn enclosure.

ASCENT *from Ambleside and Rydal*

The Fairfield Horseshoe makes high demands on limited car parking space so one needs to know the choice. The largest car park is Rydal Road in Ambleside, but arrive late and it's full to the brim. **7** The way to Rydal is simple enough, follow the roadside footway to the gates and lodge for Rydal Hall and follow the drive to, and through, the hall complex (summer season tea-room). Smaller parking places exist on the

Loughrigg side of Pelter Bridge GR365059 and up the broad lane leading up to Rydal Mount in Rydal.
8 The main route leads up by the Mount to be drawn half-left into a walled lane above a barn conversion. This leads via a stile onto newly restored zig zags climbing the ridge-end to the ladder-stile and the top of Nab Scar. The worn way continues past Lord Crag direct-ly to the south top. **9** The Blind Cove route is for walkers looking for something a little out of the ordinary with Heron Pike is treated as the sole peak to climb. Stick with the track leading up from Rydal Mount – perhaps taking advantage of a brief detour right to visit the wooded delights of Rydal Falls (*following Rydal Estate access area waymarking*). Passing through a series of gates and the exciting rocky turbulence approaching Buckstone's Jump, proceed to where the Blind Cove gill spills over the track, divert upstream for minimal bracken interference. Climbing above a rocky knoll find a hurdle gate in the traversing fence. Continue into Blind Cove, a steep grassy strip in the headwall between runs of scree leading to the ridge-top saddle with the summit close to the right.

south top

Alcock Tarn

NAB SCAR

Blind Cove

Erne Crag

Rydale

9

8

Rydal Beck

Rydal Falls

A591

RYDAL

13 **7** *route from* AMBLESIDE *via Rydal Hall drive*

SOUTHERN APPROACHES

Erne Crag Quarry's yawning cavern

(below) wild Rydale

Great Rigg
Fairfield
Hart Crag

The Summit

A neat little rocky top, with the ruins of a wall, fashioned into a rough cairn. The remainder of the wall runs down the slope eastwards coming to a severe termination above the Erne Crag obviously built to deter sheep from false stepping o'er the brink. To set your mind at rest regarding the height, glance at the photograph above showing the cairnless quartz south-top in the foreground and the clearly higher (by twenty-nine feet) and pikish north-top in the middle distance.

Safe Descents

The ridge path due south to Rydal is as safe as houses. For Grasmere a pathless descent south-west leads to Alcock Tarn, where paths are picked up leading north to the foot of Greenhead Gill and south-east to Town Head. One may reasonably safely slip down into Blind Cove from the dip on the ridge between the two tops, steepness and bracken lower down being the only caution, go right, along the Rydale track for little more than a mile to enter Rydal, descending the lane by the Mount.

Ridge Routes to....

GREAT RIGG   DESCENT 150 feet   ASCENT 580 feet   1.5 miles

Head N, the path never in doubt as it gently dips and weaves along the undulating ridge until above Greenhead Gill the ground steepens to Greatrigg Man.

NAB SCAR   DESCENT 500 feet   0.7 miles

Head S crossing the depression and slip over the south-top. The ridge path all too palpable, stepping down by Lord's Crag, is particularly badly eroded into a gravel stumble. A broken wall clinging to the ridge outcropping leads down to the large cairn to the right of the path.

PANORAMA from the south top

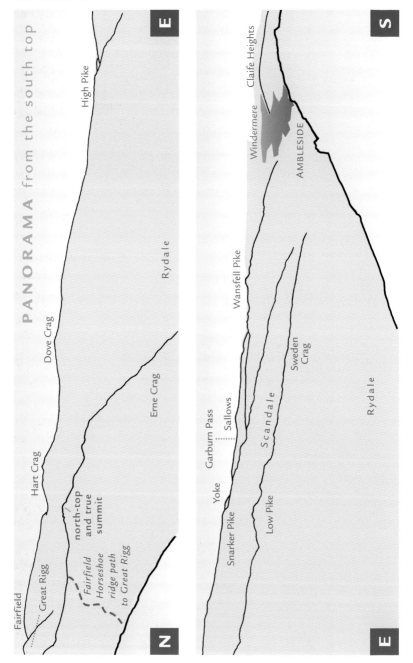

E

High Pike

Rydale

Dove Crag

Erne Crag

Hart Crag

north-top
and true
summit

*Fairfield
Horseshoe
ridge path
to Great Rigg*

Great Rigg

Fairfield

N

S

Claife Heights

Windermere

AMBLESIDE

Wansfell Pike

Sweden
Crag

Rydale

Garburn Pass

Sallows

Scandale

Yoke

Snarker Pike

Low Pike

E

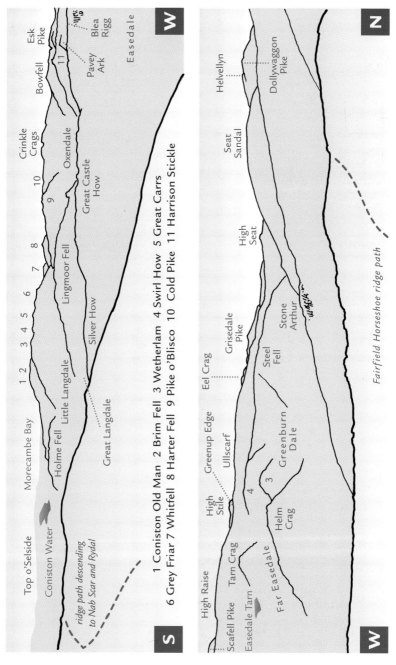

W

Esk Pike
Bowfell
11
Pavey Ark
Blea Rigg
Easedale
Crinkle Crags
Oxendale
10
9
Great Castle How
8
7
6
5 4 3
Lingmoor Fell
Silver How
1 2
Little Langdale
Great Langdale
Morecambe Bay
Holme Fell
Top o'Selside
Coniston Water
ridge path descending to Nab Scar and Rydal

S

1 Coniston Old Man 2 Brim Fell 3 Wetherlam 4 Swirl How 5 Great Carrs
6 Grey Friar 7 Whitfell 8 Harter Fell 9 Pike o'Blisco 10 Cold Pike 11 Harrison Stickle

N

Helvellyn
Dollywaggon Pike
Seat Sandal
High Seat
Grisedale Pike
Stone Arthur
Steel Fell
Eel Crag
Greenup Edge
Ullscarf
Greenburn Dale
High Stile
4
3
Helm Crag
High Raise
Tarn Crag
Scafell Pike
Easedale Tarn
Far Easedale

Fairfield Horseshoe ridge path

W

HIGH HARTSOP DODD

Taking its name from the lost community of High Hartsop, the fell swells to form the conclusive divide between two contrasting valleys, embracing the delights of Dovedale to the west, and the simple symmetry of Caiston Glen to the east. The fell is the abrupt spur end of Little Hart Crag, a conical lure for any red blooded fell-walker relishing a horseshoe ridge walk from Cowbridge or the Brotherswater Inn. Such a tour may also feature Dove Crag, Hart Crag and Hartsop above How in a seven-mile circuit. By common convention this circuit would be taken widdershins (anti-clockwise), when the descent of this lovely ridge forms a superb finale, the eye constantly drawn into the lovely Hartsop vale - a sublimely Lakeland scene *(see picture overleaf)*. There is next to no scope for varied ascent, with steep grass and precious little rock to cling to on the short steep climb. The flanking slopes give the fell a special texture, high on the shadowed eastern slope juniper thicket flourishes, while to the west, open native woodland lingers to the lower banks providing shelter, not merely for coy sheep, but timorous roe deer too.

ASCENT *from Cowbridge or the Brotherswater Inn*

1 The modest National Trust car park at Cowbridge has a terrible knack of filling in anything like fair weather, so an early start is to be recommended. Follow the level track through the fringe of Low Wood beside Brotherswater, a joyous preamble to any fell day. Pass on by Hartsop Hall, and the farm-track approach from Sykeside and the Brotherswater Inn. **2** Branch left over the ditch duck-board, signed '*footpath to Kirkstone Pass and Scandale Pass*'. From the wall gate, short of both sheep pen and barns enter a meadow. The path links up with an open track advancing

519 metres   1,703 feet

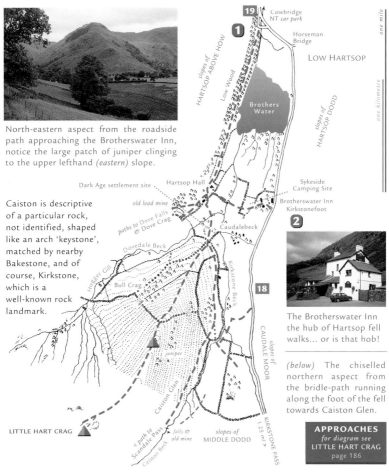

North-eastern aspect from the roadside path approaching the Brotherswater Inn, notice the large patch of juniper clinging to the upper lefthand *(eastern)* slope.

Caiston is descriptive of a particular rock, not identified, shaped like an arch 'keystone', matched by nearby Bakestone, and of course, Kirkstone, which is a well-known rock landmark.

Map labels:

19   Cowbridge NT *car park*

1

Horseman Bridge

LOW HARTSOP

one mile

one kilometre

slopes of HARTSOP ABOVE HOW

Low Wood

Brothers Water

slopes of HARTSOP DODD

Dark Age settlement site

Hartsop Hall

old lead mine

paths to Dove Falls & Dove Crag

Caudalebeck

Dovedale Beck

Hogget Gill

Bull Crag

Kirkstone Beck

18

Sykeside Camping Site

Brotherswater Inn

Kirkstonefoot

2

juniper

slopes of CAUDALE MOOR

Caiston Glen

LITTLE HART CRAG

< path to Scandale Pass

Caiston Beck

falls & old mine

slopes of MIDDLE DODD

1.25 m >

KIRKSTONE PASS

The Brotherswater Inn the hub of Hartsop fell walks... or is that hob!

(below) The chiselled northern aspect from the bridle-path running along the foot of the fell towards Caiston Glen.

APPROACHES
for diagram see
LITTLE HART CRAG
page 186

from the barns, diagonally across the pasture to a farm-bridge spanning Dovedale Beck. The next pasture contains a ring earthen bank and several massive standing stones, remnants of an old enclosure, probably associated with the lost farmstead of High Hartsop. Go through a gate beside an outbarn, with the bridle-track bearing left beside the left-hand wall. However, our task is at hand, 'thar's na'but for it', head down and right foot forward to begin the stiff climb initially with a broken wall right. The path keeps resolutely to the leading edge, via a fence stile, mounting without respite until a broken wall strapping the ridge-top spells an end to rigours and the final grassy rise.

The Summit

Determining which is the true summit on a rising ridge can only be a matter of personal whim or inclination. The small heap of stones, on a grassy knob up from the wall, can be taken as a summit of sorts. Particularly as it makes a fine excuse to pause after the hard climb and take in the view, most notably the stirring westward angle on Hogget Gill backed by Dove Crag *(here seen in wild snowy winter raiment)*.

Safe Descents

Stick to the ridge path heading NE, cross the broken wall descending to a fence stile, a subsequent broken wall guides down to a barn where the dale meadows begin.

Ridge Route to....

LITTLE HART CRAG   ASCENT 350 feet   0.5 miles

A narrow ridge path on grass and sedge leads steadily up the ridge, with a few peaty hollows to step through before climbing onto summit outcrop, resting on the ridge like a mock bastion.

Place Fell

Angletarn Pikes

PANORAMA

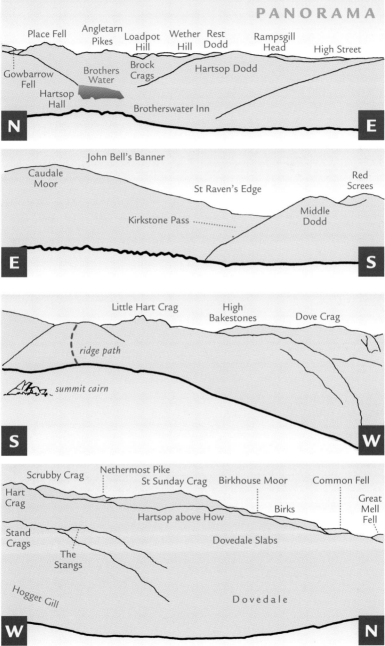

N

Place Fell
Angletarn Pikes
Loadpot Hill
Wether Hill
Rest Dodd
Rampsgill Head
High Street
Gowbarrow Fell
Brothers Water
Brock Crags
Hartsop Dodd
Hartsop Hall
Brotherswater Inn

E

John Bell's Banner
Caudale Moor
St Raven's Edge
Red Screes
Kirkstone Pass
Middle Dodd

S

Little Hart Crag
High Bakestones
Dove Crag
ridge path
summit cairn

W

Scrubby Crag
Nethermost Pike
St Sunday Crag
Birkhouse Moor
Common Fell
Hart Crag
Birks
Great Mell Fell
Hartsop above How
Stand Crags
Dovedale Slabs
The Stangs
Hogget Gill
Dovedale

N

HIGH PIKE

Viewed from Low Pike *(above)*, the continuing rough edge soars to an exalted peak, in the manner befitting a real mountain. This is virtuous flattery, for although the scrambly way is fun, despite showing fatigue from countless descending boots, once underfoot the summit does not quite match the expectancy of the long view. The plateau of Dove Crag tapering at its southern extremity as a pencil tip on High Pike.

It is pretty unusual to find anyone arriving on the summit from any other direction than alongside the Great Wall of China ridge wall. However, the author did encounter a couple clambering to the top directly out of Rydale. They were from the Czech Republic engaged upon a literary coach tour that had parked up for the night at Rydal. Perhaps being cooped up with over-much rubber-necking had been more than enough for them as they had set out aiming vaguely for the skyline. Needless to say they were quite relieved to meet someone who could direct them safely back in the failing light of evening, guiding them off Low Pike, via Buckstone's Jump. I well remember them exuding much delight in the 'Swallows and Amazons' stories - which might explain their unorthodox expedition and youthful sense of energetic adventure.

ASCENT *from Ambleside*

1 Route to Low Pike described on page 236 and the continuing ridge path page 237. By common practise this is the return leg of the Fairfield Horseshoe, normally undertaken clockwise via Nab Scar, Heron Pike, Great Rigg, Fairfield, Hart Crag, Dove Crag, High and Low Pikes.

612 metres   2,152 feet

Approaching the summit from Dove Crag

Low Pike and High Pike from the headstream of Scandale Beck on the Low Bakestones ridge above Thack Bottom.

This fence line is a reliable guide in mist to Scandale Pass and from the first fence junction left into Dovedale via Hunsett Cove

DOVE CRAG

> ridge paths to Little Hart Crag & Scandale Pass

High Bakestones

Low Bakestones

Scandale Pass

Far Swine Crag

Thack Bottom

Rydal Beck

Near Swine Crag

APPROACHES
for diagram see
DOVE CRAG page 81

Scandale

Buckstones Jump

LOW PIKE

Scandale Beck

> lane to AMBLESIDE

one kilometre   one mile

High Bakestones

Thack Bottom

Sunlit High Pike and the Scandale Head flank of Dove Crag

The Summit

The ridge wall slices through the summit. A cairn rests on a rocky perch, a fine spot to peer down into Thack Bottom and across Scandale Head to High Bakestones and Little Hart Crag. Through

an enlarging wall-gap *(see right, looking to High Street)*, marginally higher ground, brings in Rydale and, looking westwards, the Scafells.

Safe Descents

All hangs on the wall. In descent do not deviate until beyond Low Pike. The 'bad step' of Sweden Crag situated precisely beside the wall. With no wish for personal 'in descent assault', it is safer to follow the popular path swinging left, bound for Low Sweden Bridge and Nook Lane en route to Ambleside.

Ridge Routes to....

DOVE CRAG   ASCENT 446 feet   1.2 miles

The ridge wall continues N, the popular path keeping to the east side for shelter from prevailing winds, a lesser path exists on the west side, this is fine on sunny days as the views are just that bit better. The detour to High Bakestones is recommended. A clear path diverging from the popular east side path after half-a-mile, runs along the edge to the landmark currick (*cairn*). Approaching the summit of Dove Crag the ridge wall becomes intermittently broken.

LOW PIKE   DESCENT 45 feet   ASCENT 490 feet   0.7 miles

Again there is a path on either side, the main way has a knack of switching sides early on to avoid the worst erosion. Crossing a peaty depression, cross the ladder-stile and climb the bluff to the summit. The west

side path is actually the more pleasant to follow, the only hiccup is on top, there is no stile and the only option is to climb over... *oh, so very carefully!*

The sturdy ridge wall making the final pull to the summit includes two stout step stiles. They remain as new, for neither have value for contemporary visitors and it would appear down the years shepherds' have had little use for them either, so why were they built side by side?

PANORAMA

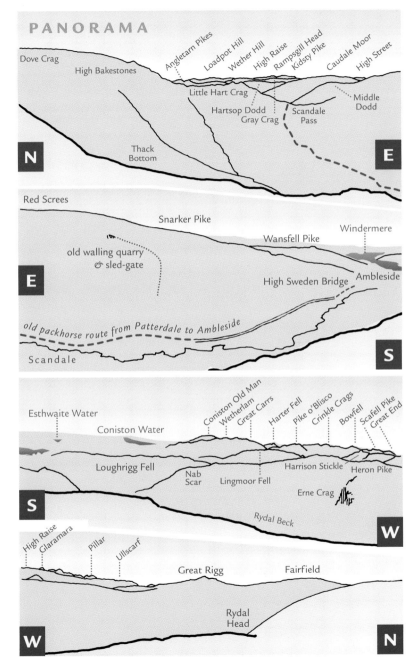

LITTLE HART CRAG

The best view of this fell is on the climb beside the wall, eastward, to Red Screes (*above*) and from Middle Dodd, from where the summit outcrop looks like a volcanic plug. It lies at an intermediate point, on an otherwise nondescript ridge, between higher and more noted brethren.

Dove Crag's east ridge falls to Bakestone Moss, levels, kinks and steps up onto this rocky knot, before sweeping as a sickle north-eastward, down the grassy High Hartsop Dodd rigg then steeply to Hartsop. The summit outcrop is reminiscent of a battleship riding the high seas, there is something of a fantasy castle about this little bastion too, here spectral watchmen may be thought to lurk, scrutinising innocent, unsuspecting travellers as they slip over the ancient Scandale Pass.

To the west of the summit the broken northern edge of Black Brow sends long shadows into the depths of Hogget Gill, while on the south side of the ridge, Scandale Tarn sits serenely in a sunny lap.

Just one step up from High Hartsop Dodd physically and meta-phorically. Fellwalkers are unlikely it set out with the sole intention of climbing this modest top, with Red Screes and Dove Crag in proximity the day has greater thrills in store. The sense of inferiority, veiled in the fell-name, perhaps reveals the former natural range of particular herds of deer, hunted across Dovedale.

The roughest and most rewarding way to the top climbs from half-way up Hogget Gill onto Black Brow, though few will have sampled this line.

Most commonly it is visited en route upon the Dovedale Horseshoe, though it is so convenient to the Scandale Pass that many may be tempted, on a whim, to nip to the top as 'a quicky' during an otherwise leisurely inter-dale tour. It is a splendid fell-top viewpoint.

637 metres   2,090 feet

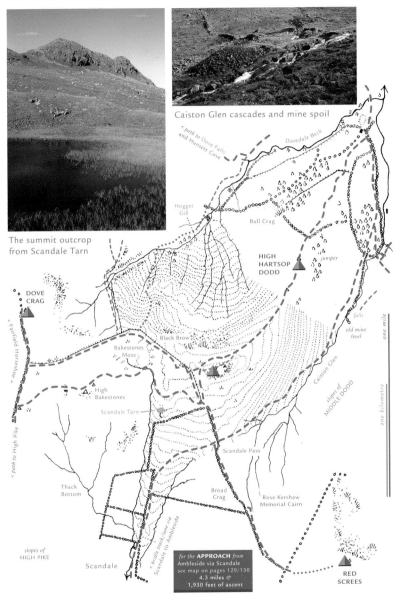

Caiston Glen cascades and mine spoil

The summit outcrop
from Scandale Tarn

The dale-name Caiston Glen is intriguing, does the original 'key-stone' still exist? Scottish influence betrayed in the latter-day switch from glyn to glen. The Caiston Lead Mine appears to have been a short venture, to judge from the trifling heap of spoil below the trial level, which is situated close to a eye-catching cascading waterfall midway up the dale *(see picture above)*. The old miners' approach can still be traced leading on the east side of the dale.

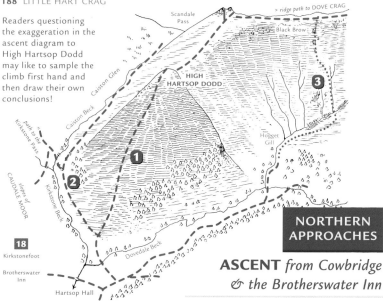

Readers questioning the exaggeration in the ascent diagram to High Hartsop Dodd may like to sample the climb first hand and then draw their own conclusions!

NORTHERN APPROACHES

ASCENT *from Cowbridge & the Brotherswater Inn*

There are two obvious and commonly followed lines of ascent and one natural, pathless route, expressly suited for those inquisitive fell wandering types who like to sneak up on their prey. **1** The head-on, belts & braces, ridge route is described in HIGH HARTSOP DODD pages 176/7. **2** Caiston Glen will be welcomed by walkers seeking a steadier gradient, the age-old cross-ridge bridle-path leading to Scandale Pass. Reaching the ladder-stile at the pass, turn right, following the wall and subsequent fence to the summit outcrop. **3** The Black Brow route. Follow the track leading into Dovedale from Hartsop Hall. Keep the wall left, pass a solitary out-barn, the open track forks, either ford Hartsop Beck here or continue to a footbridge. Bear left to re-join the track leading to a gate. Pass the sheepfold and up the boulder-strewn open gill. Keep right, avoid entering Hogget Gill (*serious scramblers' only*). Clamber up the rock rib and bracken rigg to a natural weakness in Hogget Gill, cross through and ascend the tributary gill bearing up left as it forks onto the steep naze to reach Black Brow, go left to reach the summit.

(*left*) Caiston Glen   (*below*) The Scandale outgang

The Summit

For all its modest elevation, peering down the length of Scandale and north-eastward looking into the depths of the Hartsop Vale does lend this place real appeal. The summit outcrop has two small tops each with cairns, the westernmost, set on the lip of a rock platform is the actual summit. Both tops are defended by short rock walls on the south side, while a cleft splits the whole crag.

Marsh on the ridge fence
directly above Black Brow

Safe Descents

When mist threatens to suddenly envelope or heavy clouds portend rain (*as in the view of Claiston Glen opposite left*), head due W, a matter of fifty yards to reach the broken fence. Follow this and the succeeding wall S down to Scandale Pass. Turn left at the ladder-stile (N) for the Brotherswater Inn 2 miles, or cross it right (S) for Ambleside 3.5 miles via Scandale.

Ridge Route to....

DOVE CRAG
DESCENT 50 feet
ASCENT 540 feet   1.3 miles

A marshy ridge leads W, the ridge path keeping company with the broken boundary fence. After the right-hand junction with the fence from Hunsett Cove, the path climbs more steeply to meet the ridge wall, turn right to reach the summit.

Summit cairn looking north

HIGH HARTSOP DODD   DESCENT 350 feet   0.5 miles

Leave via the eastern cairn, picking a route onto the grassy ridge. The path descends easily by some peat hollows, with the most inspiring of views west towards Dove Crag at the head of Dovedale.

RED SCREES   DESCENT 404 feet   ASCENT 865 feet   1.5 miles

Join the broken fence and succeeding wall heading S down to the ladder-stile at Scandale Pass. The wall is the sure guide, climbing steadily onto the high plateau, nearing the top the wall deserts its duty at a wall T-junction and leaves you to find your own way due E to the summit.

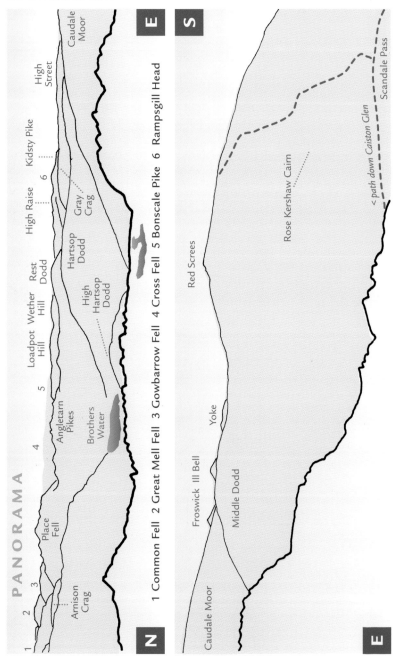

P A N O R A M A

1 Common Fell 2 Great Mell Fell 3 Gowbarrow Fell 4 Cross Fell 5 Bonscale Pike 6 Rampsgill Head

E

S

N

E

Caudale Moor

High Street

Kidsty Pike

High Raise

6

Rest Dodd

Wether Hill

Loadpot Hill

5

Gray Crag

Hartsop Dodd

High Hartsop Dodd

Angletarn Pikes

Brothers Water

4

Place Fell

3

Arnison Crag

2

1

Red Screes

Yoke

Froswick Ill Bell

Middle Dodd

Caudale Moor

Rose Kershaw Cairn

Scandale Pass

< path down Caiston Glen

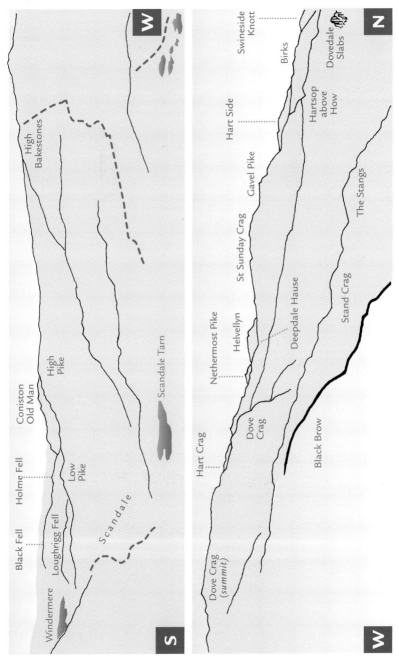

W

High Bakestones

Coniston Old Man

High Pike

Holme Fell

Black Fell

Loughrigg Fell

Low Pike

Windermere

Scandale

Scandale Tarn

S

N

Swineside Knott

Hart Side

Birks

Hartsop above How

Dovedale Slabs

Gavel Pike

St Sunday Crag

The Stangs

Nethermost Pike

Deepdale Hause

Helvellyn

Stand Crag

Hart Crag

Dove Crag

Black Brow

Dove Crag (summit)

W

LITTLE MELL FELL

In earliest references Melloc, *'the lesser bald hill'*, revealed in Watermillock. While the nucleus of the present-day settlement lies close to Ullswater, the first part of the parish-name actual refers to *'the pasture of wether sheep'* - matched by Wether Hill in the Far Eastern Fells. Little Mell Fell in all its unabashed modesty, remains a simple sweep of fell neatly parcelled by straight fences, inferior by name and nature. By definition no hill to be climbed is without merit, its just a matter of degrees, Little Mell graduates with honours about even. Nonetheless, the summit is a fine place to survey the neighbouring worlds of Eden and Lakeland, wherein may lie its greatest virtue.

In symmetry with the greater Mell, the walker may happily encircle the fell, a pleasant four mile tour conducted upon minor roads and quiet lanes - best begun from the vicinity of Thackthwaite and undertaken clockwise. One wonders who planted all those crab apple trees.

ASCENT *from The Hause*

There are three lines of ascent - the shortest route being the best. **1** GR 424235 Lay-by parking serves this, the quickest ascent. Cross the stile beside the covered reservoir compound, traverse the paddock to a stepped stile (a slate sign indicating the course of the Lowthwaite footpath left). A groove slants directly up the fellside, as an option one may follow the easier line of a graded path right, though this switches left to regain the groove with only a modest height gain.

505 metres   1,657 feet

Complete the incline to meet a shepherd's path running across the fell towards the saddle, go left, as this path levels the route to the summit breaks up the slope right.

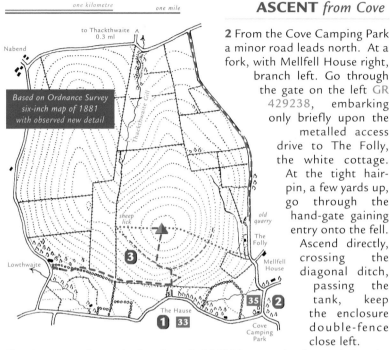

one kilometre   *one mile*

to Thackthwaite
0.3 ml

Nabend

Based on Ordnance Survey
six-inch map of 1881
with observed new detail

Thackthwaite Gill

sheep
lick

old
quarry

The
Folly

Lowthwaite

Mellfell
House

The Hause

Cove
Camping
Park

ASCENT *from Cove*

2 From the Cove Camping Park a minor road leads north. At a fork, with Mellfell House right, branch left. Go through the gate on the left GR 429238, embarking only briefly upon the metalled access drive to The Folly, the white cottage. At the tight hairpin, a few yards up, go through the hand-gate gaining entry onto the fell. Ascend directly, crossing the diagonal ditch, passing the tank, keep the enclosure double-fence close left.

Continue steeply up the bracken-clad hillside, a path of sorts being the product of Cove visitors making for the crest of their prize 'mountain'.

ASCENT
from Thackthwaite
No!

Formerly an access agreement existed permitting fellwalkers to approach Little Mell from GR 42225 off the minor road above the little shy farming community of Thackthwaite. Currently this is not operative, but when all the open access legislation is in

Lane leading to Thackthwaite

Springtime at Lowthwaite

place there is every likelihood that this line may become freely available once more. Not that it has much going for it, anyone who has tackled it recently, in error, will probably accord it the accolade "dullest climb of the range". Keeping company with the headstream of Thackthwaite Gill up, a fenced green lane, the crucial stile half-way up set in a marsh replaced with a multi-strand barbed-wire obstacle. So the advice is give it a total miss and enjoy the orbiting lanes to The Hause - t'is far better.

The Summit

CLOUGH HEAD   BLENCATHRA   GREAT MELL FELL

An impoverished grassland rapidly losing its heathery content culminates on an old Ordnance Survey triangulation pillar *(see westward view left)*. Only the lower reach of Ullswater makes a grudging appearance, Gowbarrow claiming praetorial rights as the lake's gallery. There are views towards Helvellyn, Martindale and into east Cumbria across the wide Eden vale backed paternally by the mighty wall of Cross Fell.

Little Mell Fell from Great Meldrum

Safe Descents

One's safety is unlikely to be in question, to avoid entanglement with barbed fencing, however, retrace the ascent from The Hause due south.

Ridge Route to....

GOWBARROW FELL   DESCENT 622 feet   ASCENT 460 feet   2.2 miles

Follow the path S to The Hause, cross the road via a gate and follow the track to a gate into forestry, keep the wall close right and conifers left to a stile. A path winds SW through the heather, crossing Great Meldrum to a ladder-stile at the wall corner entering National Trust land, a path ascends directly to the summit knot.

PANORAMA
120-degree horizon featuring the Far & Near Eastern Fells

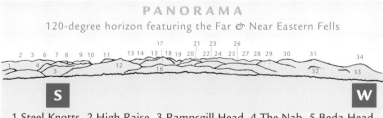

1 Steel Knotts 2 High Raise 3 Rampsgill Head 4 The Nab 5 Beda Head
6 High Street 7 Thornthwaite Crag 8 Gray Crag 9 Caudale Moor
10 Angletarn Pikes 11 Red Screes 12 Place Fell 13 Dove Crag
14 Hart Crag 15 Scrubby Crag 16 Gowbarrow Fell 17 St Sunday Crag
18 Fairfield 19 Seat Sandal 20 Dollywaggon Pike 21 Birkhouse Moor
22 Nethermost Pike 23 Sheffield Pike 24 Helvellyn 25 Helvellyn Lower Man
26 Common Fell 27 White Side 28 Raise 29 Hart Side 30 Stybarrow Dodd
31 Great Dodd 32 Dowthwaite Crag 33 Wolf Crags 34 Clough Head

LOW PIKE

While it may be true, Low Pike tends to play a 'bit-part' in the Fairfield Horseshoe grand tour, there is no denying its splendid individuality. With a couple of hours in your pocket for a fun climb then Low Pike makes a fine mini-Matterhorn escapade. Forming the final exuberant peak on the chiselled ridge running south from Dove Crag, the fell is a natural objective from Ambleside. Once attained, few will not look up to its big brother High Pike with eager relish and submit to the temptation of continuing up the sharpened edge.

The overwhelming majority of visitors climb direct from Scandale by either Low or High Sweden Bridges, the latter a charming structure, purely pedestrian, that has received many an adoring glance down the tourist age. Precious few climb the undistinguished western slopes from Rydale, though this line gives a good excuse to inspect Buckstones Jump. As the picture on page 237 shows a resistant band of ice-smoothed igneous rock forms a convincing dam across the dale floor, forcing the beck to twist and squeeze through a weakness at the eastern end. Stepping stones assist walkers' progress, a curious and pleasing event on the otherwise plain climb up't fell.

The natural ridge, continuing south from the summit, has one mischievous trick up its sleeve. Sweden Crag hugs the sturdy ridge wall forcing it to take a giant rock step in its stride, the wall builders achieved this with aplomb but many walkers will think seriously before following suit. No doubt knowledge of this obstacle has caused most walkers to trudge up the winding green trail east of the edge at this early stage.

507 metres   1,663 feet

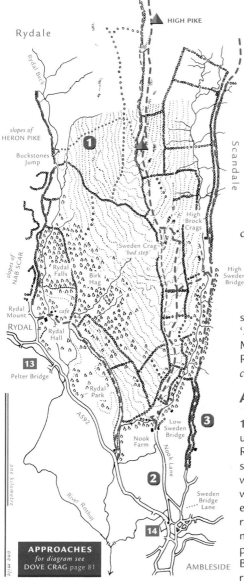

The ridge-wall *'bad step'*
scramble at Sweden Crag

Sweden is an unlikely country-name to find here-abouts and, in common with many another instance, this place-name is not quite what it appears. Pronounced s'we-dun it originally meant *'land cleared by burning'*. Much as Birk Hag (above Rydal Park) meant *'newly cleared birch woodland'*.

ASCENT *from Rydal*

1 Follow the village street up between the Hall and Rydal Mount. Pass through several gates on a track which leads into the lonely wilds of Rydale proper. The excitement of falls app-roaching Buckstones Jump making this a particularly pleasant walk. Access to Buckstones Jump has recently been made less welcoming, the gateway awkwardly fenced. However, carefully slip through and stroll down to the falls, walk along the rim of the rock band and stride over the stepping stones at the rear of the falls. The ensuing fell-side has a few small outcrops to avoid achieved by slanting slightly left of a natural direct line, only latterly adjusting right to reach the ridge wall *(easily crossed - showing due respect for the wall & wallers' craft)*.

ASCENT *from Ambleside*

Two lanes lead into Scandale from the old town. **2** From the Rydal Road car park, cross the mini-roundabout into Smithy Brow, turning left into Nook Lane. Tarmac is sustained to Nook Farm, go through the gate and cross Low Sweden Bridge. The ensuing track switches up right above the bank then goes left keeping the wall to the left. Beyond the next gateway the path forks, with a way bearing up left accompanying the ridge-top wall, via ladder-stiles and negotiating the awkward Sweden Crag 'bad step', which is the most minor of ascent problems. Nonetheless, some walkers chicken-out via an alternative scarp path to the right. The main way leads on through two further gateways before bearing up through High Brock Crags onto the ridge, skipping over some peaty ground before climbing by the wall to the summit. Folk dscending Fairfield Horseshoe tend to 'skip' the summit on a path to the east. **3** From Smithy Brow continue with the Kirkstone Road taking the next left, Sweden Bridge Lane. This becomes a walled lane, the former drove way to Hartsop. Passing through woodland the track forks, go left crossing the picturesque High Sweden Bridge, take the ascending path to join the green trail from Low Sweden Bridge.

High Sweden Bridge with Low Pike on the right-hand skyline

Ice-smoothed rock-band dam and stepping stones at Buckstone's Jump

The Summit

The ridge-wall so conclusively muscles in on the act that it claims the summit for itself. There is little room left, though passing walkers have erected a small cairn as a mark of respect for the fell top. Fortunately, the wall is exceedingly well-made for occasionally visitors clamber over at this point en route to/from Rydale and in following the ridge to/from High Pike on the sunny, less eroded, west side. A popular path by-passes the top to the east to reach the ladder-stile. Not all engaged upon the Fairfield Horseshoe are purist enough to touch each and every summit on that famous round - though why miss Low Pike? *It's probably the best of the bunch!*

Safe Descents

Ordinarily a ridge wall is a friend in a time of need, and while this is basically true, the Sweden Crag 'bad step' brings a peculiar caution into this equation. The popular route prudently bears left short of this feature, slipping through a breach in the outcropping at High Brock Crags. Wind down through a series of gateways to Low Sweden Bridge and the security of Nook Lane leading into old Ambleside.

Ridge Route

HIGH PIKE DESCENT 45 feet ASCENT 490 feet   0.8 miles

With the wall as the guide. Proceed via a ladder-stile in the depression. As height is gained tread easy as the path is suffering foot 'wear' fatigue.

Ambleside backed by Windermere from the summit

Ridge wall and therefore not-quite-the-summit cairn, looking to High Pike

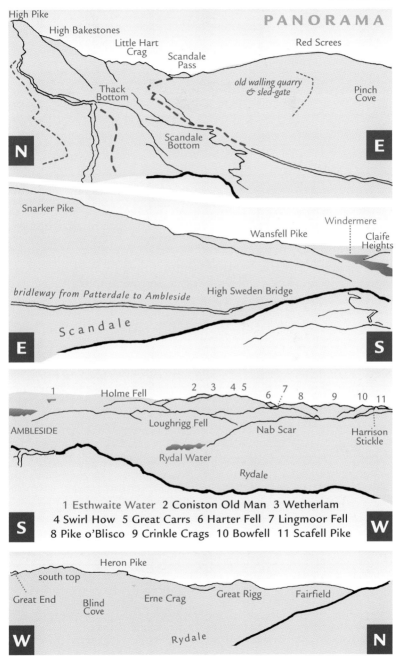

PANORAMA

High Pike

High Bakestones

Little Hart Crag

Scandale Pass

Red Screes

old walling quarry & sled-gate

Pinch Cove

Thack Bottom

Scandale Bottom

N

E

Snarker Pike

Windermere

Wansfell Pike

Claife Heights

bridleway from Patterdale to Ambleside

High Sweden Bridge

S c a n d a l e

E

S

1

Holme Fell

2 3 4 5

6 7

8

9

10 11

AMBLESIDE

Loughrigg Fell

Nab Scar

Harrison Stickle

Rydal Water

Rydale

1 Esthwaite Water 2 Coniston Old Man 3 Wetherlam
4 Swirl How 5 Great Carrs 6 Harter Fell 7 Lingmoor Fell
8 Pike o'Blisco 9 Crinkle Crags 10 Bowfell 11 Scafell Pike

S

W

Heron Pike

south top

Great End

Blind Cove

Erne Crag

Great Rigg

Fairfield

W

Rydale

N

MIDDLE DODD

In common with the adjacent High Hartsop Dodd, this is a spur ridge, though it has a more certain and quite delectable summit. Gaining distinction and appearing separate by its abrupt conical profile. Indeed, when viewed from Kirkstonefoot it contrives to obscure the considerable bulk of Red Screes, no mean feat. Indeed, it takes no mean feet to climb! The ridge forming a really stiff approach to Red Screes from the Hartsop vale, makes the summit a place of some jubilation and relief. Quirky routes to the top may be attempted from Scandale Pass **1** on a rough pathless traverse and **2** out of the depths of the Kirkstone Pass from the vicinity of Smithy Brow. Along its base runs the old cross-range bridle-path between Hartsop and Troutbeck. A humble trail stemming from Hartsop Hall, superseded by the snaking Kirkstone road but surviving as a reminder of the nature of old Lakeland roads.

Of the flanking watercourses Caiston Beck has the most striking waterfalls, these lie beside the spoil of Caiston Level, a briefly worked lead mine. The fell-name derives from its position sandwiched between High Hartsop Dodd and (Low) Hartsop Dodd.

A summer's evening view of Place Fell beyond Brotherswater from the summit of Middle Dodd

653 metres   2,143 feet

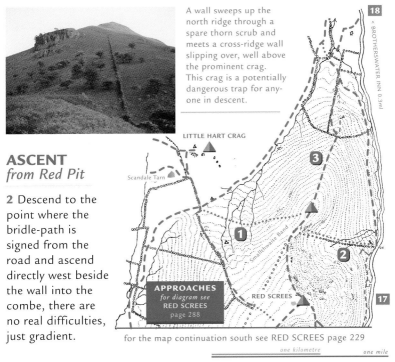

A wall sweeps up the north ridge through a spare thorn scrub and meets a cross-ridge wall slipping over, well above the prominent crag. This crag is a potentially dangerous trap for anyone in descent.

LITTLE HART CRAG

Scandale Tarn

ASCENT
from Red Pit

2 Descend to the point where the bridle-path is signed from the road and ascend directly west beside the wall into the combe, there are no real difficulties, just gradient.

APPROACHES
for diagram see
RED SCREES
page 288

RED SCREES

for the map continuation south see RED SCREES page 229

one kilometre   one mile

ASCENT *from Kirkstonefoot*

3 A third of a mile south of the Brotherswater Inn find a large lay-by with bus stop notice. GR402111. A footpath is signposted via a wall stile, this takes a clearly marshalled course by two sharp turns through the moraine pasture to a footbridge spanning Kirkstone Beck. Cross the ladder-stile beyond, originally on the old path to Caiston mine. Join the path from Hartsop Hall, crossing the adjacent footbridge over Caiston Beck. Go left, slipping through the wall to begin the ascent in earnest.

Keep the wall close right. At the top drift left to go over the cross-ridge wall with a clear path climbing the prow of the ridge to the summit. No sweat – umm plenty of the stuff!

The curious stone dyke feature close to the summit, not replicated on any other fell-top.

Middle Dodd from the summit of Red Screes

The Summit

As the ridge melts away underfoot, a solitary cairn leaves no doubt as to the top, a lofty place of scenic respite after the steepling climb. Let the pulse settle and the senses calm, suffcient to eye the shattered northern face of Red Screes ahead of the final pull to that ultimate perch. Close by what appears a man-made trench gives cause for scrutiny. Walkers who have explored Hadrian's Wall will know Limestone Corner and the litter of large boulders set beside the unfinished north ditch. They will see the same chaos in microcosm and wonder how nature contrived such a curious feature, or was it simply a drystone waller's dig?

Safe Descent

Even against a northerly breeze the steep north ridge is secure but there is one severe caution. Once the cross-ridge wall has been crossed veer sharp left and keep the partially broken descending wall close left. This is to avoid the 'blind' cliff sinisterly lurking down the ridge, a death-trap plunge for the unwary, or those engrossed in conversation!

Ridge Route to

RED SCREES   ASCENT 406 feet   0.65 miles

Head SW, the grassy ridge drawing tighter to meet the wall emerging from the eastern combe on Smallthwaite Band. The ridge path rises steadily away from the wall due S to the summit.

PANORAMA

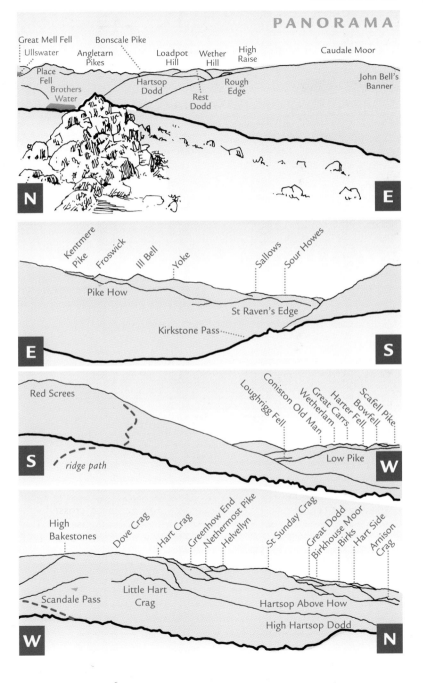

Great Mell Fell
Ullswater
Place Fell
Brothers Water
Angletarn Pikes
Bonscale Pike
Hartsop Dodd
Loadpot Hill
Rest Dodd
Wether Hill
High Raise
Rough Edge
Caudale Moor
John Bell's Banner

N **E**

Kentmere Pike
Froswick
Ill Bell
Yoke
Pike How
Sallows
Sour Howes
St Raven's Edge
Kirkstone Pass

E **S**

Red Screes
ridge path
Loughrigg Fell
Coniston Old Man
Great Carrs
Wetherlam
Harter Fell
Bowfell
Scafell Pike
Low Pike

S **W**

High Bakestones
Dove Crag
Hart Crag
Greenhow End
Nethermost Pike
Helvellyn
St Sunday Crag
Great Dodd
Birkhouse Moor
Birks
Hart Side
Arnison Crag
Scandale Pass
Little Hart Crag
Hartsop Above How
High Hartsop Dodd

W **N**

NAB SCAR

Not a fell by any proper measure, rather the first station or last knot on a famous ridge walk, with the term Nab, akin to nib or nose, *'the pointed ridge-end'*. The fell-name refers to the attractive craggy hillside overlooking Rydal Water and more significantly Nab Cottage. Associated with the Lake Poets, the house appropriately continues in its literary tradition now a centre for English language tuition - the potentially tranquil lakeside situation sullied by the busy through road.

With such singular emphasis on the ridge path the decades of wear and tear have taken their toll. Walkers descending from Heron Pike experience a jangling discomfort among the trail shingle, the steep ascent from Rydal Mount *(the central zig-zagging feature of the portrait above)* is currently recipient of major paving restoration works. Hats off to the work teams, they are doing a fine job that will endure and the ever popular Nab Scar path will be a scar no more. In due course the continuing way to Heron Pike should receive similar consolidation.

A circular walk exists which dignifies its perculiar virtuosity as a view-point, not only from its summit, but from the lower bridleway (known as the Corpse Road), the former thoroughfare between Rydal and Grasmere which leads through the wooded western slopes, providing a delightfully sylvan esplanade with lovely views across Rydal Water.

455 metres   **1,490 feet**   *(estimated height)*

ASCENT *from Rydal*

1 Strictly there is but one way, well marked and furnished, from the head of the village, above Rydal Mount. A walled lane leading onto the paved way *(works in progress left)* a welcome firm footing winding onto the ridge-top nab. For the majority of foot soldiers, providing a solid start to a day on the Fairfield Horseshoe. Notice the block of tooled stone resting beside the path as the ridge makes a turn north, there is no certain explanation to its origin or status - the silence of stones! Cross the ladder-stile and bear off the ridge highway half-left to the large crumbling cairn at the brink.

ASCENT *from White Moss*

The National Trust car park makes a fine springboard for a three-mile round walk embracing Nab Scar. **2** Begin as with HERON PIKE route **1**, climbing in sympathy with Dunney Beck to the stile at the entry to the Alcock Tarn enclosure. Ignore this, keeping up the fell, a clear path drifting right to largely contour across the slope, now above the beck's headstream, to link up with the ridge path, at two cairns west of the broken ridge

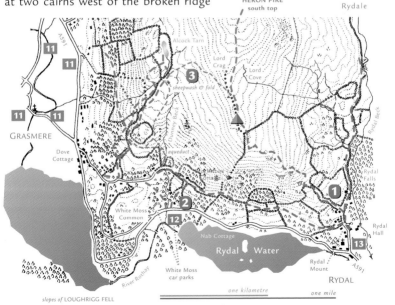

wall. The summit lying some 150 yards due south. The circular tour follows the ridge path down, over the ladder-stile, bound for the head of the village street above Rydal Mount, bearing right along the lane signposted to Grasmere. The gated bridle-path leads on for a smidgen under one mile above meadows and through woodland, with views over Rydal Water - watch for the path in the lane left at Brockstone Cottage.

The Summit

Once a fine cairn marking a pleasantly picturesque viewpoint. The passage of time and a tide of casual visitors have rendered the edifice a rather sad crumbling heap. This is the first significant pause on the great ridge leading inexorably to Fairfield. Take a breather and scan the tight cluster of fine fells which encircle Great and Little Langdales. The greatest pleasure being upon Loughrigg Fell, with its famous cathedral-proportioned Cavern, and down over Rydal Water with its wooded island sanctuaries *(see opposite)*.

From across Grasmere - a lovely mix of rock, scree, trees, meadow and glistening water

Rydal Mount, home of William Wordsworth until his death in 1850 and remains part of the family estate.

Safe Descent

The over-worked path leading south to Rydal is the surest route in adverse weather, but be aware, the new paving will be slick when summer algae growth is dowsed by the slightest shower of rain.

Ridge Route to ....

HERON PIKE ASCENT 640 feet 0.7 miles

Even in the most grim mists the ridge path can seldom be in doubt. Though if that were the case then perhaps one might be considering retreat as the greater valour, particularly mindful that it is the wider view that engages attention most thrillingly for those completing the Fairfield Horseshoe. The path, keeps consistently right of the broken wall to Lord Crag, thereafter no such companion feature exists over the bare south top to the piked summit.

Rydal and Windermere

Rydal Water, featuring Loughrigg Cavern and Nab Cottage beside the lakeside road below

PANORAMA

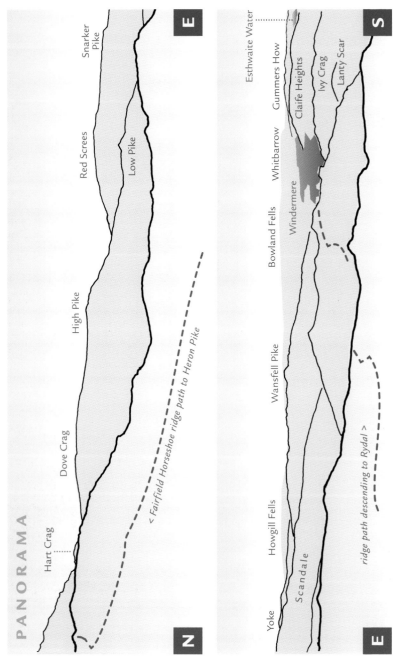

E

Snarker Pike

Red Screes

Low Pike

High Pike

Dove Crag

Hart Crag

< Fairfield Horseshoe ridge path to Heron Pike

N

S

Esthwaite Water

Gummers How

Claife Heights

Ivy Crag

Lanty Scar

Whitbarrow

Windermere

Bowland Fells

Wansfell Pike

Howgill Fells

Scandale

Yoke

ridge path descending to Rydal >

E

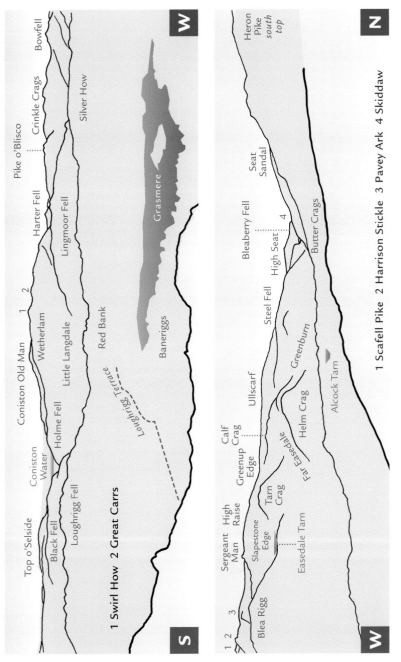

Top o'Selside — Black Fell — Coniston Water — Coniston Old Man — Holme Fell — Wetherlam — Little Langdale — Lingmoor Fell — Harter Fell — Pike o'Blisco — Crinkle Crags — Bowfell — Silver How — Red Bank — Grasmere — Baneriggs — Loughrigg Terrace — Loughrigg Fell

1 Swirl How 2 Great Carrs

Blea Rigg — Sergeant Man — High Raise — Slapestone Edge — Easedale Tarn — Tarn Crag — Greenup Edge — Calf Crag — Far Easedale — Helm Crag — Ullscarf — Greenburn — Alcock Tarn — Steel Fell — High Seat — Bleaberry Fell — Seat Sandal — Butter Crags — Heron Pike south top

1 Scafell Pike 2 Harrison Stickle 3 Pavey Ark 4 Skiddaw

NETHERMOST PIKE

A clever descriptive marriage of 'nether' the lesser peak as to Helvellyn, and 'most', the greater peak as to Dollywaggon. Viewed from midway up Grisedale this is a tantalising mountain, come winter snowy raiment it takes on alpine qualities. These are real peaks to conquer, not the swollen shoulders of giants. Enter Nethermost or Ruthwaite Coves and see one foremost peak soaring above craggy walls, wild, remote, Himalayan in its grandeur. Both corries reward exploration, with Hard Tarn a mantel-shelf pool fashioned by glacial action and frozen in time and space the one place above all to find. Tucked up under the east ridge a spot long known as Calf Hole, suggesting a place where red deer once took sanctuary with their calves. The impressive headwall of Nethermost Cove can be viewed from high on Swallow Scarth, backed by the gullied northern face of St Sunday Crag.

Hard Tarn backed by High Crag

891 metres   2,923 feet

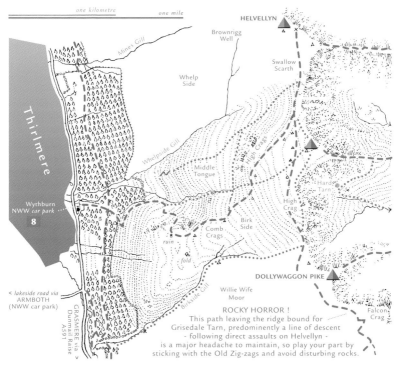

one kilometre   one mile

HELVELLYN

Brownrigg
Well

Swallow
Scarth

Whelp
Side

Thirlmere

Mines Gill

Whelpside Gill

Middle
Tongue

High Crags

Hard
Tarn

High
Crag

Wythburn
NWW car park

8

Birk
Side

Comb
Crags

ruin

fold

< lakeside road via
ARMBOTH
(NWW car park)

GRASMERE via
Dunmail Raise
A591

Birkside Gill

DOLLYWAGGON PIKE

Willie Wife
Moor

Falcon
Crag

ROCKY HORROR !
This path leaving the ridge bound for
Grisedale Tarn, predominently a line of descent
- following direct assaults on Helvellyn -
is a major headache to maintain, so play your part by
sticking with the Old Zig-zags and avoid disturbing rocks.

Looking down the east ridge into Nethermost Cove and the strath copses of Grisedale

HELVELLYN

Striding Edge

Nethermost Cove

beware! dangerous shafts

miners' path

Calf Hole

Eagle Crag (old mine)

ruin

Hard Tarn

Ruthwaite Cove

Ruthwaite Lodge

DOLLYWAGGON PIKE

Cock Cove

Falcon Crag

a trio of gullies (strictly out-of-bounds for walkers!)

Tarn Crag

Willie Wife Moor

Nethermost Cove is so thoroughly hemmed in by steepling ridges that few walkers ever trouble to find their way in, making it a place of real solitude.

View down Grisedale from the miners' path

ASCENT
from Wythburn

Tucked in behind the little church at Wythburn (in the vernacular *Wyb'n*), a North West Water car park provides a suitable launch pad for the ascent, with two interesting lines to consider. **1** Follow the waymarked and pitched path rising through the conifers, crossing a forest track to reach a stile/gate. The path runs up beside a fence shielding a triangular deciduous planting, switching left coming above the conifers, the path is presently intermittently pitched. **2** At the sharp right-hand bend follow an unusual line directly up the grassy southern bank of Comb Gill. Climbing steeply to the brink to either, join a traversing path, going left under High Crags, or more likely, continue directly to the summit plateau crossing the main Wythburn path at the next edge. **3** The forgotten shepherds' path up the Middle Tongue ridge is described on HELVELLYN page 166. This path pre-dates the conifers and flooding of Leathes Water to create Thirlmere, being an integral element of the pastoral heritage of the Wythburn valley. Gaining the Wythburn path at the Swallow Scarth depression bear right onto the plateau.

HELVELLYN

High Crag

Birk Side

Comb Crags

3
2
1

22 Wythburn car park

WESTERN APPROACHES

Thirlmere

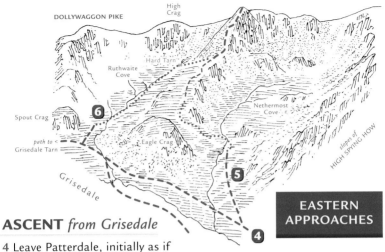

ASCENT *from Grisedale*

4 Leave Patterdale, initially as if
destined for Striding Edge, though, having left the road at the kissing-gate and climbed the pasture bank to the hand-gate the route goes left beside the wall. This path leads south-westwards up the valley, above Braesteads (*farm*) - consult the map on BIRKHOUSE MOOR page 31.

   5 Shortly after the third hand-gate, with Eagle Crag looming ahead, an old path branches half-right to a wall-stile. The path enters Nethermost Cove climbing within a bracken and boulder infested groove to top the cascades. As this old miners' path is lost, ford the beck and climb through the outcrops, admiring the fabulous views of the surrounding headwalls, on course for the ridge above Eagle Crag and all evidence of the copper mine. The ridge ascends in easy stages, with a better defined path materialising as the dramatic upper ridge commences. At this point contemplate a spur diversion to Hard Tarn, though the traverse latterly includes rough boulders (there is no direct ascent from the tarn). There is no serious hazard, other than steepness, to the ridge climb, the ultimate sharp rocks giving plenty of handhold security.

   6 The less than orthodox, but by far the more intriguing, line branches from the path at Ruthwaite Lodge. A path slants up beside Spout Crag into Ruthwaite Cove. Where this disappears, ford the cascading Ruthwaite Gill passing the two huge erratic boulders, keep to the right-hand headstream. An erosion scar just below, helping to identify the location of Hard Tarn. The crystal clear waters make a painfully slow exit through the peaty fringe. The shallow pool, on first sight, looks to have sinister depths, an illusion, created by the black algae on its bed, which must have the effect of slightly warming the waters with any hint of sunshine. Traverse the boulders north-east to the peat shoulder rising to embark upon the prow of the east ridge.

The east ridge in profile from Helvellyn backed by Dollywaggon Pike

The Summit

Many walkers 'hell bent' on Helvellyn, or descent from the same, will be unaware of Nethermost Pike, the main path taking a dismissive off-centre swipe to the west. The triangular plateau is a pasture invaded by a crop of rock, some splintered specimens pointing skyward. The summit cairn, one of several candidates among the clitter *(see below)*, stands towards the north-eastern edge. Though it has to be said the more complete panorama is enjoyed from the prim crest of High Crag, over-looking Ruthwaite Cove to the south.

Safe Descents

The east ridge should not be considered in hostile weather. Either follow the broad cairned path crossing the top in a southerly direction, thus avoiding the edge, to reach Grisedale Tarn, for either Patterdale or Grasmere. Alternatively, go straight over this path descending westwards to join the lower path leading via Comb Crag to the Wythburn car park.

The east ridge soaring over Nethermost Cove

Ridge Routes to ....

(below) Grisedale's boulder-field of erratics

HELVELLYN   DESCENT 93 feet   ASCENT 287 feet   0.7 miles

Either follow the edge for superlative views, or join the main thoroughfare rising N from Swallow Scarth to pass the cross-wall wind-shelter.

DOLLYWAGGON PIKE   DESCENT 170 feet   ASCENT 163 feet   1 mile

Join the broad way W of the summit this studiously avoids the ridge heading S, so after rounding High Crag bear half-left (SE) over easier ground to reach the neat summit ridge.

P A N O R A M A

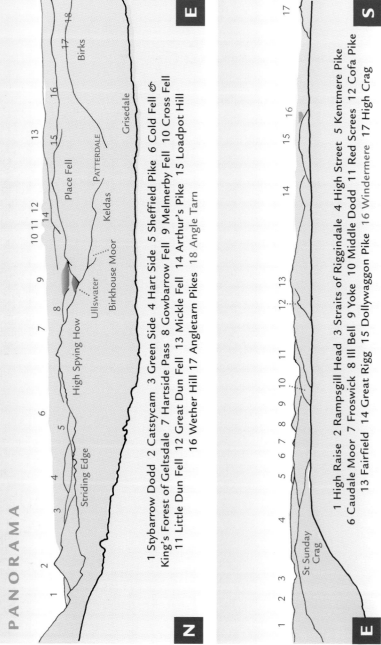

E

N

1 Stybarrow Dodd 2 Catstycam 3 Green Side 4 Hart Side 5 Sheffield Pike 6 Cold Fell &
King's Forest of Geltsdale 7 Hartside Pass 8 Gowbarrow Fell 9 Melmerby Fell 10 Cross Fell
11 Little Dun Fell 12 Great Dun Fell 13 Mickle Fell 14 Arthur's Pike 15 Loadpot Hill
16 Wether Hill 17 Angletarn Pikes 18 Angle Tarn

S

E

1 High Raise 2 Rampsgill Head 3 Straits of Riggindale 4 High Street 5 Kentmere Pike
6 Caudale Moor 7 Froswick 8 Ill Bell 9 Yoke 10 Middle Dodd 11 Red Screes 12 Cofa Pike
13 Fairfield 14 Great Rigg 15 Dollywaggon Pike 16 Windermere 17 High Crag

S **W**

Thunacar Knott   Ullscarf   Brandreth

1 Top o'Selside 2 Wetherlam 3 Coniston Old Man 4 Brim Fell 5 Swirl How
6 Grey Friar 7 Black Combe 8 Pike o'Blisco 9 Cold Pike 10 Harrison Stickle 11 Crinkle Crags 12 Bowfell
13 High Raise 14 Esk Pike 15 Scafell 16 Scafell Pike 17 Great End 18 Lingmell 19 Allen Crags 20 Glaramara
21 Great Gable 22 Kirk Fell 23 Red Pike (*Wasdale*) 24 Scoat Fell 25 Pillar 26 Iron Crag (*Caw Fell*) 27 High Crag

N

Helvellyn

Helvellyn Lower Man

Fleetwith Pike High Spy

W

1 High Stile 2 Red Pike (*Buttermere*) 3 Dale Head 4 Hindscarth 5 Robinson
6 Mellbreak 7 Whiteless Pike 8 Wandope 9 Grasmoor 10 Eel Crags 11 Hopegill Head 12 Grisedale Pike

The east ridge tapers to a stunning peak, seen here in high summer from the lonely depths of Nethermost Cove, an utterly beautiful and wild hanging valley.

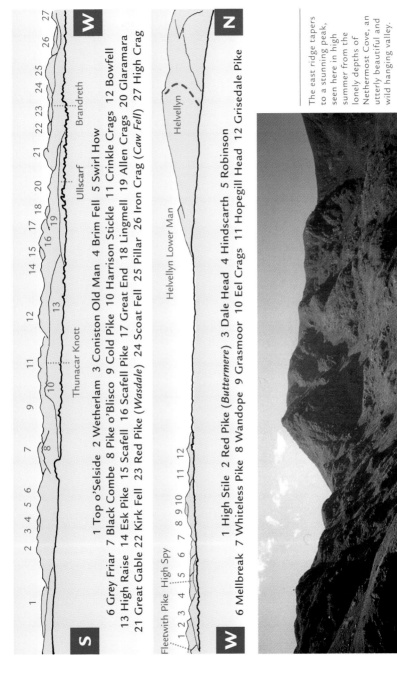

RAISE

Raise differs from its compatriots in several respects. When winter brings its alpine bloom, the upper slopes overlooking the Sticks Pass can be the scene of much revelry. There are skiers and snow-boarders at play on this, the only permanent ski-tow and piste on the high fells of Lakeland. The eastern arm of the fell is given texture by its dense spread of ageing juniper and the industrial remnants of a silver and lead mining smelter flue running up the ridge, like some strange rocky vertebrae. The fell-name derives from the Old Norse hreysi 'cairn', pockmarked rocks about the summit lending weight to the sense of this being the site of some ancient elevated burial, though there is no lingering trace to support this suggestion.

Sticks Gill West

Raise fails to reach the Thirlmere valley on the west, succumbing to the rival squeeze of White Side and Stybarrow Dodd. While to the east it fairs only slightly better, terminating on Stang End, overlooking the old Greenside Mine.

ASCENT *from*
Legburthwaite & Thirlspot

1 From the small car park close to the Thirlmere Recreation Hall at Legburthwaite. By long tradition, walkers have strode up the long shoulder of Stybarrow Dodd on the ancient path to

884 metres   2,900 feet

Rock features north of Helvellyn are sufficent of a rarity to arouse a modest interest, hence the tor east of the summit will give walkers, with an idle moment to fill, cause to drift aside to inspect.

In times past whether travellers were approaching the Sticks Pass from Glenridding or Legburthwaite they apparently saw no need to refer to the adjacent becks as anything other than Sticks Gill. Latterday writers, for navigational clarity, proffer bracketed east/west distinction.

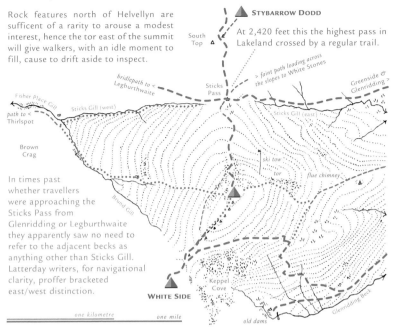

STYBARROW DODD

At 2,420 feet this the highest pass in Lakeland crossed by a regular trail.

the Sticks Pass (*see* **STYBARROW DODD** pages 279/80), breaking onto the marshy ground bound for Raise. But the more adventureous may consider variant lines from two alternative valley bases. **2** Follow the footpath signposted to Swirls, off the Sticks Pass path, directly after crossing Stanah Gill. This runs above the intake wall to cross a footbridge spanning Fisher Place Gill. A path has materialised up the steep south bank, suppressing the bracken, the tumbling waters and craggy surrounds surely bringing out even the most sparing of photographers. There are several mighty waterfalls, individually fine, but as a series magnificent - a resounding handsome and stirring sight.

Copious water was drawn to the Greenside Mine processing complex via aqueducts. Though damaged by neglect, it is fun to trace their course across the slopes of Stang

View down Glenridding from above the old Greenside Mine works

The steepness of the bank path engenders an appropriately slow pace (*see illustrations on* page 225).

3 Fisher Place Gill can also be reached from Thirlspot. However, if you choose to park at the King's Head Hotel report to reception for a parking permit, redeemable at the bar later - Theakston's Best Bitter is fine reward for the non-driver in your number. A footpath is signposted through the gated farmyard on the south side of the hotel. Passing a caravan park via gates over a channelled ditch, then straight up to a kissing-gate at the Thirlmere Leat, bear half left to a gate in the intake wall. A pitched path ensues rising by a gill and the intake wall to meet The Swirls/Stanah path. Go left, as indicated by the slate guide 'Sticks Pass', fording the gill. After 80 yards fork right, not signed, the path gently rising. At a further fork, ignore the steep path, the old pony route, instead follow the contouring path through the dense bracken to reach Fisher Place Gill. **4** Above the final waterfall, hidden from the valley and difficult to access, the gradient eases. Approaching the confluence with Sticks Gill (west) the old shepherd's path drifts right to dissolve nearing the Brund Gill ravine.

5 One might choose to ascend Sticks Gill fording at the moraine ridge following the southern bank. There are a couple of modest falls to break up the pathless journey, linking with the Sticks Pass path as it levels onto the marshy saddle. At the cairn, join the heavily used ridge path, keeping right of the natural line to minimise ankle dipping in the saturated peat. Higher up the broad path becomes a loose stony trail. **6** Perhaps a better line initially is provided by Brund Gill, ford the beck, tight by the ravine's exit, ascend the steep east bank, at an early stage peering into the narrow gorge. Above, tussocky moor-grass leads, via a leftward fork with the tributary gill, to an old sheepfold. A direct, little hindered line of ascent to the ragged summit outcropping is surprisingly swiftly achieved.

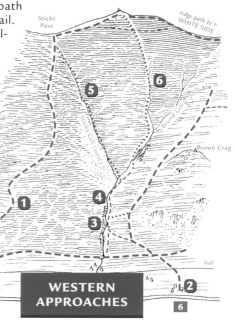

Sticks Pass

ridge path to > WHITE SIDE

Sticks Gill (west)

Brund Gill

Brown Crag

Stanah Gill

Stanah

leat

THRELKELD <
via St Johns-in-the-Vale

KESWICK A591 <

WESTERN APPROACHES

ridge path to
WHITE SIDE

Sticks
Pass

Keppel
Cove

10

8

9

ruins of the smelter flue

BIRKHOUSE MOOR

slopes of

Glenridding

Glenridding Beck

Rowten Gill

Sticks Gill (east)

Stang
End

Swart Beck

Area of orderly
mine tip adjacent to
the drained bed of
Sticks Reservoir

ASCENT
from Glenridding

There are three principal
lines of approach from
Glenridding. Again the Sticks
Pass being most popular.
But surprisingly, even
easier walking is provided

EASTERN APPROACHES

A sense of tidiness is slowly
but surely overtaking the ugly
environs of the old Greenside
Mine smelter, scree and spoil
merging as nature reclaims
the scene of man's toil.

7
slopes of
SHEFFIELD PIKE

by the old pony route to Helvellyn, which conveniently climbs over the
southern shoulder of Raise, with a third route breaking off above
Greenside Mine tracing the old smelter flue and the broad east ridge.

7 Follow the Greenside Road track to, and through, the former mine
buildings. **8** The old pony route branches left signed 'Brown Cove,
Whiteside Bank'. The track runs beneath the juniper wood clothing the
slopes of Stang, coming under an outcrop the old pony path branches
right, zig-zagging in comparatively easy stages above Keppel Cove : a
name of Norse origin which means *'high hollow of the horse ravine'*. One may
branch off almost at will up the pathless grassy slopes, or continue to

the saddle bearing right with the
strongly cairned ridge path.

9 Alternatively, follow the Sticks
Pass path above the mine buildings at the edge of the juniper.
Nearing the top, bear off left,
accompanying the ruined lead
smelter flue, the ground beside

ski-tow and shelter quietly relaxing in
summer sunshine awaiting winter duties.

Striding Edge · Catstycam · Helvellyn · Helvellyn Lower Man

Cairn on Stang looking south-west

this piece of industrial archaeology is poisoned and lifeless. The quarried spoil, fanning from beneath Green Side, filling the space beside the long drained Sticks Reservoir weir, is obvious. The two hollows above, originally opened as galleried mines, were later thus quarried. One may choose to visit the cairn on Stang ['*boundary pole*'] for its fine view both down Glenridding and to Catstycam *(above)*, and study the effects of glaciation on the smoothed rocks. The flue ends at the remains of a chimney stack. However, a green path continues on a gentle gradient ultimately, inexplicably disappearing at a minor spring. From this point ascend, keeping left of the boulder slopes, in passing close to a prominent rock tor and the top of the ski tow. **10** The Sticks Pass route crossing Swart Beck above Lucy's Tongue Level entrance, via a footbridge, then weaves through the stony spoil and redundant reservoir outflow relief channel, before forging on up above Sticks Gill (east) to the hause. This is the highest pass in Lakeland crossed by a regular path. Bear left, initially keeping a wide western birth to avoid the soggy ground.

The Summit

Here be rocks! Quite a radical admission for any summit in the Helvellyn chain. Distinctive rocks, suggestive of gruyere cheese, fashioned by air bubbles during vulcanisation. In common with all else in the range, Catstycam excepted, this is a place where grass predominates, the rocky top a pleasant contrast. As a viewpoint it has a notable command of Lakeland fell tops, inevitably only bettered in extent by Helvellyn. The fell's one visual flaw, caused by the cairn-builders trait, an excessive line of cairns beside the ridge path running south to the saddle.

Safe Descents

summit cairn

Mist and torrid weather are not a cause for undue panic, the fell harbours few natural perils. The simplest line of retreat is north, down to the Sticks Pass, though a general westward line eventually leads to safe territory, mindful of the Brund, and particularly, Fisher Place Gill ravines.

Ridge Routes to ....

STYBARROW DODD   DESCENT 440 feet ASCENT 394 feet   0.8 miles

Descend N upon the common way to the cairn at Sticks Pass. Continue N rising to the south top cairn from where angle NE taking 370 *yards* to the flake of slate and stones marking the true, if lack-lustre, summit.

WHITE SIDE   DESCENT 210 feet ASCENT 142 feet   0.7 miles

A plethora of cairns litters the ridge path S from the summit. Descend to the saddle where the old pony route from Glenridding joins the ridge from the east. The pinky-brown gravelly trail continues undisguised up to the solitary cairn.

Two sections of the Fisher Place Gill drama

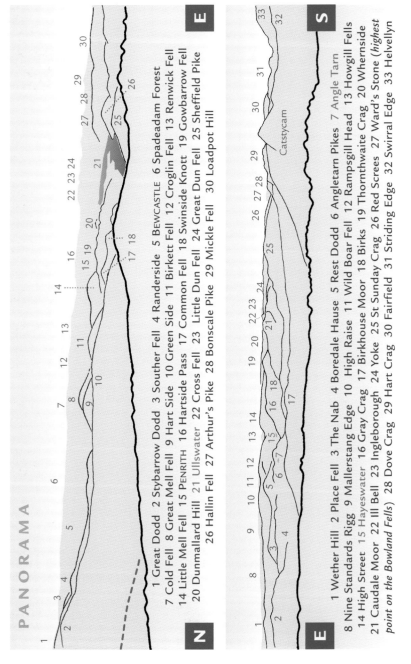

PANORAMA

E

N

1 Great Dodd 2 Stybarrow Dodd 3 Souther Fell 4 Randerside 5 BEWCASTLE 6 Spadeadam Forest
7 Cold Fell 8 Great Mell Fell 9 Hart Side 10 Green Side 11 Birkett Fell 12 Croglin Fell 13 Renwick Fell
14 Little Mell Fell 15 PENRITH 16 Hartside Pass 17 Common Fell 18 Swinside Knott 19 Gowbarrow Fell
20 Dunmallard Hill 21 Ullswater 22 Cross Fell 23 Little Dun Fell 24 Great Dun Fell 25 Sheffield Pike
26 Hallin Fell 27 Arthur's Pike 28 Bonscale Pike 29 Mickle Fell 30 Loadpot Hill

S

E

1 Wether Hill 2 Place Fell 3 The Nab 4 Boredale Hause 5 Rest Dodd 6 Angletarn Pikes 7 Angle Tarn
8 Nine Standards Rigg 9 Mallerstang Edge 10 High Raise 11 Wild Boar Fell 12 Rampsgill Head 13 Howgill Fells
14 High Street 15 Hayeswater 16 Gray Crag 17 Birkhouse Moor 18 Birks 19 Thornthwaite Crag 20 Whernside
21 Caudale Moor 22 Ill Bell 23 Ingleborough 24 Yoke 25 St Sunday Crag 26 Red Screes 27 Ward's Stone (*highest
point on the Bowland Fells*) 28 Dove Crag 29 Hart Crag 30 Fairfield 31 Striding Edge 32 Swirral Edge 33 Helvellyn

Catstycam

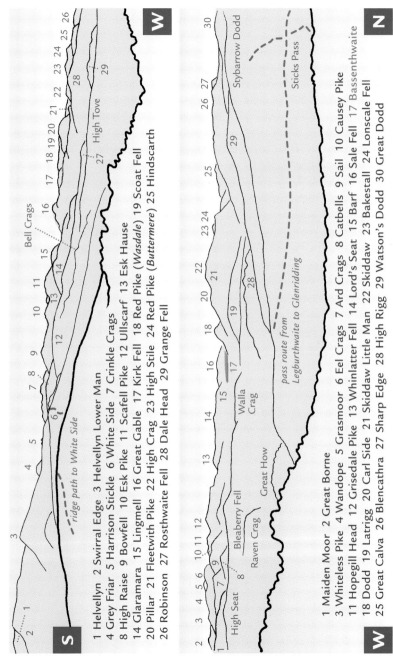

S / **W**

1 Helvellyn 2 Swirral Edge 3 Helvellyn Lower Man
4 Grey Friar 5 Harrison Stickle 6 White Side 7 Crinkle Crags
8 High Raise 9 Bowfell 10 Esk Pike 11 Scafell Pike 12 Ullscarf 13 Esk Hause
14 Glaramara 15 Lingmell 16 Great Gable 17 Kirk Fell 18 Red Pike (*Wasdale*) 19 Scoat Fell
20 Pillar 21 Fleetwith Pike 22 High Crag 23 High Stile 24 Red Pike (*Buttermere*) 25 Hindscarth
26 Robinson 27 Rosthwaite Fell 28 Dale Head 29 Grange Fell

Bell Crags High Tove

ridge path to White Side

N / **W**

Stybarrow Dodd Sticks Pass

pass route from
Legburthwaite to Glenridding

Walla Crag Great How Bleaberry Fell Raven Crag High Seat

1 Maiden Moor 2 Great Borne
3 Whiteless Pike 4 Wandope 5 Grasmoor 6 Eel Crags 7 Ard Crags 8 Catbells 9 Sail 10 Causey Pike
11 Hopegill Head 12 Grisedale Pike 13 Whinlatter Fell 14 Lord's Seat 15 Barf 16 Sale Fell 17 Bassenthwaite
18 Dodd 19 Latrigg 20 Carl Side 21 Skiddaw Little Man 22 Skiddaw 23 Bakestall 24 Lonscale Fell
25 Great Calva 26 Blencathra 27 Sharp Edge 28 High Rigg 29 Watson's Dodd 30 Great Dodd

RED SCREES

The fell has obvious attraction, it's a real individualist, the Mohammed Ali of the range. Packing a punch structurally, in every dimension a mountain, while it can honestly brag the best skyline view of the High Street range, with a brilliant vista towards Helvellyn to boot. At fifteen hundred feet the Kirkstone Pass, forming the bridgehead with the Far Eastern Fells, elevates at least one ascent to such an extent as to bring the 2,500 foot fell on a par with lowly Arnison Crag in terms of a climb. A smidgen over one thousand feet of, it has to be said, torrid climbing, caused by the tide of walkers on a route ill-suited to the burden, puts the walker on a superb fell-top. This apart it is no wonder so many walkers make Red Screes a regular expedition, such discerning folk would only countenance the climb from Ambleside either via Scandale or, best of all, the south ridge via Snarker Pike. In these enlightened times the climb direct from the Kirkstone Pass deserves to be considered a black mark for the environmentally conscientious fell-walker... readers of this guide!

The Kirk Stone, looking north to Brotherswater and Place Fell

777 metres   2,549 feet

for the map continuation north see page 230

Scandale Bottom

fold

old quarry

The Horn

Raven Crag

Kirk Stone

Kilnshaw's Chimney

16

Kirkstone Pass Inn

Walling quarry & shop ruins

Scandale out-gang lane

Pinch Cove

The Struggle

15

Snarker Pike

TROUTBECK 2 ml >

one mile

Scandale Beck

Pets Quarry

High Sweden Bridge

Kirkstone Road

one kilometre

High Grove ruins

Scandale

Peel Wood

Low Sweden Bridge

Nook Lane

Stock Ghyll

Middle Grove

The south ridge path transformed by winter chill to a solid river of ice

Sweden Bridge Lane

Ellerigg Road

Roundhill Farm

slopes of WANSFELL

14

Mountain View *(a bungalow with the most beautiful view)*

path to Troutbeck via WANSFELL

AMBLESIDE

Stockghyll Force

Stockghyll Force may not rival Aira Force as a pictur-esque composition, but resides in a lovely micro-wood-land environment, the stuff of romantic evening strolls.

From whichever direction one climbs the fell, one cannot but notice the sheer amount of drystone walling sub-dividing the fell. Probably no other comparable fell in Lakeland is partitioned more thoroughly. Stone is plentiful right enough, even today Pets Quarry, etching into the flank of Snarker Pike, is an active source of superb green granite.

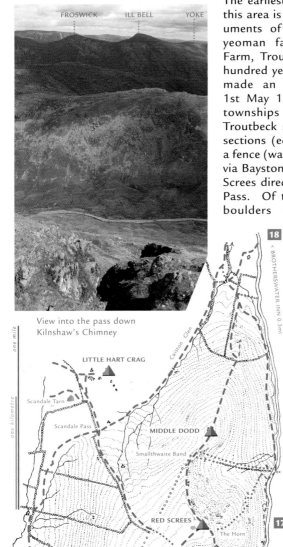

The earliest record of walling in this area is 1551 within the documents of the Browne family, yeoman farmers of Townend Farm, Troutbeck for over three hundred years. At this time they made an agreeemnt that by 1st May 1553 the men of the townships of Ambleside and Troutbeck should build in rood sections (equivalent to 7 yards) a fence (wall) over Wansfell Pike, via Baystones climbing onto Red Screes direct from the Kirkstone Pass. Of the array of tumbled boulders beneath Kilnshaw's Chimney one is a landmark without question. The Kirk Stone, so named from its appearance, linked with the superstitions of a goblin's church. Kilnshaw's Chimney itself *(left)*, reached at the top of the over-popular climb from the Kirkstone Inn, is easily picked out when viewed from the pass. A dark gully spewing copious red scree, the cleft is now ill-suited to exploration, the name suggests association with an early ascendant.

View into the pass down Kilnshaw's Chimney

one mile

one kilometre

18

< BROTHERSWATER INN 0.3ml

Caiston Glen

LITTLE HART CRAG

Scandale Tarn

Scandale Pass

MIDDLE DODD

Smallthwaite Band

RED SCREES

The Horn

17

for the map continuation south see page 229

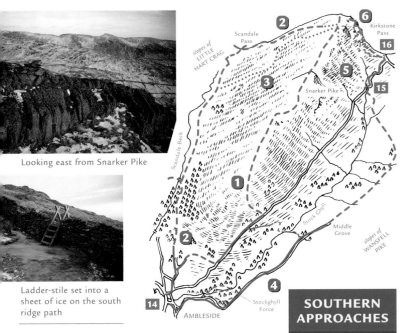

Looking east from Snarker Pike

Ladder-stile set into a sheet of ice on the south ridge path

SOUTHERN APPROACHES

ASCENT *from Ambleside*

Most visitors will know Ambleside for its bustling lakeside setting, its shops, cafes and yes, the traffic! The fellwalker lifting their eyes will consider more the town's situation at the foot mighty Red Screes. A fell of stature and independence, commanding attention from a distance to the north or south. Unquestionably the most attractive approach to this great whale-back of a fell begins apparently remotely here in this urban setting. Valley approaches lead via Stock Ghyll and Scandale. But pride of place goes to the south ridge. In fact it is so steady a climb that thoughts of the objective can easily be forgotten with attention drifting first back into the valley, then to the tantalising western horizon, and latterly, as higher ground is gained, eastward to a skyline of yet more fells. Only when Snarker Pike is reached does one's attention focus back on the original purpose of the expedition.

1 Starting from the Rydal Road car park, cross into Smithy Brow. Ascend beyond The Golden Rule via Kirkstone Road, go left into Sweden Bridge Lane, and right into Ellerigg Road. Bear right on a footpath by Eller Beck Cottages, which leads via wall gates to a stile and on into a gated lane, with a pleasing view down over Ambleside. The lane leads to a gate re-emerging into the Kirkstone Road above the town. Ascend the road, and, a matter of 300 yards beyond Sunny Bank Cottages, find a wooden hand-gate to the left. Pass through the cattle crush, ascending the broad irregular walled drove lane winding up to a stile, where a holding pen intervenes in the lane. Keep within the lane enjoy extensive views over Rydal Water to a backdrop of Coniston and Langdale Fells. Pass through a hand-gate in a wall, the broad green lane, frequently challenged by marshy ground, rising to a ladder-stile. One may go up, immediately right by the wall, then left once on top of the ridge, or continue ahead rising more steadily onto the ridge. The ridge makes a definite grassy sweep up to Snarker Pike, the cairn sitting on a bare patch of rock on the far (east) side of the wall. The name Snarker is intriguing and rare having been the dialect for snake, and meant *'the place of adders'*. Encounters must always have been exceptional events and the chances of anyone seeing one here in present conditions is so remote as to merit mention on the World Service! The ridge path leads on through a gap in a wall, strapping the ridge to reach a cairn above Raven Crag. Overlooking a rough combe, the eyes are naturally drawn down to the Kirkstone Inn. From this stance it is easy to spot the runs of burnt ochre-coloured scree from which the fell-name derives. Several pools lie on the plateau leading to the summit, the last being a very definite tarn.

View over Rydal Water from the south ridge path leading to Snarker Pike

2 Alternatively, continue along Sweden Bridge Lane and the succeeding out-gang lane leading up the length of Scandale. Rise to the ladder-stile in the saddle of Scandale Pass, go right with the wall, climbing via the slabs of Broad Crag onto the summit plateau. **3** Or, with some thought for the walling tradition of the fell, bear right immediately after passing through the gate at the end of the out-gang rising to a hand-gate. Skirt to the left of a small outcrop, climb the fellside drifting left on the trace of a sled-gate leading to a prominent wallers' quarry. Follow the wall up, at the wall junction slant half-left to the summit.

4 Via Stock Ghyll. From Rydal Road car park go right along the footway into town, branching left from the street between the Market Hall and Barclays Bank. Bear left, signed '*to the waterfalls*'. The road rises beside Stock Ghyll. One may enter Stock Ghyll Wood (park) follow a circular path clockwise via footbridges embracing the falls, exiting at the turn-stile. The unenclosed road advances beyond the cattle-grid. Pass 'Mountain View', a bungalow which enjoys an enviable exclusive view towards the Langdale Pikes. Directly after Low Grove one may bear left on a footpath that traverses the valley to the menagerie of domestic stock at Roundhill Farm, joining route **1** at Sunny Bank Cottages. Otherwise, continue to Middle Grove Farm. Passing through gates tarmac is replaced by a rough tracked lane, yielding to a partly cobbled green lane. The track fords a gill as green way passing the ruins of High Grove, sheltered by sycamores. The track continues, via gates, to meet the Kirkstone Road over by a stile.

Go right. Either follow the road all the way up to the Kirkstone Pass Inn

Summit reflections

(see route **6**), or **5** making light of the daunting slope, embark directly from the foot of The Struggle. As the road shapes to make its first tight hairpin, there is a padlocked gate is seen to the left. Cross the gate, ford the beck and begin the steady pathless (breathless) climb in the company of the wall. As height is gained place the wall to the right, in parts it is crumbling, but is there any wonder on this steep rise. Hats off to the dogged industry of the wall-builders of Red Screes. This wall is really old dating from circa 1680, when the Troutbeck Painable Fence Book was first written. This records a fence (wall) ascending from The Struggle "between the Forest and Woundale". The "Lords Jury of Troutbeck" saw to it "that every tenant shall maintain their painable fences in good repare or else shall be in pain" that is, fined six shillings and eight pence. There is no difficulty in the climb, though it is not your average line of ascent, nor best suited for descent. Just short of the wall junction drift left to a breach, then cross the wall straddling the ridge, angling north over easy ground, to reach the cairn at the top of Raven Crag.

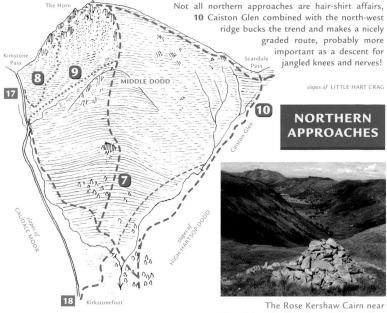

Not all northern approaches are hair-shirt affairs, **10** Caiston Glen combined with the north-west ridge bucks the trend and makes a nicely graded route, probably more important as a descent for jangled knees and nerves!

The Horn

Kirkstone Pass

Scandale Pass

MIDDLE DODD

slopes of LITTLE HART CRAG

NORTHERN APPROACHES

Caiston Glen

slopes of CAUDALE MOOR

slopes of HIGH HARTSOP DODD

Kirkstonefoot

The Rose Kershaw Cairn near Broad Crag looking down Caiston Gken

ASCENT *from the Brotherswater Inn*

The northern aspect of Red Screes is consistently steep, to some eyes formidably so. **7** The blunt Middle Dodd ridge (see **MIDDLE DODD** page 203) contrasts strikingly with the long south ridge. From the Hartsop vale fellwalkers' have to dig deep into their energy reserves for a big pull.

This is no bad thing if, like the author, you prefer ascents to descents, in this instance the quality of the ultimate view made all the more sweet by the labour and commitment of the climb. One may park at Cowbridge following the track by Brothers Water, or begin from the Brotherswater Inn (Sykeside camp site). Both routes converging at Hartsop Hall, from where a bridleway leads south, across meadowland, to the foot of Caiston Glen. Alternatively, start from the large lay-by at GR 403112. A footpath is waymarked south-eastward to a footbridge over Kirkstone Beck. Crossing the subsequent ladder-stile join the old Kirkstone bridle-path. **9** One may choose to follow the bridle-path up the Kirkstone Beck valley, at the point it meets the serpentine road, bear right and follow the steep wall climbing up through the combe to the col at Smallthwaite Band (see **MIDDLE DODD** page 203).

ASCENT *from the Kirkstone Pass & Red Pit*

8 From Red Pit car park GR 403089, an exciting and novel line of attack may be undertaken that reveals the full drama of Red Screes ascending the blunt north-eastern ridge, though good weather is obligatory. Cross the bottom stile and walk down on the fell with the road wall to the right to find a faint shepherds' path slanting uphill short of where the bridleway from Hartsop steps up onto the road. Rising to meet the wall descending from the combe, switch sharp left. Now climb pathless is steps and stages, defly avoiding small outcrops. Rise impressively above Red Pit to reach a rock tor, what might be described as The Horn of Red Screes *(see below)*, a startling viewpoint, adjacent to the summit.

'The Horn' rock tor at the top of the NE ridge

6 From the National Park car park opposite the Kirkstone Pass Inn, go through the kissing-gate at the north end and, before crossing the marsh, take a good look at the rocky fellside ahead. This is useful as the potential trials and tribulations ahead will then be anticipated and not come as any form of surprise. In fact, a two-way system has evolved. Descending walkers having found an easier line than the trail of the multitude, keeping more closely to the stubby south ridge. The cruel erosion of the obvious direct route, notably nearing the top of Kilnshaw's Chimney, should be a call to caution. So while most walkers will set the heads down and wind ever upward upon the first path, smart cookies will keep left a little longer and pick up the 'descending' ascent, which though showing wear gives steadier footing. The paths meet up on the grassy shelf at the top and, passing a pool, wanders serenely to the summit.

The Summit

A rough wind-shelter is tucked under the summit cairn *(see right)* and a few yards west a redundant Ordnance Survey column constructed, with longevity in mind, in good walling stone adds further architectural detail to this popular viewpoint. Back from the edge a shallow tarn fills a large hollow, further south the plateau top runs away via several smaller pools. To the north and east the fell falls away shockingly giving airy depth to the view. On warm summer afternoons one may delight in seeing ring ouzel, swift and skylark enliving this most marvellous fell-top.

Safe Descents

For Ambleside, 5 miles, simply head SE and from Snarker Pike S, the ridge path obvious and secure. For Hartsop, 3 miles, head E to follow a wall NE beside the wall to Scandale Pass, turning E then N down Caiston Glen. The Middle Dodd ridge leading N is safe enough, the previso being that during the steep descent from Middle Dodd make sure you bear half-left on crossing the wall straddling the ridge to avoid the ridge-end cliff! All other routes are rough and unsatisfactory for descent.

Ridge Route....

LITTLE HART CRAG   DESCENT 865 feet   ASCENT 404 feet   1.5 miles

The link with the Fairfield range. Cross the plateau due W to a wall junction, descend NW with the wall left, passing the ladder-stile in the saddle of Scandale Pass keep by the wall and then broken fence to mount the summit outcrop.

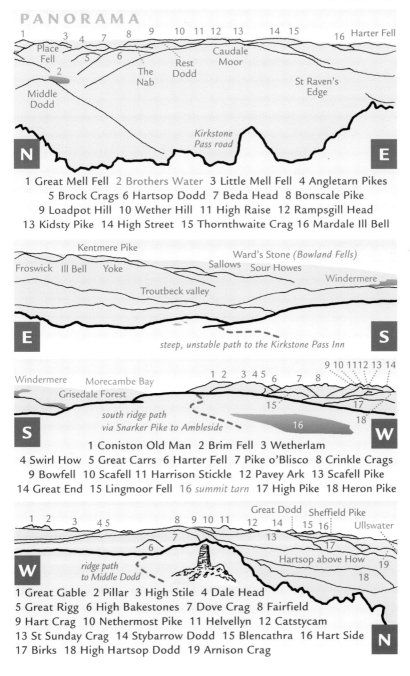

PANORAMA

1 Great Mell Fell 2 Brothers Water 3 Little Mell Fell 4 Angletarn Pikes
5 Brock Crags 6 Hartsop Dodd 7 Beda Head 8 Bonscale Pike
9 Loadpot Hill 10 Wether Hill 11 High Raise 12 Rampsgill Head
13 Kidsty Pike 14 High Street 15 Thornthwaite Crag 16 Mardale Ill Bell

steep, unstable path to the Kirkstone Pass Inn

1 Coniston Old Man 2 Brim Fell 3 Wetherlam
4 Swirl How 5 Great Carrs 6 Harter Fell 7 Pike o'Blisco 8 Crinkle Crags
9 Bowfell 10 Scafell 11 Harrison Stickle 12 Pavey Ark 13 Scafell Pike
14 Great End 15 Lingmoor Fell 16 summit tarn 17 High Pike 18 Heron Pike

1 Great Gable 2 Pillar 3 High Stile 4 Dale Head
5 Great Rigg 6 High Bakestones 7 Dove Crag 8 Fairfield
9 Hart Crag 10 Nethermost Pike 11 Helvellyn 12 Catstycam
13 St Sunday Crag 14 Stybarrow Dodd 15 Blencathra 16 Hart Side
17 Birks 18 High Hartsop Dodd 19 Arnison Crag

SEAT SANDAL

Being set apart has its benefits, as anyone who strides onto the summit of Seat Sandal, to comprehend the marvellous panorama, will quickly judge. There is a sense of being in the centre of something, which is real enough in terms of its waters at least for they have a far-flung destiny. Water shed into Grisedale Tarn flows to the Solway Firth, that entering Tongue Gill spills into Morecambe Bay, while the precipitation that timorously runs down Raise Beck is intercepted by Thirlmere and, as like as not, gravitates down the pipes to Manchester. Whence in the fullness of time and digestion Seat Sandal water enters the Liverpool Bay via a Mersey-mission. Only a token few pints make it through the dam buffers to the Derwent and the Irish Sea, some may even make it to Jennings Brewery where they indeed will become pints, now there's a refreshing thought!

Seat Sandal is marshalled by two ancient passes, Grisedale Hause and Dunmail Raise. Defined by a huge cairn or raise, the latter is an historic landmark its purpose and significance has been veiled by time and nurtured by legend. We should be grateful that it was not swept away in the guise of highway improvement.

The fell forms a eye-catching northern backdrop to the Grasmere vale and correctly will be considered a good climb from that direction. The Tongue Gill path to Grisedale Hause providing the popular approach, in its latter stages coming under the shadowed eastern scarp where hangs the awful arete, Gavel Crag. Correctly followed, the age-old bridle-path

736 metres   2,415 feet

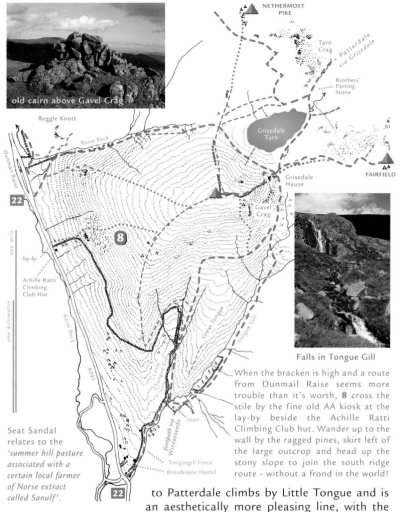

old cairn above Gavel Crag

Reggle Knott

NETHERMOST PIKE

Tarn Crag

Patterdale via Grisedale

Brothers' Parting Stone

Grisedale Tarn

FAIRFIELD

Grisedale Hause

Gavel Crag

Dunmail Raise

Raise Beck

22

one mile

lay-by

Achille Ratti Climbing Club Hut

Raise Beck

one kilometre

A591

Little Tongue

Great Tongue

Tongue Gill

resvr.

footpath via Winterseeds

Tonguegill Force

Broadrayne Hostel

22

Falls in Tongue Gill

When the bracken is high and a route from Dunmail Raise seems more trouble than it's worth, **8** cross the stile by the fine old AA kiosk at the lay-by beside the Achille Ratti Climbing Club hut. Wander up to the wall by the ragged pines, skirt left of the large outcrop and head up the stony slope to join the south ridge route - without a frond in the world!

Seat Sandal relates to the *'summer hill pasture associated with a certain local farmer of Norse extract called Sanulf'*.

to Patterdale climbs by Little Tongue and is an aesthetically more pleasing line, with the option of a direct climb to Gavel Crag as spice. Of other routes, that via Raise Beck is quickest, via Grisedale slowest, but a good alternative to avoid over-populated summits. While the south ridge will be found to be the most satisfying of all, a steady climb with excellent 'over the shoulder' views to Grasmere and the Coniston and Langdale Fells.

ASCENT *from Grasmere*

The ancient cross-range bridle-path from Grasmere to Patterdale leaves the equally antique north/south road, the present-day A591, at Mill

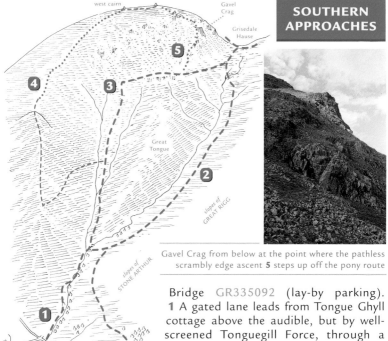

Gavel Crag from below at the point where the pathless scrambly edge ascent **5** steps up off the pony route

Bridge GR335092 (lay-by parking).
1 A gated lane leads from Tongue Ghyll cottage above the audible, but by well-screened Tonguegill Force, through a sheep handling pen to a ford and wooden footbridge spanning Little Tongue Gill.

Four routes stem from this point.
2 Tongue Gill – the preferred modern path.
Cross the second footbridge and, rising by a small fenced reservoir, follow the clear bracken-lined path running up the valley. As the ground steepens at the head paving secures footing. Pass beneath a particularly handsome waterfall, climbing to join the old pony path from Little Tongue, now over rougher ground, beneath Gavel Crag, to reach Grisedale Hause. Turn left (west) keeping the wall to the left, passing an incorporated fold, outcropping forcing the path to swing right, up loose scree. Regaining the partially broken ridge wall, the path leads to the summit beyond the wall corner.

3 The original pony path via Little Tongue Gill, from which two attractive variant routes diverge. From the bottom ford/footbridge keep to the path rising left, ford a second gill, now mount the shallow ridge – the green track, close to the gill is basically only for field access. Little Tongue is less annoyingly smothered in bracken than its big brother Great Tongue - which has a rigg-top sheep trod too, but makes an inferior line of ascent and so deserves to be ignored.

4 Via the south ridge. Coming above the walled enclosures across the gill find a contouring path branching left. Ford Little Tongue Gill, the path runs across the fell-side to ford a tributary gill above the enclosure corner, the path dips a little, then contours on to reach the foot of the south ridge. A bleached waymark post with white arrow confirms your correct approach - old guidebooks have erroneously intimated a walkers' way down from the adjacent hurdled gap, through the enclosures to the barn at the walled lane by Tonguegill Force. A thin path, with several cairns, climbs the initially undulating and narrow ridge. As the ridge merges with the greater mass of the fell the path becomes ever less apparent, though odd cairns exist as the route curves from north to east, with excellent views back over a sweep of southern Cumbrian heights. Pass a spring among a ruckle of rocks, a tiny fenced enclosure and a pool, with a lovely view the Grasmere vale and Easedale Tarn. Continue to a pair of cairns at the western end of the ridge, en route to the large summit cairn. **3** The grassy rigg of Little Tongue flattens as it rises, where the southern slope of Seat Sandal steepens and the path veers sharp right, contouring to run as a shelf above small outcropping and link to the Tongue Gill route. **5** The more intrepid may like to work their way steeply up the southern edge via Gavel Crag, to reach the old shepherds' cairn - the author descended by this route and therefore assumes it is easier as an ascent! The top of Gavel Crag an impressively airy spot, suitable for walkers with fiery blood running through their veins! The edge itself is in no way difficult, just steep, but give it a miss in the mist.

Grisedale Tarn, a classic hanging valley corrie lake, looking to St Sunday Crag, with the Old Pony route to Helvellyn climbing onto Dollywaggon Pike on the left and Cofa Pike right

Grisedale Tarn lies in the hollow beyond

west cairn

south ridge route to Grasmere

< KESWICK **9** A591 GRASMERE >

Seat Sandal from Fairfield

ASCENT *from Dunmail Raise*

WESTERN APPROACHES

6 Via Raise Beck GR 327116. On the eastern side of the traffic island containing the historic Dunmail Raise cairn, cross a ladder-stile beside a field-gate (poor verge parking, lay-by further south). A green trail leads beside the dry (original) bed of Raise Beck, diverted to infuse Thirlmere. Bracken abounds. The path leads into the confines of Raise Beck, the watershed wall falters as water-shoots and cascades to excite attention. Sections of the path are sorely eroded on the climb, the water scenery compensates, most notably the upper fall above the confluence of a beck flowing from Willie Wife Moor. The path duly bears up right to a cairned path junction, keep left to reach the isolated metal straining post at the watershed. Ahead is Grisedale Tarn, and a contouring path leading right to Grisedale Hause. However, turn right from the pass, climb beside a part broken wall to the summit.

7 West shoulder - the direct route from Dunmail Raise. Branch right from the green path as bracken intensifies GR329117; a clear path heads straight up the fell-side through the confounded stuff, wrestling clear as a zig-zagging shepherds' path materialises, negotiate the corner outcropping above the Raise Beck ravine. A cairn on a rock marks the top of this steep section, a steady pathless progression ensues up the fell pasture to the western cairn and the plateau top path to the summit. Frequent halts rewarded by improving views, notably to south and west.

(left) The upper section of Raise Beck. Dunmail Raise immersed in bracken

The Summit

The cairn rests a matter of 25 yards west of the wall corner, elsewhere small areas of rock and much grass characterise the table-top. The best view of grisedale Tarn is from the summit's eastern brink beyond the wall. While Grasmere can be enjoyed from the old shepherd's cairn 200 yards east of the summit above Gavel Crag, or the west cairn a similar distance in the opposite direction.

Safe Descents

Craggy hazards lurk beneath the southern and eastern edges. The right-angle wall corner offers a confidence-boosting guide north to the head of Raise Beck for Dunmail Raise and east, to Grisedale Hause for Grasmere and Patterdale; but be mindful that the path steers to the left of a rock step near the foot. For a direct route to Dunmail Raise one may head slightly north of west from the west cairn, the easy moor giving way in its latter stage to an abrupt declivity directly above the foot of the Raise Beck ravine, concluding with a dense bracken tussle. Alternatively, and with some joy, one may follow a curving and scenic line towards Grasmere onto the emerging south ridge. Reaching the wall contour left to join the Old Pony path descending Little Tongue.

Ridge Routes to ....

FAIRFIELD   DESCENT 473ft   ASCENT 922ft   1.25 miles

Head E following the wall down to Grisedale Hause, stride straight across at first undulating, then climbing quite steeply. The wall ceases as the gravelly, eroded trail continues rising via a cairned path onto the plateau, thus neatly avoiding a boulder-field to reach the wind-shelter.

DOLLYWAGGON PIKE   DESCENT 532ft   ASCENT 932ft   1.4 miles

The natural ridge connection is quite trying. Sane council suggests one heads for the outflow of Grisedale Tarn via Grisedale Hause, or the N wall and a soggy moorland route, across the north side of the tarn, to link up with the Old Pony Path zig-zags. Irrepressible folk with an eye for simplistic straight lines on maps, will deem the descending wall to the head of Raise Beck and the subsequent, neigh-on lost, fence-line N-N-E fair game. *The author undertook to give it a 'whirl' on an outing from Grasmere when he should have read the weather and aborted on the summit — perhaps you too have experienced horizontal rain in winter!*

PANORAMA

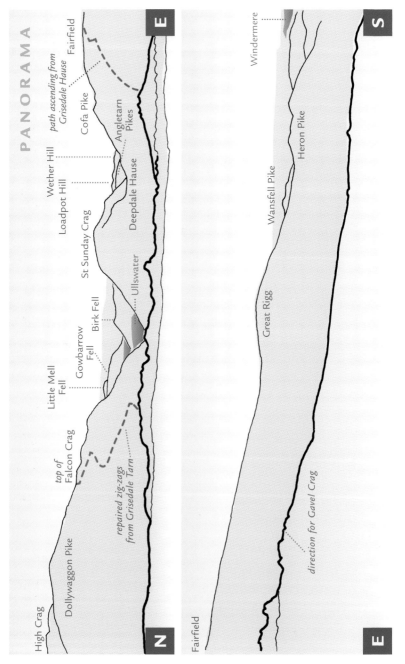

E

Fairfield

path ascending from Grisedale Hause

Cofa Pike

Angletarn Pikes

Wether Hill

Loadpot Hill

Deepdale Hause

St Sunday Crag

Ullswater

Birk Fell

Gowbarrow Fell

Little Mell Fell

top of Falcon Crag

repaired zig-zags from Grisedale Tarn

High Crag

Dollywaggon Pike

N

S

Windermere

Heron Pike

Wansfell Pike

Great Rigg

direction for Gavel Crag

Fairfield

E

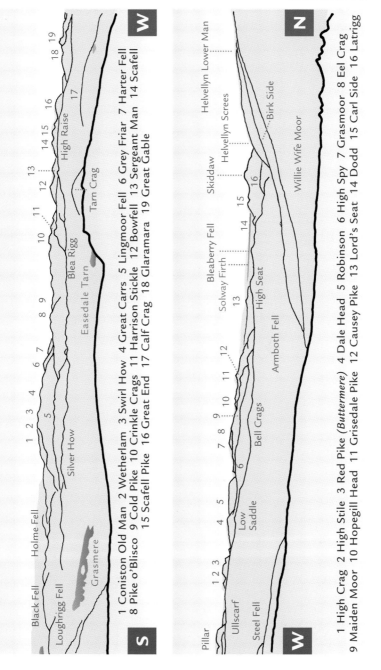

W

Black Fell

Holme Fell

Loughrigg Fell

Grasmere

Silver How

1 2 3 4 6 7 8 9 10 11 12 13 14 15 16 18 19

17

High Raise

Easedale Tarn

Blea Rigg

Tarn Crag

S

1 Coniston Old Man 2 Wetherlam 3 Swirl How 4 Great Carrs 5 Lingmoor Fell 6 Grey Friar 7 Harter Fell
8 Pike o'Blisco 9 Cold Pike 10 Crinkle Crags 11 Harrison Stickle 12 Bowfell 13 Sergeant Man 14 Scafell
15 Scafell Pike 16 Great End 17 Calf Crag 18 Glaramara 19 Great Gable

N

Helvellyn Lower Man

Helvellyn Screes

Skiddaw

Birk Side

Helvellyn

Bleaberry Fell

Solway Firth

High Seat

Willie Wife Moor

Armboth Fell

Pillar

Ullscarf

Steel Fell

Low Saddle

Bell Crags

1 2 3 4 5 6 7 8 9 10 11 12 13 14 15 16

W

1 High Crag 2 High Stile 3 Red Pike (*Buttermere*) 4 Dale Head 5 Robinson 6 High Spy 7 Grasmoor 8 Eel Crag
9 Maiden Moor 10 Hopegill Head 11 Grisedale Pike 12 Causey Pike 13 Lord's Seat 14 Dodd 15 Carl Side 16 Latrigg

SHEFFIELD PIKE

The spoil and ruins of the old Greenside Mine are slowly, but surely, settling down, becoming less of an eyesore, the renovated buildings finding sterling purpose as lodgings for a new generation seeking the personal challenge and freedom these fells bestow. For many centuries the scene of fuming industry, the clatter, dirt, dust and grim now replaced by happier emotions, with the anticipation and reward of fullfilling days in high fell country stirring the thoughts.

Most fellwalkers leave Glenridding their minds filled with thoughts of Helvellyn. But in Sheffield Pike, they may find much to equal the mighty patriarch; certainly as a viewpoint it is well blessed. As the rugged out-stretched eastern arm of Stybarrow Dodd, Sheffield Pike is robustly defended by crags and scree it lies like some mini-Munro, between two great glens - Glencoyne and Glenridding. Heron Pike means *'eagle's peak'* and recalls a time when this majestic bird commanded Ullswater skies, and how grateful are we that the distinguished bird has regained a ten-uous claw-hold in the Far Eastern Fells, though the most recent seasons their eggs have been sterile which is far from a good omen.

Two subservient ridges complete the high ground towards Ullswater, Glencoyne Wood partially shrouds the northern member adding to the verdance of Glencoyne, with Glenridding Dodd standing more openly and strategically above Glenridding. Neither shrink from the pattern of the parent fell, so much so that the valley road is forced to the lapping shore of the lake beneath the impending Stybarrow Crag.

Sheffield Pike is thought to be a corruption of *'Sheep Field Peak'*, though there are no similar word warpings in coroboration, perhaps it derives from a mischievious cartographer with steel-town connections.

675 metres   2,215 feet

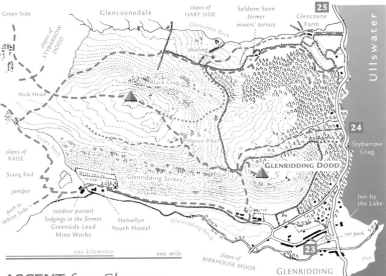

ASCENT *from Glencoyne*

Start from the National Trust car park, beside Ullswater, 100 yards north of the lane to Glencoyne Farm. Walk south, over the road bridge built of handsome Eden sandstone. Before Local Government reform established Cumbria in 1974, this would have meant walking from Cumberland into Westmorland, as the old county boundary swept out of Ullswater at this point, following Glencoyne Beck onto Green Side, to gain the high watershed ridge upon Stybarrow Dodd.

There are two options for the initial approach. **1** The firm track to Seldom Seen being the least intrusive. **2** The footpath via the lane to Glencoyne Farm has the merit of providing a close up view of this classic vernacular C18th farmstead.

Heron Pike
the Matterhorn of Mossdale

Pass on to the gate on the left between the farmhouse and byre. Ascending a grooved path, take a moment to look back for a fine view of the house backed by Ullswater. This waymarked pasture path runs under Seldom Seen (left), a terrace of ten holiday cottages, originally miners' lodgings. Fording a open gill, the path is guided left, up the slope, to run beneath the wall at the top, to reach a cobble-stepped gate, thus joining

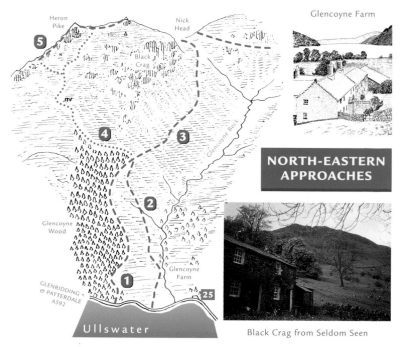

Heron Pike

Nick Head

Glencoyne Farm

Black Crag

5

4

3

Glencoyne Beck

NORTH-EASTERN APPROACHES

2

Glencoyne Wood

1

Glencoyne Farm

GLENRIDDING & PATTERDALE A592

25

Ullswater

Black Crag from Seldom Seen

the path from Seldom Seen, as it emerges from Glencoyne Wood at a stile. Take a glance down the rough pasture directly below, picked out in stones is the outline of a late medieval shieling, the simple thatched summer dwelling of a shepherd and his family, conveniently sited for him to tend the flock on the high fell.

Route **3** was probably the line taken by miners of Seldom Seen to the upper galleries of the Greenside Mine. The path follows the tall wall right, to a gate, bear up left a few yards, the old path has been built over by the re-instated wall, before continuing diagonally up Bleabank to Nick Head. The breached remains of a stone-built dam, far below, being the only feature to catch the eye in the otherwise tree-less basin. The valley-name Glencoyne was once thought to mean *'beautiful valley'*, the contemporary beauty expressed in the peace of this high 'hanging valley'. Prosaically the more likely meaning is *'reedy valley'* from British word cawn for reed-grass. Spongy peat hags shawl Nick Head. Branch left at the cairn, intermittently encountering further peat en route to the summit.

Route **4** follows the rising wall south-east, bear off right on a natural line, to either **5**, climb onto the south-east ridge to claim the striking subsidiary peak of Heron Pike (right), or make a way over the brow on a direct line to the summit cairn.

ASCENT *from Glenridding*

6 From the large National Park (*pay & display*) car park follow Greenside Road to the cattle-grid giving access to Glenridding Common. Bear off immediately right, switching left on the green track leading above the upper terrace of former miners' cottages, branching up above the gorse bank before the terrace, onto an eroding path which climbing just to the west of Blaes Crag.

On gaining a natural respite shelf, either continue up The Rake, to the dip in the ridge, or **7** take the more interesting line lassoing Glenridding Dodd. Bear right, contouring beneath the scree, seek the one grassy relent, ascend to the prominent vantage cairn. From this brink enjoy the splendid bird's eye view over Glenridding, a village which owes its origins and growth to the centuries old mining adventure, for all its subsequent adaptation to the economy of the transient tourist and fellwalking fashion. The semblance of a path winds west to Glenridding Dodd's pivotal cairn. Heron Pike is the next objective, from this station appearing a formidable climb. Follow the ridge path west, to gain the saddle, straddled by a wall, en route passing a small stone 1912 boundary marker in a shallow dip [the initials on either face indicate the family names

Ullswater from Heron Pike

M = Marshall of Patterdale Hall *and* H = Howard of Greystoke Castle].

8 This point can also be reached via Mossdale, on a far more covert route, which begins at the lay-by (*National Trust sign and post box*) beneath Stybarrow Crag. Follow the gill with the fence of Hawkhow to the right. A pronounced path draws left, this diversion should not be dismissed lightly, for it leads up to a rocky cutting and so onto the oak and bilberry crown of Stybarrow Crag, a sumptuous picture

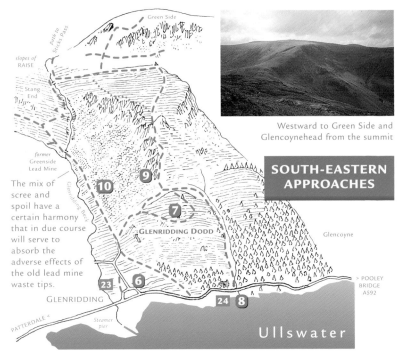

Westward to Green Side and
Glencoynehead from the summit

**SOUTH-EASTERN
APPROACHES**

The mix of
scree and
spoil have a
certain harmony
that in due course
will serve to
absorb the
adverse effects of
the old lead mine
waste tips.

postcard view. Either backtrack to the gill at the bottom or, less satis-
factorily, follow the old wall (no path) reaching a stile at the wall corner,
keep on up to meet Mossdale Beck. The gill route continues beside the
Hawkhow estate fence, via a stile, until forced left by the Mossdale Beck

Sheffield Pike from Park Brow Foot

Helvellyn, Catstycam and White Side the headwall of Glenridding

ravine. Ascend, with no hint of a path, beside fine cascades passing a manhole cover at a water extraction point. Weaving through the mature larches onto a strong sheep path which leads to the hand-gate in The Rake depression.

9 Keep the wall to the right, rising to a gap and embark on the steady clamber up the south-east ridge, less daunting when under foot. Perhaps spotting a second boundary stone early in the ascent, periodically chancing a look down Glenridding Screes to Greenside Road and across to Blea Cove on Birkhouse Moor, foreground heather adding vibrant colour in summer months. At the top, the path leads by a cluster of small tarns, it is all too easy to inadvertently miss the rocky crest of Heron Pike. The summit-bagging urge must not prevent you from taking a few

Sheffield Pike from the head of Deepdale Slack

moments aside to soak in this immensely gratifying view over Ullswater, the Far Eastern Fells and beyond to the Pennines. The summit of the fell is in view from the Pike, but is all but indistinguishable from other knolls. Take one of two natural lines to the summit, holding to the higher ground along the southern or northern side of the ridge, the latter offering a fine view over Glencoyne Brow from the top of Black Crag.

10 A less attractive, and by dint of progressive gradient, easier route to the top heads up the Greenside Road track. Pass through the converted complex of buildings at the old smelter works. Follow the waymarks as to 'Sticks Pass', zig-zagging by the juniper bank of Stang End, rising to a footbridge over Swart Beck, short of the stone spoil and weir of the old Sticks Reservoir. Head north-east to Nick Head, branching right onto the peat and rock ridge to the summit.

The Summit

An undulating plateau of marsh and rock, with a modest spread of heather characterise this fell-top. The haphazard pile of a summit cairn, surmounts a splintered outcrop. Casually lying in its midst, an old estate boundary stone of 1830 with the Marshall/Howard initials and a cryptic ER. Nearby a wind-break gives limited succour when a fierce wind blows.

As a panoramic station, notably of the exquisite Ullswater scene, it has to concede to Heron Pike on the easternmost rim. In settled weather head due south, no path, for the best of all views of upper Glenridding with the thrilling backdrop of Catstycam and Helvellyn. Stop short of where Glenridding Screes break precipitously, conveniently a well-marked sheepwalk follows this edge to either Heron Pike or Nick Head.

Ullswater from the edge above Black Crag

Safe Descents

Go west young man, to California.... and Nick Head, thereby assuredly avoiding the fierce rim of rock on all other fronts. In mist there is no substitute for such caution in escaping this stronghold of a fell-top.

Ridge Routes to....

STYBARROW DODD
DESCENT 108 feet
ASCENT 920 feet
1.9 miles

Descend W over peaty ground to Nick Head. Cross the path in the depression rising on a narrow path up the peat, follow the balcony path, continuing to the unprotected edge of the quarried slope. Keep up right onto the grassy ridge, plodding to the cairns on Green Side (correctly the summit is called White Stones, though there is little evidence of quartz). Head W with a clear path which diminishes on the final rise to the summit.

HART SIDE   DESCENT 105 feet   ASCENT 656 feet   1.5 miles

Take a similar course to the preceding description, though in ascending from Nick Head, skirt the craggy rim of Glencoyne Head N, there being no necessity to traverse Green Side - except in misty conditions, when the security of the cairns can aid navigation and avoid the peril of the aforementioned crags, on such occasions bear NE to the depression, then head due N.

PANORAMA

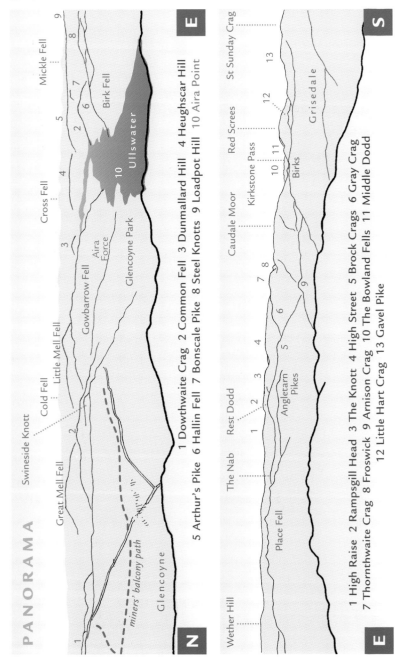

N

Great Mell Fell Cold Fell Little Mell Fell Cross Fell Mickle Fell

Swineside Knott

Gowbarrow Fell

Aira Force

Glencoyne Park

Glencoyne

miners' balcony path

Birk Fell

Ullswater

E

1 Dowthwaite Crag 2 Common Fell 3 Dunmallard Hill 4 Heughscar Hill
5 Arthur's Pike 6 Hallin Fell 7 Bonscale Pike 8 Steel Knotts 9 Loadpot Hill 10 Aira Point

S

Caudale Moor Kirkstone Pass Red Screes St Sunday Crag

Rest Dodd The Nab

Place Fell Wether Hill

Angletarn Pikes

Birks

Grisedale

E

1 High Raise 2 Rampsgill Head 3 The Knott 4 High Street 5 Brock Crags 6 Gray Crag
7 Thornthwaite Crag 8 Froswick 9 Arnison Crag 10 The Bowland Fells 11 Middle Dodd
12 Little Hart Crag 13 Gavel Pike

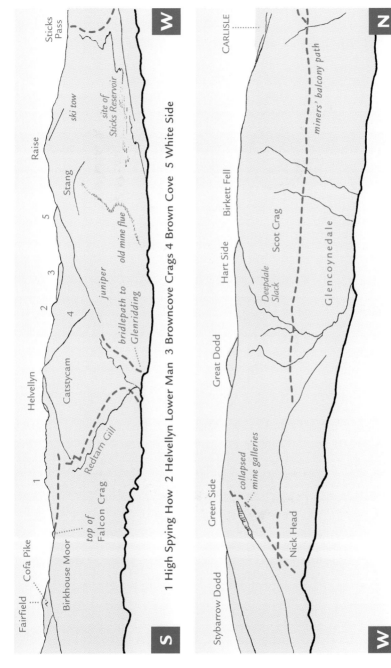

S

Fairfield
Cofa Pike
Birkhouse Moor
top of
Falcon Crag
Helvellyn
Redtarn Gill
Catstycam
1
2
3
4
5
juniper
bridlepath to
Glenridding
old mine flue
Stang
ski tow
site of
Sticks Reservoir
Raise
Sticks Pass

W

1 High Spying How 2 Helvellyn Lower Man 3 Browncove Crags 4 Brown Cove 5 White Side

W

Stybarrow Dodd
Green Side
collapsed
mine galleries
Nick Head
Great Dodd
Hart Side
Deepdale
Slack
Scot Crag
Glencoynedale
Birkett Fell
miners' balcony path
CARLISLE

N

ST SUNDAY CRAG

Travellers along the shores of Ullswater will be familiar with the shapely outline of St Sunday Crag indeed it is often referred to as the Ullswater fell *(see 'A precious place' at the end of this book)*. The bond between valley and heavenward height emphasised in the fell-name, linking St Patrick's valley with Lord's Day observance, associated with St Dominic from the Latin *Dies Dominica*, colloquialised as St Sunday. This Patterdale Patrick a different priest to the Irish patron saint. The name Lord's Seat attributed to a shoulder of the fell beneath Gavel Pike probably reveals nothing more than secular manorial ties.

Visitors to Patterdale wishing to buck the seemingly irresisible trend to climb Helvellyn, will turn with due relish and reverence to this handsome and tantalising objective. Few make both summits in the day for the gulf between is quite profound. The formidably dizzy northern slopes spilling rock and scree at an alarming angle into deepest Grisedale.

The fell has a high, narrow union with Fairfield at Deepdale Hause. Broadening its girth, in a north-easterly direction, in a great triangular wedge over the summit helm, before narrowing again above Cold Cove then dipping to the long shoulder of fell pasture on Birks. Most ascents follow the worn and torn Thornhow End approach, but there are other lines that well merit consideration. The Elmhow zig-zags emphasise the Grisedale decivity, while the route out of Deepdale via Gavel Pike, glories in the majesty of Fairfield. The quiet path up the southern flank of Birks from Trough Head is perhaps the most pleasingly sneaky of all.

841 metres   2,759 feet

(left) Looking down the Pinnacle Ridge

The quartz cross
which lies on the edge directly
above East Chockstone Gully

ASCENT *from Patterdale*

1 Via Thornhow End - the way of the many.   Take the valley road branching from the A592 at Grisedale Bridge. Turn left at the stile GR 386158, ascend the pasture to a fence stile to meet Mill Moss/Thornhow path - an attractive alternative approach along the foot of Glemara Park. Climb straight ahead up the ridge, a low stile crosses the park wall on Thornhow End, a grooved path continues rising across the slopes of Birks to the saddle between Cold and Blind Coves. Either continue up the north-east ridge, or slant left on an easier gradient making for The Cape, the saddle between Gavel Pike and the top.

2 Via Blind Cove - the way of the few. Follow the valley road, bearing onto the gated-track leading past Elmhow *(farm)*. Directly after going through the gate beyond the ruined barn, break up left from the track climbing beside the walled plantation. Ford the gill at the top and swing round the lefthand side of the little knoll to a green path which becomes more apparent as height is gained. This, the Elmhow zigzags, climbs the fellside into Blind Cove.

Grisedale

Grisedale Beck

Pinnacle Ridge

East Chockstone Gully

West Chockstone Gully

Y Gully

Ruthwaite
Lodge

Spout
Crag

Falcon
Crag

Tarn
Crag

Deepdale
Hause

Sleet Cove

Deepdale

5

Grisedale
Tarn

Cofa Pike

one kilometre

one mile FAIRFIELD

The ridge path from Fairfield to the NE cairn above Blind Cove is a beautiful causeway of sustained scenic drama.

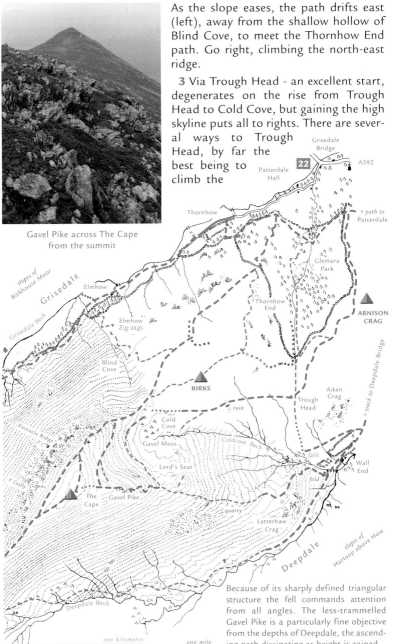

As the slope eases, the path drifts east (left), away from the shallow hollow of Blind Cove, to meet the Thornhow End path. Go right, climbing the north-east ridge.

3 Via Trough Head - an excellent start, degenerates on the rise from Trough Head to Cold Cove, but gaining the high skyline puts all to rights. There are several ways to Trough Head, by far the best being to climb the

Gavel Pike across The Cape
from the summit

Because of its sharply defined triangular structure the fell commands attention from all angles. The less-trammelled Gavel Pike is a particularly fine objective from the depths of Deepdale, the ascending path dissipating as height is gained.

north ridge of Arnison Crag (see page 19), the ascent of Glemara Park offers less generous views. A further option climbs out of Deepdale using the old shepherds' path above Wall End (see page 20). From Trough Head, a narrow path sets course across the flank of Birks, half-way up passing a curious ruin among a rash of rocks, with internal dimensions only a courting couple would find adequate. Reaching Cold Cove, either ford the head-stream angling south across Gavel Moss climbing onto the Lord's Seat saddle and ascend the heather and bilberry ridge to Gavel Pike, or go west to meet up with the

The steep northern slopes above Elmhow

main ridge path; this latter has two options to the summit, the north east ridge, or the path slanting across to the Gavel Pike saddle, which offers greater shelter on a windy day.

Gavel Pike means *'the gable-shaped peak'*

As a viewpoint at the heart of a grand gallery of rugged peaks the fell has pre-eminence. The key stations are Gavel Pike for Fairfield, the north cairn for Ullswater and the narrowing ridge towards Deepdale Hause for Dollywaggon Pike, Nethermost Pike and Helvellyn. The craggy north-western facade of the fell is superbly seen whilst descending the east ridge of Nethermost Pike and from within Ruthwaite Cove. An obvious fan of scree pin-pointing Pinnacle Ridge.

The Cape
Gavel Pike
Lord's Seat
Pinnacle Ridge
Latterhaw Crag
Cold Cove
Blind Cove
Elmhow zig-zags
BIRKS
Deepdale
Trough Head
Black Crag
Glemara Park
ARNISON CRAG
Grisedale
Bridgend
20
21
PATTERDALE

EASTERN APPROACHES

From High Spying How with Eagle Crag at the foot of Nethermost Cove bottom right

ASCENT *from Deepdale*

Secretive and wild Deepdale is a world apart. There is every chance of walking its full extent and not seeing another walker. In fact, surprisingly few actually give it consideration, preferring the high ridges. The solitary fellwander will love the looming presence of Greenhow End, the grandeur of lonely Sleet Cove and, once above the scored final bank onto Deepdale Hause, the thrill of the ridge as an ultimate scenic reward.

4 Via Lord's Seat - the quiet alternative, the gregarity of the summit coming as quite a shock! Follow the lane from Bridgend to Lane Head, the subsequent open track leading, via gates, above Deepdale Hall to Wall End. This lower quarter of verdant Deepdale is alive with birds and farm stock. The flagstone bridge spanning Coldcove Beck spells a striking change in the character of the dale. The track ahead soon diminishes to a narrow path en route to the drumlins beneath Greenhow End, (for the route to Deepdale Hause see Fairfield pages 85 and 86).

Turn directly at the flagstone bridge, passing up through the old

Gavel Pike from Lord's Seat

sheep-wash fold on a path mounting through the bracken, close to the beck. Above the second confluence watch for a leftward turn. The green path, rising above Latterhaw Crag onto the ridge seems to evaporate into a tiny trod. Part way up the steepening slope find a small, long abandoned slate quarry now a 'shelf' feature *(see picture bottom left)*, the stone will have been drawn down on sledges. Keep east up the ridge to the modest cairn on Lord's Seat. Continuing to Gavel Pike, soak in the fabulous views across Deepdale to Link Cove and mighty Fairfield.

Deepdale Hause - see what popularity can do for a scenic ridge way

ASCENT *from Grisedale Tarn*

5 From the outflow of the tarn a thin path angles east-north-east, gradually climbing the rough slope of Fairfield to reach Deepdale Hause at its lowest point. Advice: anyone thinking of dropping over into Sleet Cove should be mindful that the path into Deepdale descends at the next, slightly higher dip, towards Cofa Pike. Go left, the south-west ridge of St Sunday Crag broadens as it reaches the domed summit.

The Summit

The chiselled architecture of the fell culminates upon an ecclesiastical dome. Two decrepit cairns hold to the highest point, further sullied by loose rock litter, such distractions quickly transcended by the beauty of the all-round mountain view. The advent of Wainwright's Coast to Coast Walk has elevated the popularity of this summit, so if peace is sought take deliverance upon Gavel Pike, a marvellous viewpoint for Greenhow End and the wild fastness of upper Deepdale.

While it is the established habit of sheep to traverse edges in search of Spartan grazing, over-hasty walkers have fallen prey to the same trait above the western scarp. But even this shameful denial of the summit fails to locate the solitary old quartz cross, situated well below the north cairn on the fringe of a mass of scree GR 368137, progressively being devoured by bilberry. Experienced rock-scramblers find sport in their ascent by climbing the impressive Pinnacle Ridge. This can be viewed from above, by cautiously descending the steep ground north-westward from the north cairn. Caution must be emphasised, the long north-western brink of the fell is underpinned by crags and gullies posing possible calamity for the unwary.

Safe Descents

To keep the prevailing weather to your back, the highway to Patterdale is preferable. Though the best path begins due east to the saddle approaching Gavel Pike, a more sheltered path slants down northward, above Cold Cove, to the col. Re-join the main path, drifting down the west side of Birks to Thornhow End and into the verdant reassurance of Glemara Park. The south-west ridge to Deepdale Hause offers a focused line, though the rough traverse down to the outflow of Grisedale Tarn can be a trial on the ankles. However, the valley paths down Grisedale offer assurance and comfort on a fierce or unfriendly day.

Ridge Routes to....

BIRKS   DESCENT 770 feet   ASCENT 40 feet   1.25 miles

Cross the summit plateau to the N cairn, descend the N.E. ridge, at the depression, above Cold Cove. Bear half-right onto the narrow path leading along the grassy crest, a pleasing leg-stretcher to Birks.

FAIRFIELD   DESCENT 490 feet   ASCENT 650 feet   1.5 miles

Follow the narrowing SW ridge down to Deepdale Hause, pausing from time to time to marvel at the stupendous views. Keep to the roughening ridge, clamber over the shapely peak of Cofa Pike (*peak of the coves'*), upon reaching the plateau the subsequent loose, stony path eases at last.

Grisedale, Ullswater and the distant Pennines from the north-eastern brink

PANORAMA

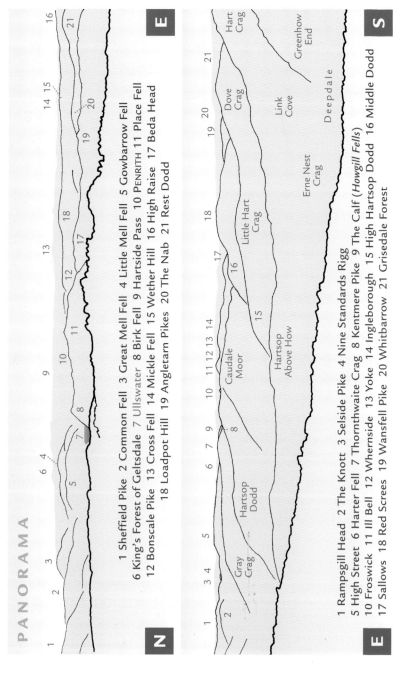

N

E

1 Sheffield Pike 2 Common Fell 3 Great Mell Fell 4 Little Mell Fell 5 Gowbarrow Fell
6 King's Forest of Geltsdale 7 Ullswater 8 Birk Fell 9 Hartside Pass 10 PENRITH 11 Place Fell
12 Bonscale Pike 13 Cross Fell 14 Mickle Fell 15 Wether Hill 16 High Raise 17 Beda Head
18 Loadpot Hill 19 Angletarn Pikes 20 The Nab 21 Rest Dodd

E

S

1 Rampsgill Head 2 The Knott 3 Selside Pike 4 Nine Standards Rigg
5 High Street 6 Harter Fell 7 Thornthwaite Crag 8 Kentmere Pike 9 The Calf (*Howgill Fells*)
10 Froswick 11 Ill Bell 12 Whernside 13 Yoke 14 Ingleborough 15 High Hartsop Dodd 16 Middle Dodd
17 Sallows 18 Red Screes 19 Wansfell Pike 20 Whitbarrow 21 Grisedale Forest

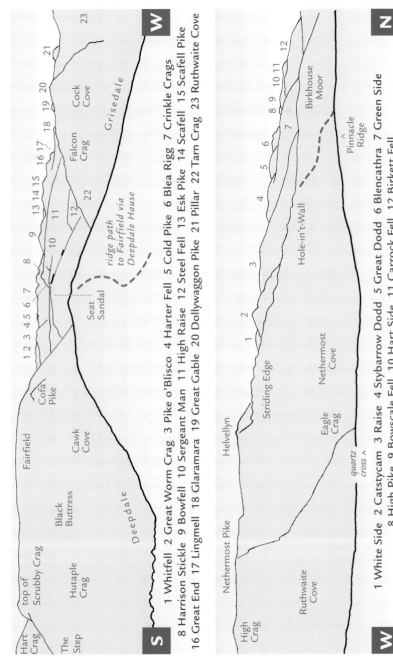

W

Cock Cove

Grisedale

Falcon Crag

21 20 19 18 16 17 13 14 15 11 12 10 9 8 7 6 5 4 3 1 2

1 2 3 4 5 6 7 8 9

ridge path to Fairfield via Deepdale Hause

Seat Sandal

Cofa Pike

Fairfield

Cawk Cove

Deepdale

top of Scrubby Crag

Black Buttress

Hutaple Crag

Hart Crag

The Step

S

1 Whitfell 2 Great Worm Crag 3 Pike o'Blisco 4 Harter Fell 5 Cold Pike 6 Blea Rigg 7 Crinkle Crags
8 Harrison Stickle 9 Bowfell 10 Sergeant Man 11 High Raise 12 Steel Fell 13 Esk Pike 14 Scafell 15 Scafell Pike
16 Great End 17 Lingmell 18 Glaramara 19 Great Gable 20 Dollywaggon Pike 21 Pillar 22 Tarn Crag 23 Ruthwaite Cove

N

12 10 11 9 8 7 6 5 4 3 2 1

Birkhouse Moor

Pinnacle Ridge

Hole-in't-Wall

Nethermost Cove

Eagle Crag

quartz cross ∧

Striding Edge

Helvellyn

Nethermost Pike

Ruthwaite Cove

High Crag

W

1 White Side 2 Catstycam 3 Raise 4 Stybarrow Dodd 5 Great Dodd 6 Blencathra 7 Green Side
8 High Pike 9 Bowscale Fell 10 Hart Side 11 Carrock Fell 12 Birkett Fell

STONE ARTHUR

APPROACHES
for diagram see
GREAT RIGG
page 144

GREAT RIGG

slopes of
SEAT SANDAL

old pony path
to Grisedale
House

Tonguegill
Force

Broadrayne
Hostel

KESWICK via
Dunmail Raise

Mill
Bridge

Travellers'
Rest

Raise Beck

fold

5

10

4

Swan
Hotel

1

GRASMERE **11**

RYDAL

path to Alcock Tarn

2

old copper mine

Greenhead Gill

Arthur's Chair

Brackenwife
Knotts

3

ridge to
HERON PIKE

one kilometre   one mile

The high ridges of Lakeland provide the best a fellwalker can get. This judgement derived not merely from the undouted potential for breathtaking views, but reflects the likelihood of an ease of progress - the continuing ridge to Great Rigg being a case in point. Breathless climbs are best reserved for the early stages of a fell walk when energy levels are still in store, as is certainly true with the 1,400 foot steep pull out of the Rothay vale to this ridge-end.

Parking in high summer can be 'Lotto' for late starters, there are three large car parks, but they do fill up quickly.

Nuthouse Farm white-washed house and barn combined, situated on the back road beneath Greenhead Gill

503 metres   1,650 feet

Standing at the foot of Easedale Road *(see below)*, at the heart of Grasmere village, the rocky battlements of Arthur's Chair draw the eye to the brink of the near eastern horizon. Compulsive or impulsive, whatever your mood, from this sighting Stone Arthur is clearly a fine short, stiff fell walk objective. Only as height is gained does the fell melt away beneath one's feet with the realisation that this is nothing more than a hoary hoaxster. Stone Arthur is nought but the abrupt scarp-top to Great Rigg's long and otherwise rather plain south-west ridge. So while claims for separate fell status rest on shaky ground, subsidiarity clearly has its virtues. The stiff climb is rewarded with a superb view over the Vale of Grasmere towards the central fell heights backing Easedale.

The fell wears bracken to empire-line subsuming the head-on approach. Not that one should assume there to be just the one way to the top, the canny fell explorer can outflank the fondling fronds by angling up from either the Tongue Gill or upper Greenhead Gill valleys. By such means one may turn the ascent into a tidy round trip with no implicit requirement to plod up the remainder of the ridge to Great Rigg Man.

Stone Arthur suggests association with another 'man' of legendary note, the fabled King Arthur. Perhaps the fell-name can be explained as a later borrowed likeness to other commanding outcrops. Though it should be understood that the word Arthur never referred to one charismatic person, being a British term for *'a leader'*. So, in fact, the fell-name probably meant commanding rock, which is most apt.

Seen in splendid isolation in this view, the apparent summit a worthy and peerless viewpoint

ASCENT *from Grasmere*

Invariably this handsome ridge-end viewpoint is visited en route to Great Rigg, linking with the Fairfield Horseshoe. **1** The normal approach begins from the Swan Hotel GR 339083. Follow Swan Lane east, taking the second turning right, signed Allcock Tarn (*sic*). The tarmac lane rises to a gate gaining entry to the fell at the foot of Greenhead Gill. Bear left on a path that climbs initially close to the wall and plantation, damaged by water action the path leads to a padlocked metal gate. Hereon it draws up and across the bracken

The Easedale fells from a summit pool

slope within a drove lane, the flanking walls largely in ruin. Coming to the ridge-edge above Greenhead Gill, a faint path emerges to meet the drove way. Switch up left, climbing eventually out of the dense bracken to reach and surmount the summit outcrop. **2** Greenhead Gill provides a super-shy approach. From the gate go right, over the footbridge and follow the Alcock Tarn path. At the top of the rise wall corner, contour into the gill on a tangible path. Passing the remains of an old copper mine find a groove that switches steeply up the facing fell-side (difficult to determine when bracken is at full vigour), to join with route **1** on the brow. **3** A better expression of this approach is to keep company with the narrowing gill, via its minor spills and tumbles, compensating for a lack of a path, to where a strong sheep path leads through the gill somewhere near the 1,600 foot contour. Follow this confidently left onto the ridge, to gain the summit.

4 Follow the footway beside the A591 north, with two options into the Tongue Gill valley. Either turn right, up the drive to Meadow View, a waymarked footpath passes left of the house and up the pasture to a gate. Bear up right at the waymark post to a hand-gate in the wall at the top and go left, within the lane, through a sheep pen to a gate above the small fenced reservoir thus entering the Tongue Gill valley. **5** The second option being to continue to the Mill Bridge junction (lay-by parking), follow the bridle-lane right, by the white-washed cottage 1 Tongue Ghyll. This rough lane leads above Tonguegill Force to a gate by sheep pens, crosses two footbridges and rises by the fenced reservoir to link with the Meadow View route. At the wall corner divert from the main valley path climbing right (south-east) initially with the enclosure wall, then over Brackenwife Knotts, presiding above the mother-of-all bracken slopes, to reach the summit unhindered by bracken at all!

The Summit

The object of all ascents is the massive, broken outcrop of Arthur's Chair, not exactly Aires Rock, but a fun scrambly environment to explore. The summit is not obviously defined, how could it be on a continuing ridge?

The block shown here might have some claim to be the chosen spot. The view well rewards the effort. Take your time, gaze long and deeply, for in the westward dimension the prospect excels Great Rigg, and by a league the view from the more lowly and more popular Alcock Tarn.

Safe Descent

There is nothing other than steepness and dense bracken to cause concern or hamper progress. Keep to the popular path heading S, aligned to Alcock Tarn, then S.E. trending down by the plantation wall to the foot of Greenhead Gill bound for Grasmere and its many watering holes.

Ridge Route to....

GREAT RIGG   ASCENT 866 feet   1.2 miles

The ridge and ridge path lead on N.E. plain and simple to meet the Fairfield Horseshoe at a cairn a little below the summit.

The sun-drenched Vale of Grasmere

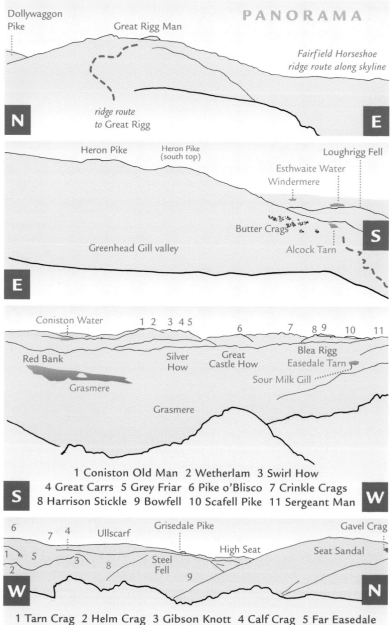

PANORAMA

Dollywaggon Pike

Great Rigg Man

*Fairfield Horseshoe
ridge route along skyline*

N

*ridge route
to* Great Rigg

E

Heron Pike

Heron Pike
(south top)

Loughrigg Fell

Esthwaite Water
Windermere

Butter Crags

Alcock Tarn

S

Greenhead Gill valley

E

Coniston Water

1 2 3 4 5

6

7 8 9 10 11

Red Bank

Silver
How

Great
Castle How

Blea Rigg
Easedale Tarn

Sour Milk Gill

Grasmere

Grasmere

1 Coniston Old Man 2 Wetherlam 3 Swirl How
4 Great Carrs 5 Grey Friar 6 Pike o'Blisco 7 Crinkle Crags
8 Harrison Stickle 9 Bowfell 10 Scafell Pike 11 Sergeant Man

S

W

6

7 4

Ullscarf

Grisedale Pike

Gavel Crag

High Seat

Seat Sandal

1
5

3

Steel
Fell

2

8

9

W

N

1 Tarn Crag 2 Helm Crag 3 Gibson Knott 4 Calf Crag 5 Far Easedale
6 High Raise 7 Greenup Edge 8 Greenburn Dale 9 Dunmail Raise

The summit tor from the west, sometimes referred to as Arthur's Chair

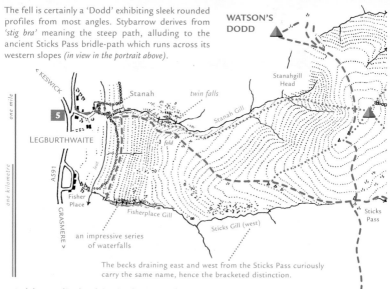

STYBARROW DODD

The fell is certainly a 'Dodd' exhibiting sleek rounded profiles from most angles. Stybarrow derives from *'stig bra'* meaning the steep path, alluding to the ancient Sticks Pass bridle-path which runs across its western slopes *(in view in the portrait above)*.

WATSON'S DODD

< KESWICK

one mile

one kilometre

Stanahgill Head

Stanah   *twin falls*

Stanah Gill

5

LEGBURTHWAITE

A591

fold

A591

GRASMERE >

Fisher Place

Fisherplace Gill

Sticks Gill (west)

Sticks Pass

an impressive series of waterfalls

The becks draining east and west from the Sticks Pass curiously carry the same name, hence the bracketed distinction.

RAISE

Seldom climbed in isolation, this is a fell held high by compatriot heights. All the eastern slopes come within The National Trust's large estate north of Grisedale Hause. Its northern ridges and the western slopes, part of St John's Common, are privately owned. Green Side holds its own secret bounty. For deep within its mass has been hewn some of the richest deposits of lead ore in the Lakes. The legacy of lifeless rock spoil languishing below Green Side and the barren slopes littering Swart Beck *'dark water'*, reminders of those former ages of hard toil in these, now tranquil, and so lovely hills.

846 metres   2,776 feet

ASCENT *from Legburthwaite*

At 2,420 feet the Sticks Pass is the highest Lakeland hause crossed by a regular path. Approaches from the Thirlmere side are normally executed via this old path which rises steadily from Legburthwaite over predominantly grassy terrain. Two variants are available, either up the pathless west ridge or, an earlier adventure, in the similarly path free environs of Stanah Gill. This latter option, though seldom undertaken, is ideal for the solitary walker who will surely savour the gill's lonesome depths. Though the end-wall climb is unremittingly steep; there is always a price to pay for an overly direct line of attack - in this case several buckets of sweat!

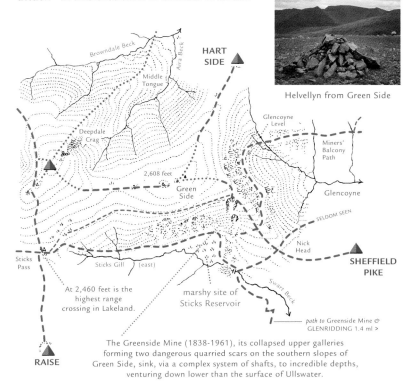

Helvellyn from Green Side

The Greenside Mine (1838-1961), its collapsed upper galleries forming two dangerous quarried scars on the southern slopes of Green Side, sink, via a complex system of shafts, to incredible depths, venturing down lower than the surface of Ullswater.

1 The Sticks Pass route begins from a modest car parking facility, with telephone kiosk, in the tiny community of Legburthwaite. Heading up the lane by the Thirlmere Community Hall, it either climbs the ladder-stile at the top, or, as a bridle-path, sweeps right around the cottages at Stanah Farm, via gates. Climb the ensuing paddock to a gate and stile beside the open Thirlmere supplementary leat, which slips beneath a giant, glacially sculpted, outcrop before capturing the aerated waters of Stanah Gill, apparently taking water uphill, flowing updale to gather several sidestreams to further placate Mancunian thirst.

The path comes to a bridle-gate and little bridge crossing the excited waters of Stanah Gill. Above, the main path rises through bracken, ignore the wooden footpath fingerpost (directing right on a predomin-antly contouring route to The Swirls car park). **3** At the point where the path bears right, up a groove, the gill-walker makes entry, thereby carefully avoiding the impregnable,

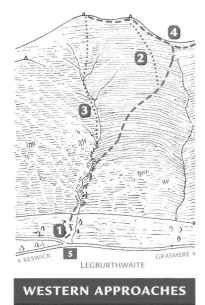

LEGBURTHWAITE

WESTERN APPROACHES

shrouded, lower ravine. A cautious traverse brings the walker into a rocky place heading up to the mighty twin falls, thereafter scrambling up the narrow valley, progressively over less taxing ground, until the final grassy rigg climb looms.

1 The Sticks Pass path climbs above the bracken to level at an old sheepfold then rising across a marshy patch before climbing on. **2** At the first, apparently casual cairn, a direct ascent can be contemplated over the grassy expanse of the west ridge this leads unfailingly to the cairn on the south top, without the comfort of a path.

Twin falls in Stanah Gill

4 In doubtful visibility continue to the cairn at Sticks Pass perched amid a marshy patch - all the more pertinent for walkers heading south to Raise - bear left, on the obvious ascending path, the destination, Stybarrow Dodd's wind-swept south top and a superb all round view subject of the PANORAMA on pages 338 & 339.

Stybarrow Dodd from Brown Crag, off the old pony route to Helvellyn

ASCENT *from High Row & Dowthwaitehead*

More often than not, and wisely too, ascents from the quiet agricultural community of Dowthwaitehead embrace Hart Side. The Deepdale route, from either High Row or Dowthwaitehead has a most promising start, but sadly deteriorates into expansive spongy mosses. The Dowthwaitehead route, via Glencoyne Head, may have the wettest start, but once the ridge is crossed matters markedly improve, contouring around the barren glaciated hollow before climbing over Green Side. NB: There is no car parking at Dowthwaitehead, hence the importance of High Row for conscientious car owners. Many visitors using this facility content themselves with a stroll along the Old Coach Road; energetic readers of this guide will know its greater value and will look to plan for a big day on the Dodd's, aware that if dusk, rain or mist should fall the old road will give a safe line of retreat.

5 Either walk along the road to the hamlet, or **6** branch onto the common where a clear path gives false confidence of a well-marked route. The footpath passing under Dowthwaite Crag gives excellent views upon the community, while the direct way, **7** over High Brow, only hastens the marshy going, the views of Hart Side, the distant Middle Tongue ridge of Stybarrow Dodd framed by Lurge Crag up the lonely

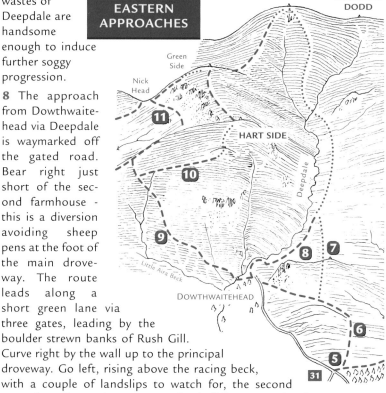

wastes of Deepdale are handsome enough to induce further soggy progression.

8 The approach from Dowthwaitehead via Deepdale is waymarked off the gated road. Bear right just short of the second farmhouse - this is a diversion avoiding sheep pens at the foot of the main drove-way. The route leads along a short green lane via three gates, leading by the boulder strewn banks of Rush Gill. Curve right by the wall up to the principal droveway. Go left, rising above the racing beck, with a couple of landslips to watch for, the second occurring above the water-works building. Dowthwaite Moss spells the end of any hint of a path. Keep your spirits up as you wade through the rushes aiming towards Lurge Crag. Come ashore (so to speak) at Randerside Fold. Contouring under Lurge Crag, ford Browndale Beck and buckle down to the pathless, featureless ascent of Middle Tongue, skirting Deepdale Crag to reach the fell top.

9 The Hart Side/Glencoyne Head route passes left from the main farm-house along a waymarked lane leading to a gated footbridge, where Rush Gill reverts to its name of birth, Aira Beck. A discernible track leads on, after a gateway, angling diagonally up the in-take bank, to reach a kiss-ing-gate directly after slipping through a shallow ravine. This old miners' path continues up through rushes, and is more evident now than was once the case, no doubt as a result of some increase in visitors to Birkett Fell. The path crosses the head-stream of Little Aira Beck to reach the broken ridge wall. **10** Consult the HART SIDE chapter for the next stage of the ridge route which sets course right, up beside the wall, bound for

Sheep gather beneath Lurge Crag in Deepdale - early spring 1999

Birkett Fell. **11** The Glencoyne route slips over the peaty ridge, dropping (metaphorically) to join the Dockray path at a tight gill. Go right, watching your footing on a narrow path. The path contours round the dalehead before climbing right, onto Green Side from Nick Head.

The Summit

Most fellwalkers take Stybarrow Dodd in their stride, an incident on a long day over the tops. But taken in its own right, it does have eminent merit as a viewpoint, and, for the majority, it is from the cairn on the south top that this bounty is surveyed. The main ridge path, naturally skirting the brink of Stanahgill Head, continues to attend to this prime view. The paltry heap of stones, huddling around a solitary flake of blue slate, constitutes the actual summit cairn *(see below, looking west)* set well back on the plateau. N.E. beyond an occasional pool are the remnants of a wall. This tumble-down structure, now partially adapted into a wind-shelter, is a curious piece of labour and seems to have been stunted at birth, terminating at the top of Aira Beck's grassy gully, it warned of the sly presence of Deepdale Crag.

Green Side headwall of Glencoyne from the verdant meadows of Glencoyne Farm

Safe Descents

The one and only hazard is Deepdale Crag. This may be a poor excuse for a crag, but it still poses a problem for woeful navigators, it lurks north-east from the summit, the ragged wall being the warning to its presence. In foul weather turn due south and head for Sticks Pass. The nearest public telephone is at the car park at the foot of the Sticks Pass path (west), a little over two miles of uncomplicated descent from the summit - Glenridding is twice this distance (east-bound).

Erosion where paths converge on Sticks Pass - looking north to Stybarrow Dodd's south top

The subsiduary summit of Green Side, forming an intermediate link with Hart Side, deserves a special mention at this juncture. It also commands a scenic situation, the view south-west to Helvellyn's northern satellite heights is particularly pleasing. The summit, known as White Stones, is one of a number of Lakeland tops so described. In this instance more for the paleness of the stone than the presence of quartz.

Ridge Routes to....

GREAT DODD   1.2 miles
DESCENT 230 feet   ASCENT 263 feet

NW to depression, then NE to wind-shelter, with the summit cairn 150 yards NW across the undulating bald top.

HART SIDE   1.4 miles
DESCENT 427 feet   ASCENT 164 feet

March ESE over grass, picking up a path from a cairn heading E, cross the pool depression mount-

Stanahgill Head

ing onto Green Side marked by four cairns. From highest point bear NNE, via grough and pool step, rising gently via the miners' trench to reach the summit.

RAISE DESCENT 328 feet   ASCENT 430 feet   1.1 miles

S from the south top cairn, descending to cross Sticks Pass 2,420 feet, avoid boggy ground to the right, climbing directly, latterly on eroded gravel, to the distinctive pock-marked rocky crest.

SHEFFIELD PIKE DESCENT 951 feet   ASCENT 394 feet   1.7 miles

Start as to Hart Side, only from highest cairn on Green Side take an E course, curving down right, to the top of the unprotected edge of the collapsed mine hollow, then SE over blanket peat to the Nick Head depression. Ascend E to the summit on a clear path with further peaty patches to reach the fine cairn perched on a rocky knoll.

WATSON'S DODD DESCENT 197 feet ASCENT 24 feet   0.6 miles

NW to a pool depression, curving round to W over level ground, to reach the lonesome cairn. Ignore the popular path contouring above Browndale, this is the ridge walkers' rat-run to Great Dodd. Watson's Dodd has only a western dimension and many walkers, oblivious of this, unwittingly miss the summit cairn striding on to its big brother, only then do they glance back down to spot this scarp spur summit.

PANORAMA from the south top

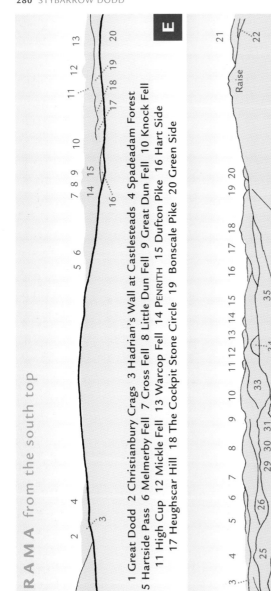

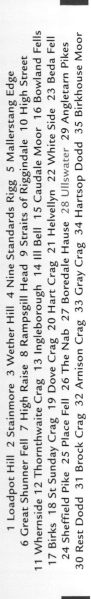

N

1 Great Dodd 2 Christianbury Crags 3 Hadrian's Wall at Castlesteads 4 Spadeadam Forest
5 Hartside Pass 6 Melmerby Fell 7 Cross Fell 8 Little Dun Fell 9 Great Dun Fell 10 Knock Fell
11 High Cup 12 Mickle Fell 13 Warcop Fell 14 PENRITH 15 Dufton Pike 16 Hart Side
17 Heughscar Hill 18 The Cockpit Stone Circle 19 Bonscale Pike 20 Green Side

E

E

1 Loadpot Hill 2 Stainmore 3 Wether Hill 4 Nine Standards Rigg 5 Mallerstang Edge
6 Great Shunner Fell 7 High Raise 8 Rampsgill Head 9 Straits of Riggindale 10 High Street
11 Whernside 12 Thornthwaite Crag 13 Ingleborough 14 Ill Bell 15 Caudale Moor 16 Bowland Fells
17 Birks 18 St Sunday Crag 19 Dove Crag 20 Hart Crag 21 Helvellyn 22 White Side 23 Beda Fell
24 Sheffield Pike 25 Place Fell 26 The Nab 27 Boredale Hause 28 Ullswater 29 Angletarn Pikes
30 Rest Dodd 31 Brock Crag 32 Arnison Crag 33 Gray Crag 34 Hartsop Dodd 35 Birkhouse Moor

S

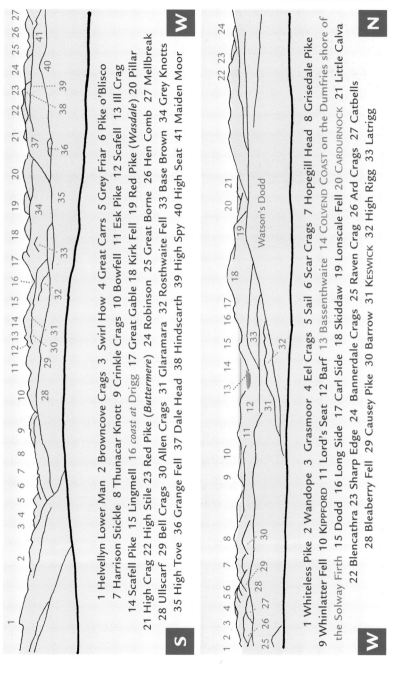

S / **W**

1 Helvellyn Lower Man 2 Browncove Crags 3 Swirl How 4 Great Carrs 5 Grey Friar 6 Pike o'Blisco 7 Harrison Stickle 8 Thunacar Knott 9 Crinkle Crags 10 Bowfell 11 Esk Pike 12 Scafell 13 Ill Crag 14 Scafell Pike 15 Lingmell 16 *coast at* Drigg 17 Great Gable 18 Kirk Fell 19 Red Pike (*Wasdale*) 20 Pillar 21 High Crag 22 High Stile 23 Red Pike (*Buttermere*) 24 Robinson 25 Great Borne 26 Hen Comb 27 Mellbreak 28 Ullscarf 29 Bell Crags 30 Allen Crags 31 Glaramara 32 Rosthwaite Fell 33 Base Brown 34 Grey Knotts 35 High Tove 36 Grange Fell 37 Dale Head 38 Hindscarth 39 High Spy 40 High Seat 41 Maiden Moor

W / **N**

Watson's Dodd

1 Whiteless Pike 2 Wandope 3 Grasmoor 4 Eel Crags 5 Sail 6 Scar Crags 7 Hopegill Head 8 Grisedale Pike 9 Whinlatter Fell 10 KIPPFORD 11 Lord's Seat 12 Barf 13 Bassenthwaite 14 COLVEND COAST on the Dumfries shore of the Solway Firth 15 Dodd 16 Long Side 17 Carl Side 18 Skiddaw 19 Lonscale Fell 20 CARDURNOCK 21 Little Calva 22 Blencathra 23 Sharp Edge 24 Bannerdale Crags 25 Raven Crag 26 Ard Crags 27 Catbells 28 Bleaberry Fell 29 Causey Pike 30 Barrow 31 KESWICK 32 High Rigg 33 Latrigg

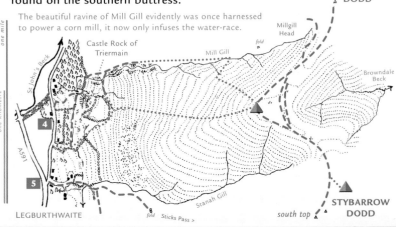

WATSON'S DODD

Side-stepped by the majority of 'range intent' ridge-walkers, and incomplete around the radius, Browndale Beck splits the spoils of its eastern slopes between Great Dodd and Stybarrow Dodd. The fell would receive scant attention but for the eye-catching Castle Rock, set low on its western slope *(see above)*.

Sir Walter Scott bestowed an aura of romance by referring to the rock in his novel *'The Bridal of Triermain'*, henceforward it has been affectionately known as Castle Rock of Triermain; Scott garnering the name from the ruined peel tower close to the Roman Wall at Birdoswald. Being west facing this handsome buttress of glacial montane basks in the late afternoon sun, its convenience to the valley road ensuring a popularity for rock sport, the easier climbs found on the southern buttress.

The beautiful ravine of Mill Gill evidently was once harnessed to power a corn mill, it now only infuses the water-race.

GREAT DODD

Castle Rock of Triermain

Mill Gill

Millgill Head

fold

Browndale Beck

St John's Beck

one mile

one kilometre

A591

4

5

LEGBURTHWAITE

fold   Sticks Pass >

Stanah Gill

south top

STYBARROW DODD

789 metres   2,589 feet

ASCENT *from Legburthwaite*

The North West Water car park GR 318195 is the obvious starting point.
1 Either follow the climbers' approach straight up to the crag. This path
climbs the pasture, from a stile off the road to a footbridge over the
Thirlmere water-race. A few yards higher, leave the canopy of trees
beneath the crag by clambering over a stile on the wall corner boulder to
the left, thereby making for the foot of the lower Mill Gill ravine. Ford
and ascend the northern bank. **2** The water-race can be enjoyed all the
more by following the road right, to a Coronation seat immediately
beyond the old Mission Room. Ascend the shepherding access, via a
hurdle gap through the fence pens, to come level with the leat - where it
runs briefly underground. A stile puts the walker tight within the leat's
fences, two further stiles draw the path out into conifers and beyond, to
run alongside the leat fence to the second of two footbridges.

3 If you're filled with gusto, and getting to grips with the fell is of
greater importance, ignore the leat and continue uphill with the gill to
the right. Ascend to the enclosure wall backing Castle Rock, follow this
right, don't enter the enclosure. At the highest point break off, burying
your head in meaningful thought, set to work on the uneventful climb
up the High Fells to the solitary cairn marking the summit of Watson's
Dodd. **4** The ascent can be alleviated to some degree by contin-

uing with the wall and gill
to traverse a narrow worn
path through the bracken,
directly above a twist in
the lower Mill Gill ravine,
to a second break in the
gill's rocky defences. Ford
and join the earlier route,
climbing along the
bracken margin beside the
upper ravine, effectively
on Great Dodd. A faint
path exists for a while, but
continue up the valley
until easier ground
suggests an opportunity
to re-ford Mill Gill. Mount
the upper slopes well
above any incidence of
rock or bracken.

WESTERN APPROACHES

Castle Rock of Triermain soaking up the late afternoon sun

The Summit

Sheep tread across Watson's Dodd's triangular plateau, fellwalkers wander around its rim. The summit cairn rests sublimely above sweeping slopes commanding a sumptuous view into the heart of the district.

From Millgill Head

Safe Descents

Descend the west ridge, keeping a right-hand bias to miss outcropping, bear down to the left of Castle Rock onto the road. Do not be tempted to venture into either Stanah or Mill Gills, they are places gill scramblers respect!

Ridge Routes to....

GREAT DODD

DESCENT 45 feet ASCENT 226 feet   0.8 miles

The ridge path has become plain enough, trending NE above Millgill Head to reach the wind-shelter (notoriously prone to litter and scrounging sheep), with a further 150 yards NNE of undulating top to gain the cairn on the true summit.

STYBARROW DODD DESCENT 42 feet ASCENT 187 feet   0.7 miles

Walk on very evident paths ESE to the pool depression, then SE, making a conscious move off the worn path to the summit, marked by its small cairn sporting a single loose flake of blue slate as a feather in its very modest cap.

Castle Rock derives its name from an Iron Age encampment that crowned the outcrop, it must have been the perfect site at times of threat with the added protection afforded by the ravine of Mill Gill and scope behind for the impounding of domestic stock.

Westward view from Mill Gill drawing the eye irresistibly towards Raven Crag, which directly overlooks the Thirlmere dam (*out of sight*).

PANORAMA *(naturally restricted)* looking west

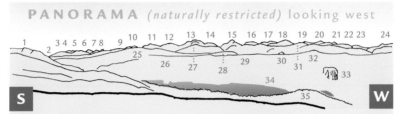

1 Browncove Crags 2 Woodland Fell (*Coniston*) 3 Wetherlam 4 Coniston Old Man 5 Swirl How 6 Grey Friar 7 Pike o'Blisco 8 Harrison Stickle 9 High Raise 10 Crinkle Crags 11 Bowfell 12 Esk Pike 13 Scafell Pike 14 Lingmell 15 Great Gable 16 Kirk Fell 17 Red Pike (*Wasdale*) 18 Pillar 19 High Crag 20 High Stile 21 Red Pike (*Buttermere*) 22 Robinson 23 Great Borne   24 Whiteless Pike 25 Ullscarf   26 Bell Crags 27 Glaramara 28 Great Crag 29 High Tove 30 King's How (*Grange Fell*) 31 Dale Head 32 High Seat 33 Raven Crag 34 Thirlmere 35 Great How

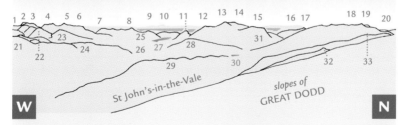

1 Wandope 2 Grasmoor 3 Eel Crag 4 Hopegill Head 5 Grisedale Pike 6 Hobcarton End 7 Whinlatter Fell 8 Lord's Seat 9 Bengairn 10 Screel Hill (*both hills lie across the Solway in Dumfries & Galloway*) 11 Dodd 12 Carl Side 13 Skiddaw Little Man 14 Skiddaw 15 Lonscale Fell 16 Forest of Ae (*Scotland*) 17 Great Calva 18 Blencathra 19 Sharp Edge 20 Bowscale Fell   21 Bleaberry Fell 22 Causey Pike 23 Outerside 24 Walla Crag 25 The Bishop of Barf 26 KESWICK 27 Bassenthwaite 28 Latrigg 29 High Rigg 30 Tewet Tarn 31 Glenderaterra valley *draining into the Greta from Mungrisdale Common* 32 Calfhow Pike 33 Clough Head

WHITE SIDE

Signs in Glenridding direct to an uninspiring Whiteside Bank, though this name is actually only specific to the north-western shoulder crossed on the ascent from Thirlspot, an otherwise nondescript and sparce patch of fractured quartz. Strictly the fell is nameless, to fell-walkers it has long been identified and dignified by the name White Side. The western aspect exhibits a fierce fringe of outcropping along the lower slopes, clearly in view from the A591 between Swirls and Thirlspot; this is a mock defence to a general grassiness higher up. By contrast the eastern slopes fall consistently steep. Best viewed from Catstycam, this aspect forms a dividing headwall for the high mountain hollows of Brown and Keppel Coves.

The subsidiary summit of Brown Crag 2,002ft/610m, situated directly above Thirlspot is a little known, little visited, little gem of a viewpoint. Particularly or views of The Dodds and Skiddaw.

Draining watercourses are a special feature, top marks to Fisherplace Gill, in spate a thrilling series of foaming falls. At such times the tight ravine of Brund Gill runs a thunderous cataract too, while Helvellyn Gill contains its own set of exquisite forces, though seldom intimately witnessed by passing walkers. The White Stones Route, now seldom followed, derives its name from the former practise of white-washing

863 metres   2,851 feet

rocks blazing the route to Helvellyn expressly to guide guests from the King's Head, Thirlspot. No longer the focus of ascents the inn has ceeded to the water authority's Swirls car park. The old route pensioned off into quiet retirement, followed only by the nostalgic and odd lone fell-wanderer. Discerning folk, like readers of this guide perhaps, who revel in the peace of former days, when to climb Helvellyn on foot was seen to be a little quirky and certainly adventurous, at least for the average mortal, if not for the mountain tourist seasoned on Chamonix.

ASCENT *from Glenridding*

One may choose to make this a breeze or a brawl. **1** The old pony track to Helvellyn, waymarked from the Greenside Mine, wanders gaily up the Glenridding glen. The juniper bank well passed, a small outcrop looms, as too a branch in the track. The recently re-affirmed and consolidated pony path turns its mind on weaving above Keppel Cove. Reaching the saddle, the ridge path to White Side could not be more certain.

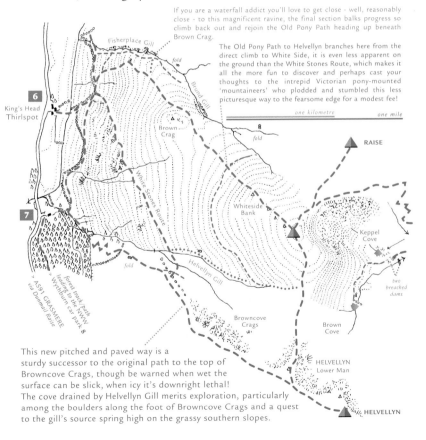

If you are a waterfall addict you'll love to get close - well, reasonably close - to this magnificent ravine, the final section balks progress so climb back out and rejoin the Old Pony Path heading up beneath Brown Crag.

The Old Pony Path to Helvellyn branches here from the direct climb to White Side, it is even less apparent on the ground than the White Stones Route, which makes it all the more fun to discover and perhaps cast your thoughts to the intrepid Victorian pony-mounted 'mountaineers' who plodded and stumbled this less picturesque way to the fearsome edge for a modest fee!

This new pitched and paved way is a sturdy successor to the original path to the top of Browncove Crags, though be warned when wet the surface can be slick, when icy it's downright lethal!
The cove drained by Helvellyn Gill merits exploration, particularly among the boulders along the foot of Browncove Crags and a quest to the gill's source spring high on the grassy southern slopes.

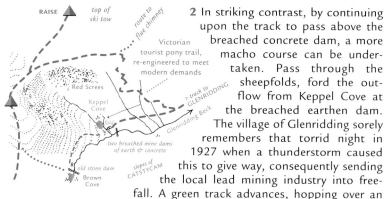

RAISE

top of ski tow

route to flue chimney

Victorian tourist pony trail, re-engineered to meet modern demands

Red Screes

Keppel Cove

track to GLENRIDDING

Glenridding Beck

fold

two breached mine dams of earth & concrete

old stone dam

slopes of CATSTYCAM

Brown Cove

2 In striking contrast, by continuing upon the track to pass above the breached concrete dam, a more macho course can be undertaken. Pass through the sheepfolds, ford the outflow from Keppel Cove at the breached earthen dam. The village of Glenridding sorely remembers that torrid night in 1927 when a thunderstorm caused this to give way, consequently sending the local lead mining industry into freefall. A green track advances, hopping over an old leat to the lost reservoir. Initially shaping towards White Side's indefinite east ridge, the track bears up to the stone remains of Brown Cove dam, backed by a sheet of water and, further on, an expanse of turf fit for a footie match. Turn smartly right keep to the one section of White Side's slope not broken by scree. There are no pitfalls, nor paths, just a steady grassy heave ho. From time to time you may chance to pause, glance back and be consoled to know the opposing north-east ridge of Catstycam is appreciably taller and quite superb from this angle. The ground duly gives way to a field, whereupon your equilibrium is rapidly restored.

Fellwalkers seldom climb directly out of Brown Cove, yet, when backed by a stout draught, the convex E slope can be an exhilarating excelsior!

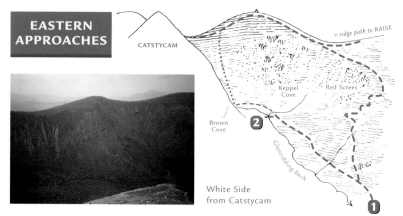

EASTERN APPROACHES

CATSTYCAM

> ridge path to RAISE

Keppel Cove

Red Screes

Brown Cove

2

Glenridding Beck

1

White Side from Catstycam

When the tops are ruled out by the weather, there is every good reason to wander up Glenridding and venture into the bowl of Brown Cove, to inspect the old stone dam, and beyond the residual tarn, an area of fine turf fit for a game of cricket - a stunning oval ignored by the crowd.

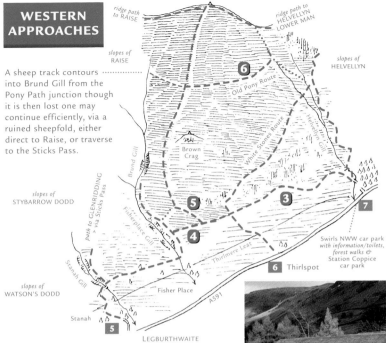

WESTERN APPROACHES

ridge path to RAISE

ridge path to HELVELLYN LOWER MAN

slopes of RAISE

slopes of HELVELLYN

A sheep track contours into Brund Gill from the Pony Path junction though it is then lost one may continue efficiently, via a ruined sheepfold, either direct to Raise, or traverse to the Sticks Pass.

6

Old Pony Route

slopes of STYBARROW DODD

White Stones Route

Helvellyn Gill

Brown Crag

Brund Gill

path to GLENRIDDING via Sticks Pass

Fisherplace Gill

5

4

3

7

Thirlmere Leat

Swirls NWW car park with information/toilets, forest walks & Station Coppice car park

slopes of WATSON'S DODD

Stanah Gill

Fisher Place

A591

6 Thirlspot

Stanah

5

LEGBURTHWAITE

ASCENT *from Swirls & Thirlspot*

Thirlspot

3 Begin from the North West Water Swirls car park beside Helvellyn Gill. Leave the enclosure upon the Helvellyn path, but key into the signposted footpath directing north (left) toward Stanah, just above the intake wall. The path has been stabilised with retaining rocks as it runs up to, and beyond a footbridge, at times close to the intake wall, at others well above. In due course merging by the wall with the footpath rising from the hotel at Thirlspot. A slate sign marks the start of the White Stones Route (directly up beside the gill), ignore this. Continue a further 80 yards to fork right, rising gently. This route breaks two ways, either, **4** contour to ascend beside the craggy rim of Fisherplace Gill, escaping right when the final fall comes into view, walking along the upper rim of

Wallside path above Thirlspot

The tight ravine of Brund Gill
beneath the Brown Crag spur

bracken growth to reach an odd 'L' shaped bield wall, or **5** ascend directly to this wall. The path continues plain enough, climbing past Brown Crag, one may strike out at a whim to embrace its cairned summit. Regain the path on the gently rising ground leading to where the Old Pony Route breaks right. A strong sheep path leads left at this point, these canny animals have adopted the largely redundant Pony Route for themselves, their path contouring and dwindling approaching a ford of upper Brund Gill. The main route now climbs directly up the barren - quartz accepted - slope of White Side. **6** Alternatively, follow the Old Pony Route right, with its impressive view of Browncove Crags, before sweeping up beside a branch headwater of Helvellyn Gill to the saddle, there joining the broad ridge path turning north for the summit.

The Summit

One modest cairn marks the brow of this gentle dome. The ease of passage has not caused a lower contouring route to develop, as is has occurred on all the summits north to Calfhow Pike.

Safe Descents

Whilst mindful of the steep mountain hollows of Brown and Keppel Coves to the east, this is not a place to fear. Follow the Old Pony Route NE take the right fork in the saddle before Raise, wind down to Glenridding in sure steady stages. Both west and south cairned paths give assured lines to The Swirls and Thirlspot. The latter ridge path enables one to join the Old Pony Route westward, down from the saddle. The old way is not obvious on the ground until one reaches the first evidence of Helvellyn Gill.

Catstycam and Brown Cove dam

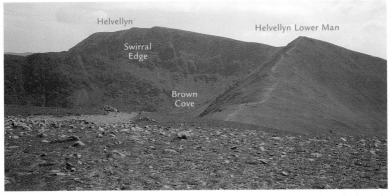

Looking south from the summit

Ridge Routes to....

HELVELLYN   DESCENT 222 feet   ASCENT 507 feet   1.2 miles

The path, always well appointed with random cairns, heads southwards crossing a depression at 2,610 feet, with Browncove Crags right, and curiously, Brown Cove itself left! The path then climbs to the prominent summit of Helvellyn Lower Man, with consistently steep ground falling to the left, trend round SE in joining the popular stroll from The Swirls to reach the summit.

RAISE   DESCENT 142 feet   ASCENT 210 feet   0.7 miles

The initially gravelly path takes a NE slant to the depression 2,690 feet, be watchful do not be lured to follow the Pony Path, which forks right. The climb to the grassy parade of Raise is soon accomplished, beside a proliferate chain of cairns.

Skiddaw from Brown Crag

PANORAMA

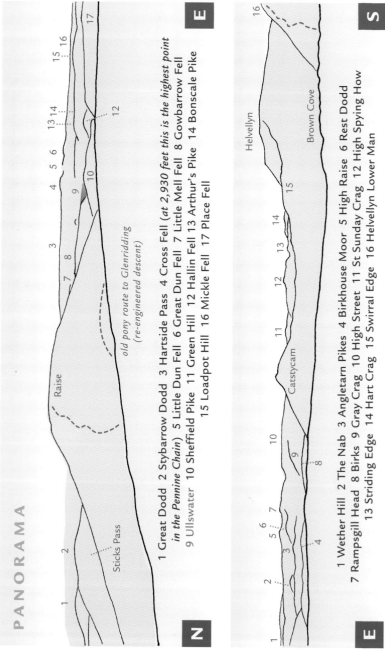

N **E**

Raise

Sticks Pass

old pony route to Glenridding (re-engineered descent)

1 Great Dodd 2 Stybarrow Dodd 3 Hartside Pass 4 Cross Fell *(at 2,930 feet this is the highest point in the Pennine Chain)* 5 Little Dun Fell 6 Great Dun Fell 7 Little Mell Fell 8 Gowbarrow Fell 9 Ullswater 10 Sheffield Pike 11 Green Hill 12 Hallin Fell 13 Arthur's Pike 14 Bonscale Pike 15 Loadpot Hill 16 Mickle Fell 17 Place Fell

E **S**

Helvellyn

Brown Cove

Catstycam

1 Wether Hill 2 The Nab 3 Angletarn Pikes 4 Birkhouse Moor 5 High Raise 6 Rest Dodd 7 Rampsgill Head 8 Birks 9 Gray Crag 10 High Street 11 St Sunday Crag 12 High Spying How 13 Striding Edge 14 Hart Crag 15 Swirral Edge 16 Helvellyn Lower Man

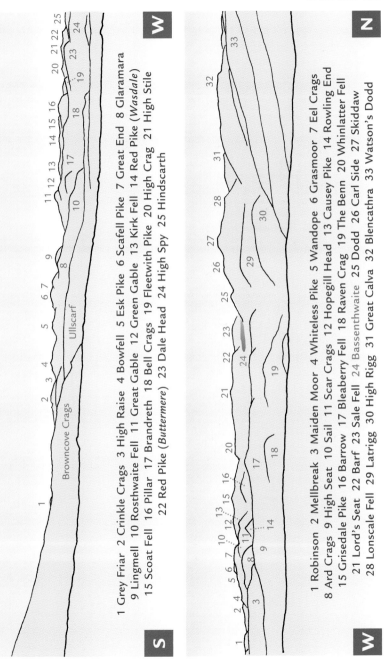

S

Browncove Crags

Ullscarf

W

1 Grey Friar 2 Crinkle Crags 3 High Raise 4 Bowfell 5 Esk Pike 6 Scafell Pike 7 Great End 8 Glaramara
9 Lingmell 10 Rosthwaite Fell 11 Great Gable 12 Green Gable 13 Kirk Fell 14 Red Pike (*Wasdale*)
15 Scoat Fell 16 Pillar 17 Brandreth 18 Bell Crags 19 Fleetwith Pike 20 High Crag 21 High Stile
22 Red Pike (*Buttermere*) 23 Dale Head 24 High Spy 25 Hindscarth

W

N

1 Robinson 2 Mellbreak 3 Maiden Moor 4 Whiteless Pike 5 Wandope 6 Grasmoor 7 Eel Crags
8 Ard Crags 9 High Seat 10 Sail 11 Scar Crags 12 Hopegill Head 13 Causey Pike 14 Rowling End
15 Grisedale Pike 16 Barrow 17 Bleaberry Fell 18 Raven Crag 19 The Benn 20 Whinlatter Fell
21 Lord's Seat 22 Barf 23 Sale Fell 24 Bassenthwaite 25 Dodd 26 Carl Side 27 Skiddaw
28 Lonscale Fell 29 Latrigg 30 High Rigg 31 Great Calva 32 Blencathra 33 Watson's Dodd

A precious place

It would be hard to imagine anyone venturing into Lakeland for the first time who, valuing landscape as a backdrop to their lives, would not be moved by its magic. Aficionados return again and again seeking to rekindle those first-sight sensations.

In preparing this guide I am ever more keenly aware of an underlying dynamic. This is a place of work as well as leisure, the National Park and The National Trust playing crucial roles. The Herdwick sheep may be little more than ornamentation, but someone cares for their needs, in so doing maintains the walls, integral with the Lakeland we love. Though, being honest, the flock needs halving and a greater diversity of plant and animal-life restored to the open fell.

For the casual visitor and fellwalking enthusiast perhaps no other organisation more surely represents their values and interests than the Friends' of the Lake District, for seventy years the ever-vigilant guardians of the whole Cumbrian landscape. My suggestion, affirm your affinity... join and lend them your much valued support - *webside*: www.fld.org.uk

That tourism has replaced farming as the bed-rock of the economy, certainly within the National Park, was made starkly evident during the disasterous Foot & Mouth Disease outbreak which hit Cumbria cruelly in 2001. Lakeland was hit so hard that it might take many years to win back some visitors to the area. Sustaining tourism demands the new thinking of 'sustainable tourism' which seeks to balance the holistic interests of people and nature. The blanket closure of the countryside also knocked my research for six. Instead of launching the first half of the series, I completed just one quarter of my mission. Still this means much pleasure awaits me, and my readership! I suppose it all goes to confirm that Lakeland is both a testing ground and a testing place, the area has challenged man for as long as he has tried to eek out a living in its thin soils and bleak climate.

St Sunday Crag, the Ullswater fell